TUNE IN TOMORROW

TUNE IN
TOMORROW

or
How I Found
THE RIGHT TO HAPPINESS
with OUR GAL SUNDAY,
STELLA DALLAS,
JOHN'S OTHER WIFE,
and Other Sudsy Radio Serials

by Mary Jane Higby

COWLES

To the memory of Kenneth MacGregor
1904–1968

Foreword

For the better part of my life I was a daytime serial star in what is now nostalgically called the Golden Age of Radio. Nobody called it that then. It is only when a thing is dead that it becomes golden. If I had allowed myself to brood about what psychologists and sociologists were saying about radio in general and daytime serials in particular, I'd have been tempted to quit my job and go straight.

Take for example the famous diatribe of Dr. Louis I. Berg, a New York psychiatrist, who, in a pamphlet issued at his own expense, said in part, "The serials just reek with twisted and morbid suggestions. They deal with the dark alleys of human corruption and appeal to the lowest instincts . . . Truly the authors have sieved the emotional sewers, drained the emotional swamps for much of their material." ("A Study of Certain Radio Programs and Their Effects Upon the Audience, Especially Adolescents and Women at the Climacterium.") Or this alarm sounded by author Worthington Gibson, writing about the children's shows, "Emphasis is placed on gore and violence . . . With the aid of radio we are doing our best to breed a race of neurotic impressionables." ("Radio Horrors for Children Only," *American Mercury*, July, 1938.) Hardly echoes from a golden age.

Now that television is drawing the critical fire and radio basks in the afterglow of "Remember when," it seems in order to take a look at the old medium and see what really went on behind those mikes. So I have tried here to present the entire radio field from the actors' viewpoint.

Most of the material has been taken from memory—my own and that of friends who have been wonderfully patient in helping me reconstruct a world now gone. Special thanks go to those who taped their reminiscences for me—Bill Adams, Keene Crockett, Betty Garde, Bill Lipton, Kenneth MacGregor, Anne Seymour, and Luis Van Rooten. Others who have been especially helpful include Walter Siegel, Hayes B. Jacobs, Nat Brandt, Mel Spiegel, Linley M. Stafford, and my husband, Guy Sorel.

Many of the most important radio actors, some of them my close friends, appear only briefly, if at all, in the book. The work itself, in taking form, seemed to impose arbitrary limits. Then, too, many of my interviews were conducted on the bus and in the supermarket. Kenny Delmar (Senator Claghorn of Allen's Alley) was not included until I ran into him among the canned goods.

I have followed a semiautobiographical form, pausing at times to explore a particular aspect of the field as it developed through the years. At such points the chronology is likely to short-circuit a bit, as in the chapter dealing with recordings, which spans the entire period—the early thirties to the late fifties.

As far as possible I have checked memory against the press and other records of the time, and I have tried diligently to separate fiction from fact. Since the demise of radio, quite a body of legend has grown up, so that many a tale that began circulation with "Wouldn't it be funny if . . . ?" finally became "I was there when . . ."

Please don't discredit my facts, however, because you find me writing "KHJ, the CBS outlet in Los Angeles . . ." I know KHJ is not the CBS outlet *now*, but it was in 1932, when this story begins. The only constant thing about radio was change. Take, for example, "When a Girl Marries," the serial in which I starred for eighteen years. It began in the New York studios of CBS, whose call letters at that time were WABC, which are now the call letters of ABC, which was then WJZ, the Blue Network station of NBC, whose other network (the Red) was represented by WEAF, now WNBC. We moved to WEAF (now WNBC) and later to WABC (formerly WJZ). Our theme song was changed from Cadman's "At Dawning" to Drigo's "Serenade" and was played by five different organists. Announcers on the show over the years were Frank Gallop, Charles Stark, Dick Stark, Dennis James, Hugh James, George Ansbro, Don Gardner, and Wendell Niles. Directors changed even more often than the announcers and every part in the piece was cast at least twice (Phil was played by Michael Fitzmaurice, Richard Kollmar, Staats Cotsworth, Karl Weber, and Paul McGrath). Elaine Carrington created and originally wrote the program, but later turned it over to Leroy Bailey, and it was he who wrote it during the peak years of the forties.

Here, then, is the story, as I saw it, of an industry that in its youth (1930–34) surpassed the growth record of any other enterprise in the history of the United States. It soared on to dizzying heights, and then sputtered out like a Roman candle.

While she lasted, though, radio was a high-stepping, if dizzy, old medium and now that she has succumbed almost entirely to "Pop" and "Rock," I must admit that she gave me the best years of her life—which I have tried to recreate in these pages.

M. J. H.
Clinton, Conn.

Contents

I.   The Early Daze 1

II.   Are Your Loved Ones Suffering From Seepage? 9

III.   The Grim Rapers and the Round Robin 18

IV.   Twinkle, Twinkle, Little Stars 31

V.   The Living End 47

VI.   The Gay Ad-libbers 56

VII.   The End of the Ice Age 67

VIII.   Flop Sweat 79

IX.   The Black Hole of Calcutta 98

X.   'Tis a Pity She's a Bore 111

XI.   The Show Must Go On—and On and On 123

XII.   The Sprained Little Pinkie 141

XIII.   Rinso—What? 151

XIV.   Who's Who in the Zoo 161

XV.   The Infernal Triangle 168

XVI.   I Hit the Fan! 187

XVII.   Help Stamp Out TV! 203

XVIII. When a Girl Commutes 213

Bibliography 225

The author and John Raby, stars of "When a Girl Marries."

CHAPTER I

The Early Daze

My sister Rita was having a bad time trying to console the gasman. He was sitting on the back steps, holding his head in his hands.

"It's terrible. It's terrible," he kept saying.

My sister had opened the door to admit this tragic figure a few minutes earlier. We hadn't paid a bill in ages. The gas company had been pretty big about it, but we knew the day of reckoning would arrive.

"I've got to turn off your gas," he said. "I don't want to, but I've got to." He hesitated. "I don't know where it is," he said.

"I do," Rita said. "Come along. I'll show you."

"I just turned off the gas in a house where there were little children. I felt like a rat."

"Well, you mustn't feel like a rat here. We have fur coats and we can keep nice and warm."

"But the woman was crying—."

"Wait a few minutes," Rita said. "I'll make you a cup of coffee while the gas is still on. You'll feel more like turning it off if you have something hot in your stomach."

While the coffee was percolating, she went to the closet and got her cocoa-dyed ermine coat and showed it to him. He felt better after that, and when he had drunk the coffee, she was able to coax him into cutting off the only means we had of heating the house.

For us, in that year of 1932, the Depression reached its lowest point. Father, who all his life had been able to earn a good living as an actor, found himself without a job and with no prospect of getting one. Mother's flurries in Hollywood real estate had come to a dismal end.

None of us really knew anything but show business, and as far as we were concerned that had slowed down to a stop. At the time it was fashionable to blame such situations on the collapse of the stock market three years before, but in fact that had nothing to do with us. My dear parents knew nothing about stocks. I refuse to contemplate what might have happened if they had. Although Mother always considered her father a wastrel (after leaving the Confederate Army he devoted the rest of his life to dealing faro in the then rip-roaring state of Texas), she inherited more of his traits than those of her saintly mother. My gray-haired Mom would take a flyer on anything. She was caught in mid-air with some fancy real estate speculation just as the Depression set in. Mother had taken the born gambler's rosy view that the boom would last forever, and her small capital had been spread thin. A few unexpected reverses, and she went under.

Father, on the other hand, was all actor. The trouble was that he refused to recognize this. He kept casting himself in different roles in life. There was the time he inherited a gold mine. He dug around in his wardrobe trunk, brought out a beautiful outfit left over from a stock production of "The Squaw Man," and headed for Bodie, once famous as the toughest town in the California gold fields. Now, sixty years later, its population had dwindled to three—an ancient Chinese cook, an even more ancient prospector, and his infant great-grandson. My father swelled the count briefly by importing an expensive engineer and three bona fide miners, and with this crew he set about locating the lost lode of the Taft mine.

It must have been a misplaced sense of humor that made the engineer send my handsome, inefficient Pop down the shaft with instructions to tie a heavy bucket onto a rope so they could start bailing out the rain water. Father tied the rope, filled the bucket with water, and shouted, "Buckets, aweigh!" When he came to, he heard one of the miners saying, "What the hell could he have tied that bucket with—a *granny* knot?"

Most of Father's savings went into that project but no gold was ever found. On his return from Bodie a few months later he went right to work on a Western with Tom Mix, but he had to make a lot of horse operas to cover the mining loss. Not long after that, the Depression set in.

At the time of the gasman's visit, we were living in a fourteen-room house, with three baths, and servants' quarters over the two-car garage. We were renting this establishment back from the bank, which had wrested it from Mother's tenuous grasp. As my sister had explained to the disconsolate gasman, we had fur coats. Mine was a gorgeous leopard

affair, which Mother had bought for me when I was fourteen. She had
let me design it myself, and the result was a slinky wraparound with a
black lynx collar. I was the only kid in my set with a coat like *that*.

This was the state of affairs when radio found me.

One day the telephone rang. (The phone was our life-link with
possible employment. We'd have taken to mugging people on the streets
before we'd have let that be turned off.) I clutched my leopard about
me and answered it. The voice on the wire asked me if I wanted to do a
radio show. I had only one interest.

"How much?"

"Seven dollars for a half-hour show."

The next day I made my way by foot (the two-car garage was by
now an empty shell) to Hollywood Boulevard and Radio Station KFWB,
which was owned by Warner Brothers Pictures and situated atop the
office building over their giant movie palace. A slight, dark-haired young
man came out to the reception room and ushered me into an office where
another, taller man was waiting. "We'll have to wait until Kay gets
here," he said. "She has the scripts."

I asked them how they happened to call me. "Oh, we saw you play
Wendy in 'Peter Pan.' You were very good."

I blushed. I am not one to blush at receiving a compliment but to
this day I am inclined to redden at the mention of "Peter Pan."

To appreciate fully any performance of J. M. Barrie's play you
must realize that all that elfin prancing and flitting is done while the
actresses are trussed up in leather-and-metal harnesses that would cause
Sonny Liston to buckle. From this harness, a tiny hook protrudes
through a hole in the back of the costume. The flying wire can be
snapped on to this hook and removed easily. There is a rope offstage
that controls each of the actors in flight, and a stagehand mans that rope.
When I played Wendy for the Los Angeles Civic Repertory Company,
I drew the most nervous, frightened stagehand who ever lived.

One of the simplest flights in the play is Wendy's entrance in the
woodland scene. The boys of Never-never Land see what they take to
be a bird and Tootles wounds it with an arrow. Wendy's soft entrance
music begins and she floats into sight, the arrow in her breast.

For this effect, the actress hangs high in the wings, clutching a guy
rope, until she hears her cue; then she lets go and swings out like a
pendulum. Her stagehand lowers her bit by bit and she sinks to the
stage.

At dress rehearsal the director noticed that from certain seats I
could be seen in the wings before the flight began, so they pulled me
six feet farther offstage. We never tested the flight again.

On opening night the first act went well. Then I was hoisted up for the slow flight. But now the arc of the pendulum was much greater. I clutched my guy rope. The dreamlike music began.

"It looks so weary," said Tootles. "How slowly it flies—."

I released my hold and WHOOSHT! I shot right across the scene and off the other side. As I slipped over his head, the voice of the director could be heard all over the theater—"Check that flight!"

He didn't need to yell at me. I was plunging toward a brick wall. I grabbed another guy rope on the other side of the stage and hung there wondering how my stagehand was bearing up in the excitement, because if he ever let go of his rope . . . I released my hold and back into view I came—twirling like a top. I hit a giant oak, which careened crazily but miraculously didn't fall. Then, as I reached center stage, still about five feet above floor level, my stagehand gave way. He just threw up his hands. I came down in my little white nightdress like a sack of rocks, with a thud that reverberated through the house—and through me.

My friends at KFWB had apparently seen a later performance, when things had gone more smoothly, and I was describing to them the problems of the airborne actress, when the person we were waiting for arrived. Kay Van Riper was of medium height, very frail, with pale blond hair, and a heart-shaped face. Years later she was to write the "Andy Hardy" films in which Mickey Rooney starred.

The four of us sat down together and they explained that they were about to produce a series of historical dramas dealing with Elizabethan England. The sight of me flying about as Wendy in "Peter Pan" had suggested to them that I would be splendid as Bloody Mary Tudor. While I was digesting this thought, Miss Van Riper leaned toward me and said, "I'm ashamed to offer this to you, because it pays so little."

I stifled an impulse to ask for an advance on my $7 and muttered instead something about how much fun it would be to do a radio show. Then, although I was unaware of it at the time, I gave my first audition. I was to give hundreds more in the years that followed, but this one was handled so adroitly that it slid by almost without my noticing it. Miss Van Riper had a deep and rather dark voice and she explained that she wanted a lighter, more silvery quality for Mary Tudor. "You'll know what I mean," she said, "if you just read a few lines." She handed me a script. They all assumed an attitude, eyes closed, brow in hand, that suggested silent prayer. I glanced at the pages and started reading aloud.

"His Most Catholic Majesty, the King of Spain—."

All three heads bobbed up and spoke simultaneously:

"Oh, she mustn't sound *English.*"

"No, no."

"Not English."

I looked at them. They were serious. I felt the muscles of my face screwing up into what I call "Radio Actors' Look"—a mixture of disbelief, resignation, and wild frustration. Wendy Moira Angela Tudor, with her west-of-the-Mississippi accent, was my first brush with the zany squareness that always characterized the radio field. It seems impossible that anything could be square and zany at the same time. Radio was.

The production staff of KFWB liked my portrayal of Bloody Mary, and it was agreed that I was to play the part.

"Come to the old Warner Brothers' lot at Sunset and Bronson at five-thirty tomorrow afternoon," Miss Van Riper said. "We broadcast from one of the sound stages there."

The following day I trudged the mile from our house to the Warner Brothers' Studio and crossed the movie lot with its cluster of sound-proofed stages, rising on every side like giant warehouses. In the last one I found the radio studio and joined six other actors for the first rehearsal. We sat around a long table. Miss Van Riper, the director, sat at the head with a stopwatch.

Time, I learned, was most important. We had to start at an exact second, and say the last word at an exact second. It was like filling a glass to the brim and walking across the room without spilling a drop. Later in the days of soap operas, the organist could help by filling in ad-lib, or by cutting his closing selection short. But in this case, an orchestra was rehearsing in another studio. The conductor had been allotted the precise amount of time for each interlude of music and he had to adhere to it as rigidly as we did to the timing of the scenes.

We were given scripts, and each actor marked every one of his speeches, outlining it in pencil. Kay Van Riper recommended that I do the same and gave me some advice about the microphone. "You'd better work not more than a foot away from the mike," she said. "If the script calls for you to scream or shout, turn your head away. If you have an intimate scene to play, lower your voice and come in a bit closer."

That was it—the sum total of my preparation for radio acting. We had no rehearsal "on mike." I never saw the thing until we were ready to go on the air. The sound-effects man, who had the charming name of Teagarden, sat through our first rehearsal and took notes. In looking back, I realize he was just plain wonderful. We never rehearsed with him either, and yet every effect was exactly right and perfectly timed. Henry VIII's period was a noisy one, full of swordplay, horses'

5

hooves, wassailings, and, of course, beheadings. Teagarden took it all in stride. He could burn you at the stake simply by crumpling a piece of stiff paper close to the microphone.

"English Coronets" went out to the radio audience every Sunday night. Kay Van Riper was its author, director, and star. She was going to play Elizabeth in the current series, but the character had not yet appeared. Henry was Hanley Stafford, who was later to become famous playing Daddy to Fanny Brice's Baby Snooks. He left this $7 "Coronets" bonanza at the end of three weeks, however, to take a job with a stock company in Arizona and was replaced by Gale Gordon. Every actor at my first radio rehearsal went on to make a solid career for himself in the years that followed. "English Coronets" was a sort of incubator for radio talent, and many of the people who reached the top later started with Kay Van Riper.

After we had read the dialogue through twice, rehearsal was over, and I gathered up my foolscap script and went home.

"How did it go?" Father asked.

"All right, I guess."

He took the script. "Good Lord," he said, "you have only two days to get up in this? You'd better start studying."

"They don't get up in it, Dad. They just read it."

"Nonsense. How can they really play it until they're free of the lines? You'd better learn it," he said. So I did.

The following Sunday night I again walked the mile to Warner Brothers and my first radio show. In the room where we rehearsed Kay was passing out new pages for the script; she asked us to throw away pages eight, nine, and ten. She had made revisions. I took a look at the new lines. They were completely different. That was the last time I ever purposely memorized a radio script. It was a doubtful practice because we were sometimes so late in getting the final draft of a show that we'd play it holding sheets still wet from the mimeograph machine.

When we went into the barnlike, main studio, where the orchestra was already rehearsing, I saw my first microphone. I had heard a great deal about mike fright, but I felt absolutely nothing. Except for one notable occasion, I seem always to have been immune. Perhaps it was because I could never quite believe in radio. I couldn't imagine that anyone was actually listening. I suffered as much as anybody before facing a live audience on an opening night, but I always had a sense of detachment when broadcasting. According to the ratings, seven million women used to tune in to hear "When a Girl Marries," but I, the Girl, could never picture those millions. So on this, my first broadcast, I looked at the thing with curiosity but without fear. I wanted to do a good job. But far more than that—more than anything in the world—I wanted those seven dollars.

The orchestra was sounding its last tune-up. Teagarden was testing his logs, his horses' hooves and the huge metal sheet he used to simulate thunderclaps. The actors had separated off into various parts of the studio and each was running over his lines to himself. Kay said, "Okay, kiddies, this is it." There were a couple of seconds of silence. Then the musicians thundered into "Pomp and Circumstance," an announcer with a fine vocal flourish intoned, "English Co-rr-o-nets," and we were off.

It went beautifully. Afterward Kay congratulated us, gave each of us a $7 check, and told me that Mary Tudor would not be in the next Sunday's episode.

"But I've just thought of something," she went on. "Can you scream?"

"Of course," I said.

"A good, big blood-curdler?"

"A whopper."

"Well, I can't," she said. "And I need a loud scream next week. So you come along and do it for me. You'll get $7. We pay the same on this show, no matter what you do."

I wasn't worried about the scream. I knew I could do that, all right.

True Boardman, one of the actors in "English Coronets," took me to the Cocoanut Grove after that first performance. In those Depression days I was astounded. He was blowing more than the whole "Coronet" check! He smiled at me across the white tablecloth. "Last week," he said, "I did fourteen radio shows."

My heart stopped, my jaw sagged, my eyes bugged out. I couldn't figure fourteen times seven but I could see that ten times seven was a nice living wage, and, of course, fourteen times seven was more than that.

"True," I said, when speech had returned, "who are the people you see about getting radio work?"

He took a pencil from his pocket. On an old envelope he made a short list and gave it to me.

"They all pay seven dollars?" I asked.

He laughed the carefree laughter of the rich.

"Oh, some of them pay ten—even as much as fifteen."

I settled into a rosy daze. True was talking, the band was playing, but above it all, though far away, I could hear the sound of coin falling in a soft, tinkly shower into a big strongbox.

The following Sunday I marched down to the Warner Brothers' lot for rehearsal and gave Kay a few sample shrieks that set her hair on end.

"That's fine," she beamed. "Save it for the show. I don't want you to get hoarse."

My contribution was to be the dramatic climax before the orchestra's final theme. The plot called for a man to jump out from behind a curtain and attack the character Kay was playing with a dagger. This wordless interlude would be indicated on the air by the sound of scuffling from Teagarden and the scream from me. The audience would know in advance that the man had hidden behind the curtain and would be breathlessly awaiting the attack. The scream would indicate that it had begun and the orchestra would cut in with the theme—all in all, a fine, dramatic ending.

The hand on the studio clock reached nine and the show was on. I took a deep breath and held my head high. This was no stopgap job till something better came along. It was my new career. The road of life stretched before me, paved with $7, $10, and $15 checks. I was a Radio Actress.

At the final scene I went to the mike and stood beside Kay while she read her last lines. Then something frightful began to take place. I was supposed to be starting a whole new career and instead I was turning to ice. Kay stopped speaking. Teagarden made a rustle of draperies and shuffled his feet. I stood. Kay looked up quickly. I stared back at her, my teeth tightly clenched. I couldn't breathe. She frowned and pointed at me. I stared at her. She turned to the microphone.

"You!" she declaimed. "And with a dagger in your hand!" She raised her arm and cued in the orchestra.

Afterward she sank, shaking, into a chair. She threw a glance at me that, if I had been capable of feeling, would have knocked me cold. I sat down beside her. She looked up and something she saw in my face changed her expression to one of concern.

"Never mind," she said as she put her arm around me. "Maybe it was better that way. Come back next week. You're a fine Mary Tudor and you really can scream . . . when you feel like it."

Then she passed out the checks. I didn't want to take mine but she just laughed.

"Don't be silly. It's already in the budget. Nobody'll ever know."

CHAPTER II

Are Your Loved Ones
Suffering From Seepage?

One Thanksgiving Day, long after he had passed the fifty mark and when he had done no consistent exercise for years, my actor father strode out of our Hollywood bungalow, turned a back somersault in the air, and landed upright on his feet. He sprained his back and tore up quite a patch of lawn where his toes dug in, but he proved his point. He had been arguing at the dinner table that most failures resulted from halfhearted efforts and that anyone—but anyone—if he threw the resources of his whole being into it, could do almost anything.

"Now," he had announced, as he moved the garden hose out of harm's way, "if I go at this halfheartedly I'll break my neck—."

Even as a small child I was a good audience for Daddy. The thought of seeing him break his neck set me quivering with anticipation. My disappointment at the prosaic outcome of the affair was mitigated by the sound of Mother's fury when she found out what sort of "damn foolishness" he had been up to while she was washing the dinner dishes. She was full of dark forebodings and she was right. As it turned out, he started work on a film version of Sir Walter Scott's "The Talisman" a few days later. Actors in those early silents often made up at home and drove to and from the studios in full costume. Prying Daddy out of his suit of armor without injuring his aching back became a ritual that engaged the entire family. I can still hear the clanging and the clatter and the loud groans as I tugged at the footgear.

The wolves of the Depression snapping at my heels gave impetus to my own version of Daddy's back flip. Five radio stations in Los Angeles employed paid dramatic talent: KFWB, KNX, KFI, KECA, and

9

The Shadow—Bret Morrison.

Ferde Grofé and Eddie Duchin at the piano on Rudy Vallee's show, top. Bottom, some famous radio personalities of 1938. The men are, from left, Jack Benny, Ed Sullivan, John Royal, and Jack Pearl (Baron Munchausen). Seated at left is Mary Livingstone.

KHJ. To these I laid siege. I sat one whole day in the outer office of KNX until the director, a charming redhead named Georgia Fifield, came in. Before I left, I had sold her a vaudeville sketch my father had written years before—and my services as an actress. The script and I, in a package deal, brought home $20.

I had been storming the other outlets with no results when a call came through from KFI, asking if I could play a part of Spanish dialect. I was not in a mood to say no. I crossed my fingers and found a weaseling reply.

"Oh, I *specialize* in dialects," I said. I meant to visit a Mexican girl friend and pick up a few pointers but I heard the voice on the telephone say, "Fine. Come right down here. We're holding auditions this afternoon."

That left me no time for preparation, so I boarded the streetcar and rode the half hour to downtown Los Angeles in a dither. KFI had its studios in dingy-looking lofts over the showrooms of the Packard dealer to whom the station belonged. When I arrived I was not cheered by the sight of two native-born Spanish actresses who were there to compete for the part. The director seemed doubtful when he saw me.

"Can you do this?" he asked. "These other girls really speak Spanish."

"I specialize in dialects," I repeated doggedly.

When the moment of truth came I had to fight down a desire to scamper right out of there. Instead, I swung my hips, wiggled my torso, changed all the short *i* sounds to *e*'s and spoke in a sing-song rhythm.

Sheer firmness of purpose must have won me that audition. I could have been nothing short of terrible. There was something in Father's theory about the back flip.

"If you make a mistake," he used to say, "make it big. Maybe they'll think you meant it to be that way. Never show indecision. Plunge."

The system has its dangers but it made me a lot of money over the years that a more timid attitude would have sacrificed. I soon discovered that I was not alone in my derring-do. Any of the thirty or so actors who were struggling to earn a living from Hollywood radio would *say* he could do anything, planning to meet the emergency of how to do it when it arose. I was astounded as I learned, during the next few months, how versatile this group really was. There was never time to prepare a detailed and searching performance, and, for the most part, the hastily written scripts did not warrant it. What was needed was a quick impression, given with broad, sure strokes. It bore the relation to a stage performance that a pencil sketch has to an oil painting.

12

The name of the KFI program was "Packard Fiesta." It featured an authentic Latin-American orchestra, an authentic Mexican chorus, and a bogus Spanish cast. The name credits at the end of the show reeled out in a flourish of Ramirez, Delgado, and Alvarez, to be snubbed up short on MacHarrie, FitzMaurice, and Higby.

Senor Don Michael FitzMaurice, who played opposite me, had come to radio by an unusual route. He had been working as a cub reporter at $16 a week on *The Los Angeles Times* when he sold KNX the idea of broadcasting a current murder trial directly from the courthouse. He had never broadcast before, but he was sure that he could. He did —with such success that the newspapers, enraged at being scooped by radio, banded together and had him and his microphone thrown out of the courthouse. When it was all over, he found that without realizing it he had changed careers. He was a radio actor.

For awhile Mike and I shared the same disability. Neither of us had a car. To get from one radio station to another twenty miles distant by means of the inadequate Los Angeles public transportation system was plain hell. The flames burned deep into Mike's psyche. A few years later, when he became the idol of millions as radio's Superman, I watched him swing from M.G. to Rolls-Royce to Mercedes-Benz in swift succession. He continued to dress modestly and he kept a simple apartment, but there were times when the Aga Khan would have bristled with envy at a peek inside Mike's garage.

My part on "Coronets" at KFWB had run its course but Johnny Murray, one of the men who had been present during my first interview with Kay Van Riper, sent for me to play the lead in an adaptation of a Warners' picture, yet to be released. The program was to serve as promotion for the film. It went by so smoothly under Murray's direction that the details are hazy after all these years. Details of the next show I did for the Warner Brothers' movie market are etched into my mind like a steel engraving.

Murray had been replaced as director by a stocky woman with startling blond hair. Her previous duties had been those of a switchboard operator. On the night of the broadcast she came forward to greet me with a warm smile, but when she spoke it was in a dull, torpid voice and so slowly that she seemed reluctant to part with each word. I was glad to see Gale Gordon in the cast. We had known one another long before either of us had heard of radio. The other two actors were Bret Morrison and Cyril Armbrister. Bret later became known as The Shadow and Cyril created and produced the popular program "Strange as It Seems." Gale became popular as the school principal on radio's

"Our Miss Brooks" and more recently as co-star with Lucille Ball on her TV show.

After we were settled around the table, our director explained in her languid way that I was to take the part Miriam Hopkins had played in the film, and we began our first reading. Before we were halfway through the page, the lady was waving her hands in the air and crying, "No, no, no!" As if by signal, the three men leaned back and dropped their scripts on the table. Gale lit a cigarette. I, alone, was still poised on the edge of my chair, willing and eager. The director pointed her finger at Cyril and read his opening speech in the plodding monotone she used in conversation. Next, she pointed at Gale and read his speech the same way. Then she applied her limp attack at my first lines.

I was confused. If I had not been, I might have noticed that my fellow players simply picked up the pages and did exactly as they had been doing before the interruption. I tried to copy her snail's pace delivery. It was sticky going because the plot was concerned with the "flaming youth" of the Prohibition Era.

The lady stopped us again to point and read some more. She frowned at me. "You're supposed to be *southern*," she said.

I added a corn-pone overtone to the whine I was developing. As air time grew near, I was sounding like Amos and Andy pushing their Fresh Air Taxi up a steep hill, and the script was running ten minutes too long. The director had to stop pointing and start cutting. Before this process was complete, time ran out and we had to plunge, ready-or-not, into the air waves.

Only one side of those early microphones was sensitive to sound. We stood in a semicircle in front of it. I was halfway through my second speech when the director sprang to my side.

"You're losing the quality!" she said in a stage whisper that could have been heard in the back benches of the Hollywood Bowl. "You're losing the quality!"

I tried to concentrate on my lines but she stood right there, cheek by jowl with me, hissing criticism and advice in my ear.

"It's Miriam Hopkins. She's southern. You've lost the quality."

When the music came in for the first bridge, I stumbled away from the microphone and into Gale. I gave him a look that, he later said, suggested the occupant of a canoe rounding the bend at Niagara. As I started the next scene I felt a strong arm around my shoulder, a reassuring "steady-old-girl" pressure. Next, I was aware that someone had moved in very near to me on my right side. It was Cyril. They stood so close for the rest of the half hour that the director couldn't get at me and had to be content to dance about on the dead side of the

14

mike and gesticulate. That was all right. I didn't have to look. I decided to hell with Miriam Hopkins, all the Warner brothers, and the Confederate States. I got a grip on myself and tried to salvage my performance.

Afterward the actors were apologetic.

"We thought you knew about her," they said. "Nobody pays any attention. We think she's tone deaf."

Oddly enough, the lady seemed pleased with what I had done. She cast me in many parts after that. On the following occasions I let my mind wander pleasantly while she droned through the rehearsal.

Weeks after my first appearance in radio, I was still struggling to get my toe in the door at KHJ. I did finally and promptly got it pinched. They were casting the part of Galatea. I wanted desperately to play it but it turned out to be the first audition I ever lost. When I heard the show on our set at home I burst into tears.

"That girl was terrible," I sobbed.

"Yes, she was," Father said.

"I couldn't have been that bad."

"No. You never could be. She's an amateur."

This judgment was not tinged with envy. The performance had been clumsy and unreal. I was overwhelmed by the injustice of it.

"I wouldn't mind losing to a good actress," I began.

"Now, listen here." Father's tone was matter of fact. "This was a mistake in judgment, that's all. And believe me, it's only the first of many you're going to meet in your lifetime. If you can't face it, you're in the wrong business and better get out right now. These things happen every day."

These words effected a permanent cure. I've since lost many roles more important than Galatea, but I've never shed a tear over any of them. "A mistake in judgment." I could see, although Father didn't mention it, that it worked two ways. I daresay those Spanish girls could have cut my throat when they heard "Packard Fiesta."

If luck played an important part at auditions, one could at least try to reduce the odds. Most of us in those early days worked constantly to increase the scope of our abilities. As soon as I learned that dialects were an asset, I signed up for French and Spanish lessons at night school. I also persuaded an old friend, a nisei, to teach me the rudiments of Japanese. For years this specialty seemed to have been a waste of time. Then the war in the Pacific set my geisha girls and oriental spies slinking through all four networks.

Many of us took pains to develop what I call "costume voices"—the radio convention for the historical drama. We sounded as if we had arrived at the station sidesaddle. It was not *English* English, but a hoity-toity accent, suggesting that the actor's undergarments had been hitched up a trifle too tight. It was useful because, at a time when Chicago was giving birth to soap opera, Hollywood was history oriented. Hanley Stafford was playing Richelieu on KFI, and Mora Martin, a girl with an exquisite, low voice was playing Catherine the Great on the same station. (Mora was the first of our group to snap up a fine contract. She abdicated the throne of all the Russias, with its $5 fee, to be swept away to Chicago by Maybelline Mascara where, week after week, the velvet voice earned an enormous sum for asking the simple question, "Do your eyes look bald?")

The life of Benjamin Franklin (played by Lindsay MacHarrie, one of the hidalgos of "Packard Fiesta") was unfolding at KHJ, and a series at KFI, called "Great Moments in History," dramatized just that.

Once in awhile a sponsor would demand a public appearance in full costume. That is how Hanley Stafford and Ted Osborne (Richelieu and Louis XIII) found themselves in lace collars and velvet knee pants, saying things like, "This course is folly—nay, 'tis madness, sire," across the hoods of Fords and Buicks at an auto show. Their sponsor was a battery company.

My favorite of the costume dramas, however, was KHJ's "Tapestries of Life." It was ushered on the air by the slow descending scale of Victor Herbert's "Ah! Sweet Mystery of Life." Then the actors did a sketch about one of the art objects at Forest Lawn cemetery. I recall plowing through some burry dialogue to stimulate trade at that chapel they call "The Wee Kirk o' the Heather." The effect we achieved each week was a bittersweet smile on life with a tear just behind. After the play, "Ah! Sweet Mystery of Life" would well up again and the KHJ announcer would inquire gravely, "Are your loved ones suffering from seepage?" or "Do your loved ones sleep on the sunny side of the hill?"

We continued "Tapestries of Life" for years, so I guess we kept business humming at Forest Lawn.

The only Hollywood program into which I never tried to brazen my way was KHJ's Kiddie Show. Although still in my teens, I was outside its strictly limited age group. It fascinated me, however, and I would often peek in on its rehearsal late of a Saturday afternoon. It was a combination of squeaky singing, uncertain concertina playing, and the then ever present tap-dancing. The proceedings remained shrill and jazzy to the end when they would take a semireligious turn. Each youngster would recite a farewell in verse sticky with bathos.

Years later, during a "Charlie Chan" rehearsal in New York, Ted

Osborne was reminiscing about the early days in Hollywood. He amazed the eastern members of the cast by ad-libbing an "Are your loved ones suffering from seepage?" commercial. Leon Janney (Charlie Chan's Number One Boy) topped him, though. He had been a child actor at KHJ and still remembered his poem:

> *May kindness, happiness, and joy*
> *Be with you all the day.*
> *And may the God who loves us all*
> *Forget not KHJ!*
> *God will not fail to watch thy sleep*
> *And wake thee with his light.*
> *And now, dear friends of KHJ*
> *I wish you all—goodnight.*

CHAPTER III

The Grim Rapers
and the Round Robin

Broadcasting was a young field in 1932 and it attracted young people. Actors, directors, producers, writers, executives—I can think of few who were over thirty. This was in sharp contrast to the heavy-jowled, paunchy officials of the motion picture studios; and it was, naturally, the young actresses who felt the differences most keenly. Instead of blocking the Forward Pass (characteristic of the older medium), the radio ingénue was likely to find herself uttering cries of delight over snapshots of the director's fiancée or the producer's children. The aging movie executives, on the other hand, seemed bent on proving that they were as attractive to women as the star of the latest Tarzan film. This put a strain both on the executives and the wits of the ingénues.

Brought up in Hollywood, I should have had a certain amount of sophistication, but my father had spent his youth on the family farm in Sand Lake, Michigan, and he had Sand Lake's idea of what a daughter's liberties should be. He raised the devil whenever he caught Rita or me wearing lipstick and when, at the age of fourteen, I went for the first time to a beauty parlor and had my sausagelike curls removed, he met me on my return with a shocked, "My God! She looks like a chorus girl!" It was the shadiest epithet he would use in my presence but I knew he meant Bad Woman. The result of Father's Victorian attitude was that I was much more naïve than I seemed and never knew how to fend off the Forward Pass, even when I saw it coming.

My most noteworthy scrimmage took place just a few months before my first and, to me, historical interview with Kay Van Riper. It had been announced in the newspaper that a showman, famous as a discoverer of new talent, had been engaged by a film studio to produce one of their musical extravaganzas. I sent him a photograph and a letter asking for an audition. My request was granted and I was told to come, not to the picture lot, but to a small public room on the second floor of the Hollywood Roosevelt Hotel. I didn't sleep the night before the appointment. I knew that this man had started more beginners on their way to fame than had even the great David Belasco. If only he would take an interest in me! The thought was so rousing that I could only lie in bed with clenched fists, staring at the ceiling, and hoping.

The next day I was much too excited to wait for the Roosevelt's elevator, but raced up the flight of stairs to keep the engagement. The room was furnished with an upright piano and a few straight chairs. The floor was bare. At one end were French doors that led to a narrow balcony overlooking the now-deserted ballroom. The Great Man proved to be a small man physically, with nearly white hair and misty, gray eyes. His overcoat was nipped in tightly at the waist and he carried a pearl gray hat. I shall never forget that hat. He put it down and ten seconds later I sat on it. I couldn't regain my composure after that, and throughout the interview and the song could feel the hysteria bubbling up in my chest. I sang "Romance" from "The Desert Song," fighting every note of the way for breath. He said I had a beautiful voice and needed only a little private coaching. He dismissed the accompanist, a world-weary fellow who gave me a knowing look, shrugged almost imperceptibly, and left. The impresario and I sat down cosily to talk over plans for my career. He mentioned his most recent discovery, a Mexican starlet, who was having what later proved to have been a very brief success in films.

"She has no talent," he was saying smoothly. "But she is willing— manageable."

His hand rested on my knee. My hysteria burst through in a giggle. His hand crept up my thigh. The giggle shot up about an octave. I leaped to my feet, still tittering. He began to laugh playfully. His arms went around me. Still laughing giddily, I put my hands on his narrow shoulders and pushed. He lost his balance and clutched at me. I teetered forward. He hung on, and we glided in a sort of reverse tango right across the smooth floor and out onto the balcony, where our progress halted at the rail. The Great Man was not only small but also limber. He went into a backbend with the agility of an adagio dancer. In this position, arched over the balcony rail, he caught a glimpse of that hardwood dance floor fifteen feet below and paled.

"For God's sake, let me go!" he cried. "Let me go!"

I released my hold and he sprang out of the danger zone and back into the room where he snatched up his mashed fedora and darted to the door.

TUNE IN TOMORROW

I never saw the Great Man again.

Nothing remotely like that ever happened to me in all the five years I worked in California radio and I never heard the other actresses complain about it, either. When I started my new career I was too young to appreciate or even notice the youthful innocence all around me, and as for the absence of the grim rapers, I never thought about it at all. Nevertheless, it was a basic condition of the radio field and it extended not only to the local stations but through the networks and advertising agencies as well.

Network radio was becoming a thing to conjure with in that year of 1932; many events occurred in the world of the unseen performer more important than my debut. Although CBS and NBC were babies of five and six years, respectively, their programming already foreshadowed the shape of things to come. It was the season that Fred Allen started his first radio series and Ed Wynn put on his Firechief's hat and sent his famous giggle coast to coast for Texaco. "The Maxwell House Show Boat," with Lanny Ross and Charlie Winninger, had its premiere in October. Jack Benny and Ethel Shutta made their commercial debuts for Canada Dry. And Rudy Vallee changed and expanded the format of his Fleischmann's Yeast program to create one of the first of the great variety shows. These star-spangled shows were produced in New York. From Chicago something less glamorous but even more enduring was seeping out. In October, backed by the folksy sound of a mouth-organ, a midwestern voice introduced "Just Plain Bill—Barber of Hartville," and one of the earliest of the soap operas was born. That harmonica was not to give its dying bleat until October, 1955. Chicago, too, saw the birth on June 29, 1932, of the delightful comedy serial "Vic and Sade." (Remember Mr. Gumpox, the garbage man, and the Lodge of the Sacred Stars of the Milky Way?)

Radio was bursting from bud to full bloom but it was doing it east of the Mississippi. Because network line charges were much higher on programs originating in the West than on those coming from the East, Hollywood was brushed but lightly by this spate of activity. This situation was not whim on the part of the networks. It had its basis in the complicated structure of the great chains. The radio programs did not go flashing through the ether from one big center to another. They went, prosaically enough, on wires provided by the telephone company. The affiliated stations in New York City were what might be called the flagships of the various chains. Each of them had a wire connected to a terminal point on West Street in New York, known as N.R. (a telegraph identification call used to clear trouble on the line). N.R. sent the sound to other terminal points in nearby cities, where it would be passed on to the following station on the hookup. The system, called the "Round Robin," was divided into segments—Eastern, Pacific Network, Dixie Leg, Rocky Mountain, and so on.

Like most great twentieth-century innovations, it functioned perfectly—except for the human element involved. In the Round Robin this margin for error was vast—thousands of technicians all over the continent awaited a signal to put this plug in or pull that plug out. Most of the line problems seemed to originate in the area around Albuquerque or Amarillo. "Having trouble getting over the Rockies," the New York engineers would say—and I used to picture atmospheric disturbances as causing the delay. Not necessarily. It could have been some drowsy engineer neglecting or confusing the plugs. One wild time in Chicago, however, the NBC and CBS radio networks found themselves simultaneously, if briefly, broadcasting the exact same comedy show. Though radio has been edged aside now by TV, and a lot of technology has changed, old-fashioned human nature has not. Modern radio listeners must have been baffled when, during President Johnson's visit to Manila in 1967, NBC's Brad Crandall said, "The next voice you hear will be that of the President of the United States." There was a five-second pause—and on came Ed Sullivan! A telephone employee in San Francisco had confused CBS *TV* audio with NBC *radio*.

Perhaps the most stimulating of all line mix-ups occurred back in 1948 during a broadcast of "The Romance of Helen Trent" when I was playing the villainous Cynthia Swanson. Helen "set out to prove that a woman can have romance at thirty-five . . . and even beyond!" She had been working on this project since 1933. Her system was to promise much and give absolutely nothing. As a result, she had had over the years a host of suitors who entered the story for a few months and then retired forever. There was one dogged soul, however, who had been in pursuit since the beginning. As played by David Gothard (a vigorous actor in everything else he did), Gil Whitney had the honeysuckle-dripping voice of a perennially suffering hero. "Helen—Helen," he would moan, "What about *us*? Don't I mean anything to you any more?"

"Gil, I don't know what to say to you," the heroine (played by Julie Stevens, an actress so accomplished that she made even Helen seem real) would counter.

"My darling, my darling," groaned Gil on this particular day, "what can I do?"

"Ah, for Chrissakes, lay the dame and get it over with," said a voice deep from the intestinal tract of the CBS Round Robin. Graphic advice followed—where, why, and with what. The voice did not reach into

Studio 21 where we were working, so none of the "Helen Trent" company heard it. Millions of American housewives did, however, and so did personnel in the control booth. After a stunned moment of suspended animation, they sprang into action, and soon men were checking channels all over the place. The romance counselor could have been anywhere—from Arkansas to Vermont—someone working on a telephone wire, an engineer, or an announcer who had left a microphone wide open, plugged in and ready to feed the entire Round Robin. Suddenly, up he popped again—this time to tell Helen some home truths about herself in his peculiarly scatological vocabulary. Then he disappeared forever from the life of Helen Trent and the homes of several million startled listeners.

The mystery was never solved and, happily, never repeated. Helen went her romance-seeking way with Gil drooling after until June 24, 1960, when she left the air—aged sixty-two, as nearly as we could figure, and still a virgin.

In fairness to the telephone and broadcasting companies, it must be said that such incidents were remarkably rare when you consider the hundreds of stations affiliated with the four major networks and the millions of feet of wire involved in the nervous system of the Round Robin. It was a smooth-singing bird, as a rule, although in 1932 it had a serious limitation. It faced stubbornly in one direction. It was not until 1937 that the telephone company could provide a reversible channel. The lines would transmit only one way, from east to west. This meant that to blanket the country from the Coast, a separate channel had to be set up to bring the program east, where it could be fed into the Round Robin. This is why the line charges were higher on shows originating from the Coast. At the end of 1932, for example, when Eddie Cantor insisted on moving his Chase and Sanborn program to Hollywood, the move added $2,100 to the weekly budget. It was no wonder that sponsors avoided West Coast broadcasting. Even so, we were beginning to get visiting shows. A star would come to California to shoot a picture, and for the duration of his movie-making his radio program would be broadcast from there.

We had one perennial representative of the Big Time, however—the "Shell Show." It began with us and it stayed with us. At first it was heard only on the Pacific wing of NBC's Round Robin, and at that time its announcer was Rush Hughes and its orchestra leader George Stoll. A comedy team, Yahbut and Cheerily (in real life, Will Wright and Jem Parker), were featured. In the spring of 1935 Al Jolson took over as master of ceremonies and Victor Young (composer of "Sweet Sue," "My Foolish Heart," and, many years later, the score for the film "Around the World in 80 Days") conducted the music. The show's name was then changed to "Shell Chateau" (or "Schelch-Toe," as Jolson used to say) and the oil company bought time on the full network, coast to coast. The format remained essentially the same. It was a variety show with some music, some comedy, and a dramatic sketch, featuring a guest film star.

Gale Gordon told me about it one day during a break in a "Coronets" rehearsal. On the back of my script he wrote the names of the two producers—Dick Weal and Cal Kuhl, care of J. Walter Thompson, Shell's advertising agency, which produced the program.

Then Gale said the words that made my pulse quicken. "Network shows pay as much as twenty-five dollars."

If anyone was passing out that much money for just one broadcast, I wanted to get right in line. The average fee for a local show was $5. Fifteen was the most I had ever received and I was currently working on two programs that paid only three. The first of these was sponsored by the Lyons Moving Company and slyly titled "Moving Stories of Life!" We recorded these dramas on sixteen-inch wax discs from which pressings were made and sent to small stations throughout the country. In areas that were not serviced by Lyons, the recording company sold the pressings to other moving-and-storage firms. We youngsters who made up the radio talent pool noticed that the owners of the recording companies were driving expensive automobiles, but it never occurred to us that, with a cost of $25 for the master record and a cast cost of $15 for five actors, a show that was sold to several hundred stations at $20 apiece would net quite a profit. So, we went on humbly accepting our minuscule salaries.

My second $3 job was a comedy series about two crotchety Civil War veterans. The author, a Mr. Dugan, who played both of the old men, also hopped about during the scenes to make the sound effects. (On one occasion, while reading aloud from a script propped on a music stand, he munched on an apple, opened and closed a door, tapped on a typewriter, rang a telephone bell, and fired a gun.) I was the daughter of one of his characters and together he and I made up the entire company. We recorded the five shows each Friday night and Mr. Dugan spent the intervening days in an old jalopy, jouncing from one small radio station to another as salesman for the series.

From where I stood with Mr. Dugan and the moving company, $25 per show looked like the mother lode of a diamond mine. So the morning after my chat with Gale I wrote a letter to J. Walter Thompson, requesting an opportunity to read for them. On a last-minute hunch, I enclosed a picture of myself, taken by an amateur photographer friend a few weeks before. The dramatic lighting, which created brooding shadows, revealed a pudgy-faced kid, her curls plastered into a vigorously unbecoming hairdo, staring malevolently into the camera. I had prettier pictures, but this, I felt, expressed the real me—a femme fatale. I can only imagine that the agency people sent for me out of curiosity.

The day of the appointment I awoke with a runny nose and no voice. But I decided to face the situation out. There is nothing like having to pay the rent to get you on the bus in the morning. With my morning coffee I developed four notes in the baritone range, then set out for the tiny private house where J. Walter Thompson, one of the largest agencies in the world, had its radio office. At that time, the full West Coast staff consisted of one secretary and two director-producers.

Dick Weal was an exception to what I have said about youth in the Hollywood radio field. I remember thinking of him as quite elderly; now I realize he must have been about thirty-eight. He was a dark, heavy-set, balding man with a ready laugh. Calvin Kuhl fell into the usual pattern. He was boyish and blond, with a cowlick that projected and, in moments of stress, trembled from the crown of his head.

The part, I learned, was the lead opposite Edward Everett Horton in a snippet culled from Noel Coward's play, "Private Lives." Dick Weal gave me a copy of it. I studied it hastily, trying to remember everything Father had said about playing comedy, and then I read it aloud for them. When I finished, both men were laughing.

"I think you're perfect," Dick Weal said, "and from the smirk I see on my associate's face, I gather he agrees with me. Come to the NBC studios tomorrow. We want you to read for Mr. Horton."

NBC had as yet no broadcasting facilities of its own in Hollywood and the studios of its affiliated stations (KFI and KECA) over the Packard showrooms were too cramped to accommodate "big name" shows with their invited audiences, so the network had rented space inside the RKO film studio, where a small auditorium was built.

When I arrived the next day, Mr. Horton was already there. We read the scene together and he said in that charming way of his, "Splendid, splendid."

They asked me to wait in an anteroom while the two agency men and the star discussed the matter. The door didn't close properly and I could hear most of what they said. It seemed that they had intended to have a double star bill that week—Mr. Horton and a film actress whose fame had steadily dwindled since the advent of talking pictures a few years before. My audition had caused them to waver in their decision. Mr. Weal believed the film star had a certain name value and would be willing to do the part for about $250. Mr. Horton said firmly, "You'll

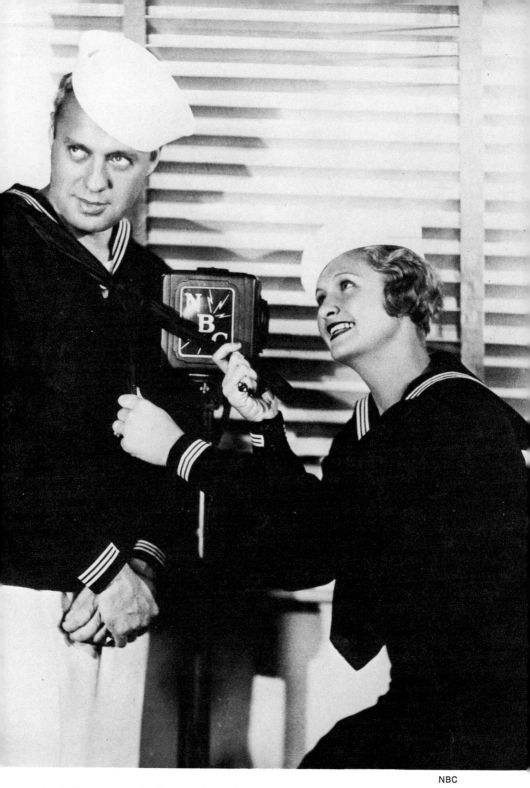

Jack Benny on his first radio series in 1932 with co-star Ethel Shutta.

Alan Mowbray as Jeeves and Edward Everett Horton as Bertie Wooster on "Forecast" in 1940.

Arthur Hughes in title role of "Just Plain Bill," the first soap opera that caught on with the public.

never get a contralto quality like the one you just heard—a beautiful voice—good actress, too."

My first thought was, Oh, that dear, dear man! My second was, Contralto quality?—Who? Me? It was the cold, of course. I struggled with my conscience. Should I tell them I had what Kay Van Riper had called a light, silvery voice, now obscured by laryngitis? I thought of how kind they all were, especially Mr. Horton. Then I thought of how unkind the landlord was going to be if the rent wasn't paid. Expediency triumphed over honesty. I said nothing. I have been sure ever since that I owed my first network show to a bad cold in the head.

The "Shell Show" was a Saturday night affair but we rehearsed for a couple of days before. In addition to the run-through on mike with the director, Mr. Horton and I went over our sketch many times. He liked to rehearse. While the orchestra or Yahbut and Cheerily were doing their bits in the studio, we would be out in the hall polishing away on ours.

Dick Weal informed me that we were going to do a "remote" broadcast from the Los Angeles County Fair at Pomona and asked me to wear an evening gown, to lend importance to the proceedings. Accordingly, late on Saturday afternoon, I put on a long, pink velvet gown and gold slippers. A friend drove me to Pomona, and I waded into the fair grounds. A good shower earlier in the day had left the place one vast mud puddle. It was the closing night of the fair. Most of the poultry had been bedded down, all the pigs had received their awards, and the great prize-winning bull was waiting to be carted off in his private car, his feet not nearly so muddy as mine. The sun had set and a sharp California frost hung in the air. The equipment for broadcasting had been set up in the big arena earlier in the afternoon.

I met Mr. Horton in one of the temporary fair buildings and we ran over our lines again. Rush Hughes, the announcer, came through on his way out to put the show on the air. There was no loudspeaker in our little room, so we couldn't hear Rush's opening, but the muted sound of Georgie Stoll's orchestra did reach our ears. About twenty minutes later Dick Weal stuck his head in the door and said, "You'd better come out now. Your spot's coming up."

Mr. Horton glanced at his script and said, "I don't think we need this, do you?" and tossed it aside. I felt it was only sporting to do the same, so I placed mine on top of the now-discarded leopard coat, which I had needed even inside the semiheated building, and stepped out into the icy air.

It wasn't until we were struggling through the slush on our way to the microphone that I realized fully what I had done. I had made no effort to memorize the lines, and had no idea whether I knew them or not. This was my first chance on radio's Big Time. If I ruined the star spot on the "Shell Show" my career would die aborning. I wanted desperately to slosh back for my script but there wasn't time. I found myself blinded by a blaze of light, and in the darkness beyond, for all I knew, were seated a thousand people. The spectators who had lingered for the trotting races (a feature of the fair) were to have the added treat of seeing Edward Everett Horton and a girl in pink velvet and ostrich feathers, standing up to their ankles in mud and reciting excerpts from Noel Coward to a low background of cackling and grunting.

When I opened my mouth I found that my laryngitic baritone had risen to a nasal whine. My head felt hot and stuffy and the huge arc lights were making rainbows before my runny eyes. I was shivering with cold and the terror of forgetting my lines. The minute Mr. Horton began to speak, however, everything came right with my world. He was such a surefooted actor, I knew that no matter what happened he could bring the thing off. It was like a strong, steadying hand. Halfway through the skit a wave of panic broke over me again. The words sounded unfamiliar. I was completely lost. Then Mr. Horton looked right at me and threw me a cue that I recognized as part of the script. I replied with my line and we went on. He had been ad-libbing and with fine effect. His digression did not interrupt the flow of a well-written scene by Coward. The scene had already been so tortured and truncated to fit into radio's arbitrary time pattern that any inspiration breathed into it from any source could act only as a restorative.

I worked with Edward Everett Horton several times afterward and the same thing always happened. He didn't change the little sketches but he embroidered around them and always with good solid laughs as a result. He never left the other actors up in the air. He changed things only within his own speeches and always came back solidly with the cue. He also had what seemed to be a built-in time mechanism. In the programs I played with him afterward we never once ran over or under the allotted time. In those early days of radio he was one of the big names most in demand.

Hollywood network radio drew largely on motion pictures for its stars. The Silent Era was but a few years behind us and some of the early players had survived in talking films only because they were allowed to make short scenes over and over until something presentable was achieved. The "now-or-never" element of the theater and radio was missing from their experience. They often were terrified of the microphone, thrown by the time element, afraid to try to read something at sight, and obsessed by a thousand other fears. Edward Everett Horton, a sound theater background behind him, wasn't afraid of anything.

TUNE IN TOMORROW

I don't know why we were out amid the livestock to do the "Shell Show." It is one of the questions about radio that have gone unanswered through the years. I have never understood the preoccupation with "remote" broadcasting. "On-the-spot" broadcasting I can see. That is different. You go to the area where an event of interest is taking place and you broadcast it as it happens—the Olympics, for example. But to gather up all the appurtenances of a radio show and produce an effect at the top of a mountain or the bottom of a coal mine that could be much better done in the network's cosy studio is a gimmick that eludes me.

In addition to a mild attack of pneumonia, I got $25 for that "remote" in Pomona. One tiny thing nagged at the back of my mind. It was that conversation about the fading movie star. She would have got two hundred and fifty had they decided on her instead of me. My gratitude for my twenty-five was somewhat, and quite literally, watered down.

CHAPTER IV

Twinkle, Twinkle, Little Stars

Memory makes strange selections. From among the programs that occupied my next twenty-five years, my mind has evidently decided to file most of the "first occasions" and, unless something regrettable or downright disastrous occurred, to reject nearly everything else.

This is not surprising when you consider the hundreds of shows a radio actor would appear on in each year. In 1949 Ted Osborne, who started his kilocycle career a few months before I did, tried with the aid of account books and publicity clippings to estimate the number of broadcasts on which he had appeared. He stopped counting when he passed the eight thousand mark.

Total recall is a helpful thing but forgetfulness has its uses, too. I should hate to wake in the night with fragments of "Linda's First Love" or "John's Other Wife" floating around in my head. The fact is that, although I talked into that microphone steadily for a quarter of a century, I have now blissfully forgotten much of what I said.

I am able to recall with photographic precision that first network program, but haven't the foggiest notion of what the second one was. It may have been another "Shell Show." That program became a good source of income for me. Whenever Edward Everett Horton was the guest star I would be given the lead opposite him without having to read for the part, but on other occasions I would find myself in competition with my best friends. The girls I faced most often were Barbara Luddy and Duane Thompson. We were the "silvery" voices. The rest of the actresses had alto and mezzo tones.

Duane was a bubbly little comedienne. Slim, about five feet two,

"Grand Hotel," top, in 1933. Don Ameche is at mike with, left, Betty Winkler (later the lead on "Rosemary") and Anne Seymour (later the star of "Mary Marlin"). Hanley Stafford, bottom, was Daddy to Fanny Brice's Baby Snooks.

Les Tremayne and Barbara Luddy on "The First Nighter" about 1940. The program, broadcast from Chicago, first starred Don Ameche and June Meredith.

with a round, pert face, she had once been a featured player in Christie comedies and leading lady for the silent film star Charles Ray.

Barbara was even tinier—just four feet eleven. She had been off on a tour of Australia in a play starring Leo Carillo. On its return to Hollywood, the company was to open at Henry Duffy's El Capitan Theater. It arrived to a great flurry of publicity, a triumphal opening, and rave reviews in the papers. The next night Barbara trotted jubilantly down to the theater to find it plastered with bankruptcy notices.

The padlocked door of the El Capitan was Barbara's introduction to the Depression. She got on intimate terms with it immediately. When her savings had dwindled to the vanishing point, Gale Gordon, an old friend from previous and more lasting Duffy productions, suggested that she turn her attention to radio. There was an opportunity for a young couple on a local station. The show went on at 8 A.M. with rehearsal at 6:30. There were no salaries attached to the enterprise, but Gale was sure that it was the open door to the entertainment world of the future. He convinced Barbara and they started their early-morning vigil. It was six months before they landed their first paying radio jobs— "English Coronets."

A few years later Barbara reached one of the most important positions open to a radio actress. She was chosen to play with Don Ameche on "The First Nighter" program and was taken by the sponsor, Campana Italian Balm, to Chicago, where she stayed on with Les Tremayne as her co-star long after Ameche had deserted radio for a film career.

We of the "silvery" tones, plus Margaret Brayton (a light mezzo), met one afternoon in the antechamber of the NBC studio to compete once more for the lead on the "Shell Show." This time the star was to be Francis Lederer. I was asked to read first.

When I entered the studio the Czechoslovakian star threw me a smile—all white teeth and dancing black eyes—that made me step back and catch my breath. What a dazzling young male! He had recently come from brilliant successes in the London and New York theaters and was already the rage of Hollywood. During the next few years he was to appear often on the "Shell Show" and Dick Weal always referred to him as the "winsome Czech."

The skit was another dehydrated and capsulated scene from a play —this time "The Pursuit of Happiness." After we had run through it together, Mr. Lederer said, "Wonderful!" pirouetted around me, picked up his belongings and prepared to leave. Dick lumbered out of the control booth.

"There are some other girls waiting to read for you," he said anxiously.

"Since the first one is perfect," said Mr. Lederer, "why waste time listening to others, who can't possibly be as good?" The star headed for the door.

"These girls have been waiting all this time, Mr. Lederer," I said. "They deserve a chance to be heard."

He paused, then gave a boyish laugh and tossed his hat and coat on a nearby chair. "Very well," he said. "We will hear them all."

I went outside and relaxed while, one at a time, the other actresses disappeared into the soundproof studio. I had the job, and I also had the smug satisfaction of having done "the decent thing." Margaret was the last to go in.

When she came back we chatted for awhile until, as time wore on, even I grew silent and nervous. At last Dick came out of the studio. He walked straight to where I sat and stood staring at me for a minute before he said flatly, "Barbara got the part."

That gave me something to think about. I decided to talk it over with Jane Darwell when we met at a rehearsal of "Coronets" that next week. Jane was an older character actress whom I had always admired. At that time she was just beginning a brilliant film career, which reached a high point a few years later when she co-starred with Henry Fonda in Steinbeck's "The Grapes of Wrath." I told her what had happened and asked for a frank appraisal of my work. She thought a long time before she gave her opinion.

"You and Barbara sound a little bit alike," she said. "Your voices have about the same pitch and timbre but you don't work alike. You are crisp and clear in your delivery of lines. And that's good. She has something different." Jane stopped for a second and thought again. "It's warmth," she said finally. "You're sincere and honest but her work is more intimate."

I made it my business to hear the "Shell Show" that week. I had to find out what Barbara had seen in the part that had escaped my notice. The story concerned a Puritan girl and a dashing Hussar. I had read it as a prim young Miss. Barbara did too—but underneath was a husky, cuddly quality that made you wonder how long the Puritan upbringing was going to hold out against nature. I had to concede it was better that way—much better.

Mother, who, since my debut in the medium, had become an avid radio listener, offered me some advice.

"There's a girl in Chicago who is marvelous," she said. "The best radio technique I've heard. The program is 'Grand Hotel' and her name is Anne Seymour."

So I began listening to "Grand Hotel." This actress, too, had that warm quality. *Intimacy*, I decided, was the keynote of radio acting.

Mother had another suggestion. "I want you to study Amos 'n Andy—especially the way Amos carries on a one-sided telephone conversation. You can tell exactly what the person at the other end of the wire is supposed to be saying."

Bit by bit, in that first year, I was laying a groundwork that would stand me in good stead many years later. Next to that intimate quality came the ability to give a feeling of action and environment through the voice alone. When I was supposed to be lifting a weight I learned to let the strain show in my voice. I would speak more loudly in an outdoor scene than I would in a fireside conversation at home. It became natural to add these little touches, which are not needed in a visual medium, and the technique was susceptible to much variation and subtlety. It was in this type of imagination that the top radio people excelled, and not one of them ever set a scene vocally better than Amos 'n Andy.

The next time Francis Lederer starred on the "Shell Show" I won the audition and played opposite him. The scene was from "Autumn Crocus." I played a young woman who is brushed by the wings of romance but who retreats before it into what you know is going to be a lifetime of loneliness and spinsterhood.

At the end of the "Autumn Crocus" skit there was a brief on-air interview with the star. Lederer wanted to add some material to this seemingly informal chat, which was actually carefully written and had been passed on by the sponsor. Dick explained that it would be absolutely impossible under the oil company's policy. Lederer seemed to acquiesce but once on the air he laughingly tossed in everything he had been told to leave out. Consternation filled the control booth. There was nothing they could do to stop him. Dick revised his estimate of the "winsome Czech" then and there. "That—that *bouncing* Czech!" he growled.

What had been said was innocent enough, I thought—a little anecdote about the actor's youth in Prague. The excitement was caused by the fact that it *had not been passed by the sponsor*. This incident was my first encounter with Corporation Neurosis. The colossal companies, suddenly flung into show business, were as skittish as an elderly maiden lady who has wandered into the men's room by mistake—always on tiptoe, always expecting the worst. Years later I used to scan with amazement the morality and clean-speech clauses that were included in even the simplest of my contracts with General Foods, wondering at what I must not say or do that would cast a blight over Post Toasties.

Prudential Life Insurance was just as jittery. During its sponsorship of "When a Girl Marries," the character I was playing once loaned a fur jacket to her maid. Corporate memos drifted down like snow. Prudential, primarily a life insurance company, offered no personal property policies but reasoned thus: If listeners started lending furs to their maids, and the maids lost them, it would react on *other* insurance companies and ultimately affect the entire field. I and my silvery tones, the company feared, would skyrocket insurance rates all over the counrty.

This overcautiousness on the part of the otherwise big and the bold was amusing in those early days. In the Joe McCarthy Era it was less so. It was the spongy soil that nourished the growth of that noxious weed, The Blacklist.

One other "Shell Show" stands out in my mind. I was listening to it in my home one Saturday night when my telephone rang.

"Mary Jane," said a calm voice. "This is Cal Kuhl. Can you do 'Shell' for me?"

"You mean next week?"

"No. Now."

"But it's on the air."

"We know that," he said. "Please get over here as fast as you can."

I scrambled into an evening gown while my sister ran next door to borrow a neighbor's car and we drove at breakneck speed to the studio. As I sprinted into the entrance hall, I could hear the sound of an orchestra and a singer from behind the closed door of the studio. A frowzy figure staggered up from a stool and accosted me. It was the star of that week's sketch—a great stage personality who had made an outstanding success in films despite the fact that she was known to have occasional bouts with the bottle.

"Whosis?" she demanded. "Another singer? Too many damn singers! When d'I go on?"

A young man who was standing by with a cup of black coffee took her elbow with his free hand and tried to lead her back to the stool.

"Now, now, now," he said.

"Now, now, now," she mimicked as I slipped past them and through the studio door.

Dick Weal's hand was shaking as he gave me the script and muttered "Penelope." But Cal Kuhl smiled placidly from the control booth and waved me out onto the stage.

The play was Maxwell Anderson's "Elizabeth the Queen." The co-star was Irving Pichel, well known as an actor and a director in both motion pictures and the theater. Margaret Brayton met me as I came out of the wings and gave me a quick briefing as we stood on the stage in full view of the audience. Little dots of perspiration lay under the black curls that fell across her forehead, and her almond-shaped dark blue eyes had widened into roundness. "You're playing my part," she murmured. "I'm doing hers. She passed out."

The announcer was already introducing the sketch.

"—one of the most brilliant of the young radio actresses, Margaret Brayton, will play opposite Mr. Pichel. The scene—."

"What do I do?" I gasped.

"Keep her sweet and young," said Margaret, and we went to join Pichel at the microphone. He threw me a quick smile and I breathed a sigh of gratitude that it was not a silent movie star that we were working with this time. After that I kept my attention on the script, looking ahead as far as I dared to see where my lines occurred and to try to figure out what they meant. I was aware, even so, that Margaret was giving a splendid performance of a difficult role. She was every inch the queen— strong, dominating, yet yearning after the man she was sending to the headsman's block.

After the scene with Penelope, which went smoothly, the two of them played the last tragic moments before the execution of Essex. Pichel's melodious voice gave added beauty to the poet's lines: "Life in prison is very quiet. It leads to thinking . . ." An off-stage door rattled violently and a female voice rose in hooting laughter. In the control booth Cal went dead white and sprang to his feet, his eye roving wildly around the studio. It lit on the drummer in the orchestra and, with a look of agonized appeal, Cal threw a cue. There was a sudden roll of drums, the soundman had the wit to start the tramp of marching feet, and without so much as a "goodby," the Earl of Essex went to his doom.

In spite of the single-mindedness of the dogged little Round Robin, more and more network shows began to drift our way. From the Olympian heights of the Metropolitan Opera, Grace Moore descended to our shore to make some outstanding films—"One Night of Love," "New Moon," and "Love Me Forever." Opera audiences had been plunged into a state of adoration by her performances in "La Boheme" and "Manon," and she was later to return to New York and still greater glory in the Met's revival of Charpentier's "Louise." But now, for the duration of her movie-making, her radio show was to be broadcast from Hollywood.

Since "The Grace Moore Show" was a musical program, the arrival of this songbird from Jellico, Tennessee, was no great boon to the radio actors. Only two of us profited from the situation. Gayne Whitman, who was sending chills up and down spines five nights a week as Chandu, the Magician, was chosen to announce Miss Moore's show, and I was called in a few times to join him in the commercial.

The program also used a local orchestra. The conductor, Harry

Opera star Grace Moore in 1937.

Jackson, was an old friend of mine, and during the six months Miss Moore was with us I saw his hair change from black with a sprinkling of silver to white with just a touch of black.

"Why are you so nervous about the show, Harry?" I asked him once.

"I never know what Grace Moore is going to do," he told me. "We rehearse it one way, and she sings it on the air another. When she gets a high note that feels just right to her she's apt to hang on to it forever. Other times she'll just graze it in passing. It all depends on how she feels."

After that, interest in the broadcast heightened for me as I began to watch for the frenzy that would come over Harry as he signaled the boys to wait—while Miss Moore clung to a surprisingly beautiful sound with the joyous abandon of an angel. She invariably brought down the house.

I never had any personal contact with Miss Moore—unless you can count a pressing of noses as a social introduction. I was standing in the wings, waiting for the dress rehearsal to start, when a voice, loud and accusing in my ear, said, "Ah-ha!"

I whirled around to find myself nose to nose with the star.

"Ah! Ha!" she repeated.

"How do you do, Miss Moore," I replied. She walked away.

"Ha! Ha!" she boomed.

"She's clearing her throat," Gayne explained. "That's all she ever says. I've been here six weeks and she has never said hello, just 'Ha.' "

Miss Moore hummed her way lightly through the "dress" but when we were on the air her voice rang out with ever-increasing beauty and clarity. During an orchestra number in the second half of the show, she retired to her dressing room. When she returned and stood waiting to go on, I noticed that her ankle-length, tight-fitting, black velvet gown had accidentally been twisted around her body and was hiked up nearly to mid-thigh.

"Her dress!" I gasped. "She doesn't *know*. We ought to tell her."

Gayne was unmoved. "She never speaks to me," he said. "Never. Not even in reply to 'Good morning.' I don't see that it's up to me to start a conversation *now*."

So the great opera star walked out to sing "Ci-ri-bi-ri-bin" with her gown pulled halfway up to her middle. Strangely, there was no reaction from the audience, but the already overwrought musicians nearly gave up. Only the string section managed to play at all. The wind instruments threw in the sponge. Their broad grins could not be puckered into playing position. I thought it would be the end of Harry Jackson, who stood waving his arms wildly, desperately, over an almost mute orchestra. Miss Moore sailed through the gay Italian song to a particularly gorgeous note at the end, the studio audience burst into applause, and she swept off. I don't think she ever knew.

One of the early shows to broadcast on a steady basis from Hollywood was the "Camel Caravan." The title is confusing because the cigarette company has used it many times over the years to describe various programs of differing content. In 1934 it followed the usual pattern for a radio variety show: musical numbers, comedy spot, and one dramatic sketch. The emcee at this time was Al Jolson. (It was not until 1935 that he moved over to "Shell Chateau.") The comedy was supplied by Martha Raye, whose mad antics had recently won a firm place for her in films, and by a small, wiry man named Sid Silvers. He had formerly written Jack Benny's show for Canada Dry, but he quit after a disagreement with Mary Livingstone and came west, where he eventually joined the Camel production as both writer and performer.

My first appearance with this group was to play the part of the little sister opposite Robert Taylor in a scene taken from "The Valiant" —a melancholy tale in which the hero goes to his execution after bidding his sister farewell. It made a mournful contrast to the general zaniness that opened and closed "Camel Caravan."

Most network productions required two or three days of rehearsal. On the first one, when I arrived at the theater that had been preempted by CBS for its audience shows, I thought the place was deserted. Then I heard a voice say, "Hello, there," from the orchestra pit.

I looked down and saw Martha Raye slumped on the end of her spine, her feet propped up on a chair. She was studying a piece of music.

"Must be early," she said. "Joint's empty." She disappeared behind her music again.

The rest of the company finally arrived and Robert Redd, the director, announced that rehearsal would begin with a trio for Miss Raye, Jolson, and Silvers—a parody of grand opera using "Yes, We Have No Bananas" as a theme. Martha sprang to her feet and into a flurry of activity that left the others dazed. She was like a high-tension wire. She never stopped.

She wore a beautifully tailored pair of gray slacks and a white silk shirt. Because of the difference in time between the West and East Coasts the night shows were always broadcast from Hollywood in the late afternoon, but we wore evening dress for the benefit of the audiences. Mr. Taylor turned up in a dinner jacket for the performance. So did Silvers and Jolson. Miss Raye, however, stayed in her slacks.

The program was a great success, to judge from the audience reaction, and after it was over I caught a last glimpse of Martha Raye, standing on a chair surrounded by a crowd of admirers in the theater alley. She was delighting her fans by singing "Bananas" as she grabbed up the autograph books, signed them, and tossed them back to their owners. Most of us who had put in a whole day in the studio were glad to relax and start wearily homeward, but she looked ready and even eager to start the entire performance over again right there in the street.

A few weeks later when I turned up to play opposite Boris Karloff in "Death Takes a Holiday" (the producers seemed determined to provide tombstone ballast for the otherwise lightweight skiff that was the "Camel Caravan"), Martha Raye greeted me as if I were an old friend.

"Hi 'ya," she said, and with no further preamble added: "They tell me I've got to dress for this damn thing from now on."

That day she rehearsed in slacks but retired before the performance to reappear in a lovely black lace dress and tiny feathered hat. Her wild energy was not affected by the change, and she still danced and clowned around right up until air time. During a sketch she was playing with Sid Silvers in which they were supposed to be having a row, he gave her, while we were on the air, a slight, unrehearsed push. She whirled around and gave him a good big push. He pushed her again. Before they reached the last line they were locked in combat and fell to the floor, where they wrestled around in front of the microphone until the startled director got himself together and cued in the orchestra.

The audience loved it. Sid Silvers seemed rather shaken, but Martha Raye didn't mind a bit. As I passed her on my way out she was cheerfully examining the torn lace of her lovely dress. "Wouldn't you know," she said, "the first time I get dressed up for the show somebody slugs me?"

The next week the "Caravan" featured in its dramatic spot a wealthy, rather haughty star. At the first rehearsal the Hollywood beauty turned up with a full retinue, including a maid, a secretary, and a chauffeur bearing a Pekinese named Fifi on a silk cushion. The glamorous lady was famous for the beautiful diamonds she possessed and she had chosen to wear a lot of them. A particularly dazzling bracelet glittered beneath the cuff of her mink coat.

The radio actors were wide-eyed. If those were rehearsal togs, they wondered, what was she planning to wear for the show?

The following day, Fifi was already comfortably established on the cushion at her mistress' feet when Martha Raye arrived. She, too, was wearing a mink coat, but over it she had draped a silver fox scarf. What looked like several pounds of dime-store jewelry adorned her bosom and she was leading a gigantic mongrel by a frayed length of rope.

Sid Silvers, Martha Raye, and Al Jolson on "Camel Caravan" in the 1930's.

"Come, Rollo," she cooed. "I want you to meet Fifi. I know you two are going to be *great friends.*"

The producer overtook the enraged beauty just as she was on the point of driving away in her limousine. After a prolonged discussion and much pleading on his part, she finally agreed to return to the studio to fulfill her obligation to appear on the show. Fifi, however, was adamant. She stayed in the car with the chauffeur.

One of the best radio programs ever broadcast from the Coast was "Kraft Music Hall," starring Bing Crosby, with John Scott Trotter's orchestra and Bob Burns—who played a bazooka and talked about his Arkansas relatives, and who would be described today as a "stand-up" comedian. My part on the program was a modest one—to help Ken Carpenter sell the cheese.

I had always listened to Bing Crosby's broadcasts because I was enamored of his silky, insinuating song style and the rolling resonance of that baritone voice. But every time he began to talk, even for the brief introduction of a number, I thought he sounded artificial and clumsy. I could picture the printed page behind every word and breath.

At the first broadcast of "Kraft Music Hall" I glanced over the script with dismay. The singer had many pages of dialogue—as host and with guest stars. If the agency people were going to let him read that material in that wooden way of his, I thought, the series was going to be one big flop.

On the air, to my amazement, a whole new personality emerged—warm, congenial, witty—a Bing Crosby I had never heard before. He didn't seem to be reading at all, but having a comfortable chat with an old friend in the privacy of his home. As his first interview with Trotter ended and the musician walked away, Bing tossed a line after him that got a big laugh from the audience. My God, I thought, he's even ad-libbing—and on the very first show! I ran through the pages of my script. No, there it was on the mimeographed page—the line that had come out so naturally I couldn't believe it had been planned in advance.

The same thing happened many times in the months that followed. I would have sworn that the star had invented a remark on the spur of the moment, but I always found it there in the script.

The authors of the variety shows invariably remained anonymous but I was eager to learn the identity of this one, so I asked Cal Kuhl at the next rehearsal. He pointed to a suntanned, smallish man, whom I had noticed wandering around, stooping forward slightly, his hands in his pockets. His name was Carroll Carroll.

Radio developed a small group of glamor writers in its day. Mostly they flourished during the war years, writing documentaries, experi-

Bing Crosby is host to Jerry Lester and Mary Martin on a 1942 "Kraft Music Hall."

mental, unsponsored "sustainers," and paeans for The American Way. Their work has been published in book form and included in anthologies and textbooks on radio writing. At their best they wrote tellingly for the ear, achieving the wonderful balance of dialogue, sound, and music that made authentic radio drama. On the other hand, much of their output might nowadays seem self-conscious, pretentious, or even windy.

The writers of the commercial shows received less acclaim. They often took the easy way out and, especially when working on the variety show, indulged in formula and gag writing. Carroll Carroll, writing a purely commercial comedy show, was hedged about with the usual agency and sponsor restrictions, yet within those narrow limits he achieved what to my mind was near perfection. From its earliest broadcast, "Kraft Music Hall" had that light and individual style of humor that we later came to associate with Bing Crosby. The lines seemed to catch the exact rhythms of the crooner's natural speech. I thought then that the "Kraft" scripts were head and shoulders above the other great variety shows, and it's my bet they would stand up today. Some of their inspired nuttiness still lingers in my mind:

"Are you implying that I'm fat?" asks John Scott Trotter.

"No," muses Bing. "I just think you might take a little Scott off your Trotter."

And Bing, on another occasion, to dashing adventurer Errol Flynn:

"Pardon me, but I think your swash is unbuckled."

Crosby was, of course, destined to be a great star no matter what the obstructions encountered on the way. But it is my opinion, based only on what I heard and saw, that his fortuitous meeting with Carroll Carroll shortened the process, removed the obstacles, and revealed a talent that perhaps even Crosby himself was not aware that he had.

In the studio Bing Crosby seemed easygoing, warm, and engaging. On holidays he invariably invited everyone associated with the show to a nearby bar for a drink all around to mark the occasion. His invitations were all-inclusive. Even the young female purveyor of cheese was not left out. This democratic generosity was in marked contrast to some of the other stars we worked with in those days. Everyone liked Bing Crosby. He was full of humor and charm. In the war he was one of the entertainers who gave generously of his time to troops overseas.

Ed Rice, an executive with the J. Walter Thompson agency, once told me about a trip the singer had made to the front lines. Crosby and his driver had gone off by themselves in a jeep. When they returned and described where they had been, the commanding officer was aghast.

"Good Lord—that's enemy-held territory," he said.

"Well, we had it for awhile," said Bing.

CHAPTER V

The Living End

It was the boast of the radio networks, in the late twenties and early thirties, that every effect heard on their facilities was *live*. Not *live* as opposed to *dead*, but *live* as opposed to *recorded*. So in the early days every sound you heard on CBS or either of NBC's chains, Red or Blue, was created just at the second you heard it.

This ruling pushed production to elaborate lengths. If a bugle call was needed, a bugler had to be brought to the studio and told to toot. If a lion's roar was required, it was not decreed that you bring a lion to the studio and twist its tail, but someone had to be found who could, literally, roar like a lion.

Before NBC moved its New York studios to Radio City in 1932, it was housed at 711 Fifth Avenue. There, one entire side of a large studio was given over to the making of railroad noises. A huge bell from a real locomotive was suspended in the room. There was an enormous apparatus to create the chug-chug of the engine and the click-click of wheels, as well as blasts of steam. And attached to the outside corner of the building, over Fifty-fifth Street and Fifth Avenue, hung an honest-to-God locomotive whistle, with a microphone placed just inside the building to pick up the sound of its blast. And blast it did, once a week, for a show dealing with the early history of the railroads called "The Empire Builders."

As time went on, and sales increased, and the pressures of production grew accordingly, the networks gradually relaxed their *live* ruling. It was never repealed, just forgotten, possibly as the networks relinquished control and the advertising agencies began to take over, sending their own directors to the studio and casting the programs in their own offices. About the same time, too, libraries of recorded sound effects first became available. The big chains remained adamant about music and the spoken word, but a railroad or the crash of a falling redwood tree could be picked up off a record.

Some of the agency people, however, clung to the old way of creating sound effects. Mrs. Dorothy McCann of McCann-Erickson, producer of "Death Valley Days," was one of these. She liked to *see* the effect as well as hear it. Keene Crockett handled sound for that show during the thirties and forties. His act consisted of balancing on his right foot while his left was stuck in a wooden box mounted on casters. He rolled the latter vigorously back and forth, simultaneously striking the table rhythmically with two coconut shells strapped to his hands and leaning perilously forward to whinny into the microphone. That gave the effect of a horse and wagon. Mrs. McCann was probably right in preferring *live* effects in this case. The speed could be better controlled than if the sound had been on a record. The horses or mules (the sponsor was Twenty Mule Team Borax) could be slowed down or spurred ahead on definite cues in the text.

While the networks were startling Fifth Avenue pedestrians with the shriek of a train whistle and making the sound of rain by pouring birdseed into a hopper on top of a monkey cage, where it fell through a small hole, bounced off a swinging Ping-Pong ball, hit a sheet of tin, fell to a whirling wooden disc, was knocked off by a windshield wiper, dropped into a berry basket, then to a box on the floor, which had to be watched carefully by one of NBC's soundmen, who dropped the seed back into the hopper at the top before the box on the floor overflowed—while all this was going on in the big, rich networks, the little independent stations, unaffiliated with a broadcasting chain, were simply dropping a needle on a record and bringing forth not only the sound of rain but complete dramatic shows and recorded commercials as well.

Syndicated recordings formed a large part of the programming in small stations all over the country. ("Chandu, the Magician," for example, was a recorded show.) The owners of these syndicated recordings accumulated great wealth. The actors who made the records accumulated ulcers.

When I started recording radio programs early in 1932, it was necessary to cut the show directly on the wax matrix. Any flaw in the wax itself, or a mistake made by an actor, engineer, soundman, or the man in control of prerecorded music, would mean stopping and starting all over again at the beginning.

If we were working at the Freeman Lang studios in Hollywood (one of the most successful recording companies on the Coast), a new wax, looking very much like a three-inch-thick cheesecake, was selected from a half dozen or so waiting on shelves in an open-faced cabinet, and the work proceeded without further delay. At some of the smaller companies, however, we would have to wait until the engineer had scraped the surface of the matrix (a very tricky job) to use it over again.

We were a busy group of actors, so in order to get a good cast together the recording companies had to set up sessions for late evening when the network shows did not compete for our talent. We were also an underpaid group of actors, so even if we had been rehearsing and broadcasting all day we usually accepted the night work.

One series made in Hollywood at the time was "Don [pronounced Doane] Hancock," a modern Robin Hood story, sponsored by the Hancock Oil Company. True Boardman played the hero, Don Hancock.

When the series had been initiated some weeks earlier, much wax had been scraped because the actors had occasionally and inadvertently pronounced the name as an abbreviation of Donald instead of as a term of address for a Spanish gentleman. The troubled author had taken to typing it phonetically—Doane—whenever it occurred in the script. This helped, but still nothing went smoothly. Nobody expected it to. John Gibson, who had been working all day on "Calling All Cars" and rehearsing another show as well, was playing a character that turned up in the first and in the last of the five programs scheduled for the night's work. While the others were recording the second script, he went out and brought back coffee for everybody. During the third recording rehearsal period, he stretched out on the top of the grand piano to rest. This was not unusual. There were no lounges provided for the talent, but every radio or recording studio had a grand piano. (So numerous were the Steinways at NBC in New York that, when two men brazenly stole one from a studio on the third floor in the middle of the afternoon, nobody missed it for several days.) So it was not exceptional, on entering a studio, to find an exhausted actor relaxing on the top of the concert grand.

The time to cut the fourth episode of "Don Hancock" arrived. The precious wax was carefully brought from its cabinet and tenderly placed on the turntable. The engineer leaned forward in the booth, his hands on the knobs that controlled the balance of sound. The director, after giving a cue to the man at the turntable to bring the needle down on the wax, started his stopwatch and gave another cue to the soundman, who started playing the recorded theme music. This was allowed to run for some time, the music from one record being poured onto the bare surface of the other disc. In this way, time was allotted for the stations to insert

NBC

CBS

"The Circle," with stars such as, top, Cary Grant, Groucho Marx, Lawrence Tibbett, Carole Lombard, Chico Marx, Ronald Colman, cost $28,000 a week. Louella Parsons, bottom, with guests on a 1938 "Hollywood Hotel"—Bob Burns, Jack Oakie, Ann Miller, Kenny Baker.

John Barrymore, Orson Welles, and Lucille Wall (Portia of "Portia Faces Life").

local commercials. Then the engineer raised the volume of sound, the music swelled for a moment, and the director cued it out. The announcer in the studio began the lead-in: "In the foothills behind the little town, a man lies motionless in the underbrush . . . tense . . . alert . . . every nerve straining—."

A loud snore from the piano.

The director groaned. "Get Gibson out of there."

While the engineer went for a new wax, Barbara Luddy shook the offender awake and pushed him out into the hall, where he promptly fell asleep on the floor. Nobody blamed him. Everybody was dog-tired.

After a series of less colorful mishaps, the fourth show was safely on wax. John came back refreshed from his nap, and at about 4 A.M. work started on the fifth and final show.

This time the first take went perfectly. The last scene had the heroine (Barbara) trapped by the villain (Gale Gordon) and, although she did not know it, about to be rescued by Don Hancock.

"If only Doane Hancock knew," she was saying. "He would save me."

An ugly laugh from Gale. "You'll never see him again," he gloated.

A clatter of hooves . . . a shout . . . a door burst open . . .

"At last!" Barbara cried.

"So, it's you," snarled Gale. "You, again, Dan Hoe-cake!"

He threw down the script, stretched out on the floor, and wept. The powers that be decided to make the last recording on another night, and the cast staggered out into the dawn to try to find an open restaurant and have breakfast.

By the end of the 1930's the recording process had improved technically. Instead of wax, acetate was used and there were no more hours of hanging around while the engineer scraped. I suppose acetate was cheaper; there always seemed to be plenty of it. The resulting product was no longer referred to as a "recording." The phrase was: "This program has come to you by means of electrical transcription."

It didn't come to you without some travail on our part. There was still no way of editing the record or correcting a mistake once it had occurred. If we "fluffed" (the trade term for making a mistake), the whole disc had to be discarded. The doors of the recording studios still swung open at four in the morning to disgorge groups of bleary-eyed actors and announcers who had been there since eight in the evening.

I never knew an actor who would not prefer to do five *live* shows to one record. But even worse than recording programs was recording commercials. Of course, all network commercials were *live*. That meant we had just one swing at the ball and if we missed we were out. We would leave the studio consoling ourselves with the thought, which NBC soundman Keene Crockett once expressed after a hideously garbled performance had gone over the air, "Well, the thing had spontanooity, anyway."

Many of the commercials heard on the independent stations were recorded on sixteen-inch discs, with each commercial on a separate band. A mistake in the first two or three bands was not serious because nobody minded doing a few commercials over again, but as the tenth, eleventh, and twelfth bands were reached, the tension in the studio would reach a point approaching spontaneous combustion.

It seems to me that I was always assigned the last two or three commercials. I would stand, white and shaking, as the other actors went through one perfect take after another, certain that when my turn came I would blow the whole night's work. As a matter of fact, these fears were largely unfounded, because I have been blessed with extremely clear speech and I very rarely fluffed. Certainly, I was never guilty of any of the famous tongue twistings, such as "Boopert's Rear is on the air" (for Ruppert's Beer), or (during the papal election) "Poe Pipus . . . er . . . Pie Popus . . . er . . . Peep . . . that is to say the late Pope," or, "There's always pree farking at Blank's Restaurant."

But there was nothing like a late-night commercial recording session to bring whatever weaknesses one had out into a glaring light. I have never forgotten the occasion when I was called, with five or six other actors, to record some dramatized plugs for a cough medicine. We all thumbed quickly through the scripts to see if we were in the last few bands. I rejoiced to note that my final commercial was number five.

We had the usual hard time getting the first three on the record. Something went wrong with sound effects on number three. Back we went to start over with number one again. The announcer fluffed the first one. Next, a music cue failed to come in. And so on. At last we cleared all hurdles; numbers four and five went smoothly, and my night's work was finished. I could not leave the studio, however, in case someone else made a mistake that would send us back to the beginning again. I went to a corner and tried not to listen to what the others were saying —for fear of hearing a fluff.

I must have been more tense than I knew, for a slight tickle began to develop in my throat. I sat in my corner and slowly turned purple as I swallowed to fight the cough down. Then, just as the announcer was saying, "No need to suffer throat irritation—," I exploded in a bark that shook the building and shattered eleven perfectly recorded cough medicine commercials.

TUNE IN TOMORROW

I recently had occasion to make a group of commercials for Westinghouse under modern conditions. Some of the veterans of wax and acetate were describing conditions in the old days to the youngsters who have joined our ranks. Don MacLaughlin, who was radio's David Harding, Counterspy and Chaplain Jim, and subsequently the star of the TV serial "As the World Turns," recounted an episode from the early acetate era.

The product was a well-known brand of soda cracker. Don had the incredibly bad luck to be in only one of the commercials—the twelfth. In those pre-union days, the actors sometimes made sound effects themselves. In this case, as each one finished his commercial with the lines, "And they're so crisp! Just listen to them crackle!" he would snap a cracker between his fingers, close to the microphone.

After the usual mishaps, they were finally well into what looked like a perfect take. Don stood through the last few bands in nervous perspiration, clutching his cracker. His moment came. He read the speech perfectly, said, "Just listen to it crackle!" and mashed a piece of silent, soggy dough in his sweaty palm. Back they went to the very first commercial, Don under strict injunction from the director that, until the last moment, he was not to touch his cracker.

Later the acetate recording process was refined to the point where we could cut one band at a time. The commercials became individual units that could be repeated singly, and it was no longer necessary to go back to number one if a mistake was made on number twelve. The dramatic shows, however, still had to be recorded without interruption; no mistakes could be corrected once the record had begun to spin.

The next and greatest improvement in recording technique was not to arrive until after World War II, when Bing Crosby brought back from Germany electronic tape. I had seen something similar demonstrated in a Hollywood recording studio back in 1936—not a tape machine, but one that registered sound on spools of wire. It had never caught on, however, and we had plugged along with the "electrical transcription" system until Crosby bettered our lot for good and for all by producing his new Philco program on tape. (Neither NBC nor Kraft would go along with the idea so he quit them for ABC and Philco.) The results, when broadcast, could not be distinguished from a live show. Best of all, the product could now be edited with a razor blade and mending tape, and it required no processing, which meant that it could be played back instantly after recording—an impossibility with the older methods of registering sound.

Reluctantly, bit by bit, the networks dropped their opposition. When, in 1951, I wanted to take the first full month's vacation I had ever had in my radio life, NBC permitted the taping of "When a Girl

Marries," the soap opera I was doing. But taping was still the exception, rather than the rule.

For commercials, tape finally just crept in. When I went to CBS in 1959 as the star of "Nora Drake," one of the last surviving daytime radio serials, I was amazed when I heard our opening plug—the taped voices of Bing Crosby and Bob Hope singing, "Sound off! Sound off! Sound off for Chesterfield!"

My mind shot back to 1934 and I pictured myself sitting alone, almost unnoticed, and certainly underpaid, on one side of the old "Kraft Music Hall" studio, waiting to say a few words about cheese. My career had made some sort of lopsided circle. Now I was the star (in the tragic twilight of the industry, once more underpaid) and Crosby was selling the product for *me!*

The NBC and CBS rulings against recorded effects are now as dead as vaudeville and nearly all the material you hear on the networks is transcribed on tape. The difficulties of producing a radio drama such as "Lux Radio Theater" or the "Theater Guild of the Air" have been reduced ninety percent by this simple device. Instead of four or five days of arduous rehearsal to perfect the whole show, it may now be done in one day, scene by scene, on tape. Any mistakes can be merely cut out of the finished product.

Gone is the strain, the stress, the ulcer-making frenzy that caused the insurance companies to rate the radio actor as a risk only slightly less hazardous than that of a construction worker on a skyscraper. The atmosphere in today's radio broadcasting studio can be completely relaxed, and delightfully cheerful.

There is only one small hitch. There are no radio dramas any more.

CHAPTER VI

The Gay Ad-libbers

ANYBODY CAUGHT TRYING TO START A UNION WILL BE
FIRED!

These words, which appeared on a sign tacked up on the studio wall
at KFI, set us all to thinking. Such an activity had never occurred to us,
but now that it had been brought up we could see that a union might not
be a bad idea. We could use one.

We did have two little social clubs. The one to which I belonged,
the Women's Radio Guild, had been started out of pique at the Men's
Radio Guild. The fellows had told us brusquely that theirs was an ex-
clusively masculine affair and to please get lost. I don't know what the
men did at their meetings, but I suspect that they invented secret hand-
shakes and passwords and sat around telling dirty stories.

We of the Women's Radio Guild pursued a loftier course. We ate
creamed chicken and quizzed each other on tricky word pronunciations.
In the two years I was a member we also queried our way through an
entire book of English grammar. So much for self-improvement. I came
away with the knowledge that a participle must not dangle, "minuscule"
is pronounced with the accent on the second syllable and not where you
think, and leftover roast pork cannot be successfully disguised as chicken
salad.

Word of these shady doings must have climbed to the upper echelon
of KFI, the NBC affiliated station, and the cry had gone forth, "Hang out
our banners on the outward walls. Behold the pinkos come!" KFI's menacing banner didn't faze us a bit because we were, in all truth, innocent.
The memory of an attempt by Actors' Equity Association five years be-

fore to organize the Hollywood screen actors was still too vivid for any of us even to breathe the word union.

When, in 1928, the "silver screen" switched from subtitles to sound, the producers looked to New York for theater-trained talent. The new importees found themselves sealed into hastily soundproofed and inadequately ventilated studios under huge, sizzling lights that made every hour on the set seem like high noon in Death Valley. They found, too, that management was solidly knit into a union of its own, called the Motion Picture Producers' Association, with Cecil B. De Mille as its president. The actors suspected that information about their salaries was being passed from one studio to another, and they noticed that if they had trouble with one employer they would suddenly find themselves "out" with all the others. Mail containing outraged complaints began to pile up in drifts in the offices of Actors' Equity Association, which ten years before had won decent working conditions for stage actors. Early in 1929 Frank Gillmore, who was then the president of Equity, came to Hollywood to "feel out the situation on the spot." My parents met him at the home of a mutual friend, and it was one of the many occasions when Mother and Father failed to see eye to eye. Through a series of probing questions, Mother ferreted out the fact that, in the event of a strike, Mr. Gillmore did not intend calling out any players who were under contract. Without the contract players, Mother insisted, the fight was lost before it began. She returned from the little gathering like Cassandra on the eve of the sack of Troy. Father, on the other hand, came home aflame with sentiments of "loyalty to my fellow actors" and "the rights of the working man."

A few months later the strike was called. Equity members were told not to accept work or sign any new contracts until the union had been recognized by the studios. True to Mother's forebodings, contract players were not called out. Any misgivings she might have instilled in Father's mind, however, were swept away at the great mass meeting held in the American Legion Stadium on Sunset Boulevard. He took me with him, and it was an experience I shall never forget.

The huge arena was packed. Performers of all sorts turned up— nearly four thousand strong. Many of the greatest stars in Hollywood (most of them former theater people, it is true) appeared on the platform and pledged to throw in their lot with the underdogs and risk their careers to help win the day. The speaker I remember best was Joe E. Brown, who had participated in the successful New York actors' strike in 1919. At the time, he told us, he had just made his first starring appearance in the Broadway theater—after long, hard years on the burlesque wheel. He was putting on his make-up, when someone came into his dressing room and announced that the actors were going out on strike.

"Oh, great!" said the comedian. "They picked a fine time for it." Angry and disgruntled, he walked outside just as some Equity members, bearing signs that read, "No more pay—Just fair play," came marching down Broadway. Brown watched for a few minutes, then impulsively grabbed a sign and joined the march.

Amid the fervent cheers that welcomed these heart-warming recollections, Father whispered, "This is what your mother doesn't understand. You can't *beat* spirit of this sort."

In addition to the many world-famous players on the platform, extras of all sizes and shapes turned up—from cowboys in ten-gallon hats to a contingent of midgets. In the midst of the rally, a long line of full-blooded American Indians marched down the aisle in feathered war bonnets. A bedlam of cheers shook the stadium. An actress in the next seat turned to me, her eyes brimming with tears of emotion. "You'd think this would strike *terror* in their hearts," she said.

But the Hollywood moguls were prepared to take a firmer stand than Custer. And they had ammunition. They had the threat of reprisal against the actors who struck; they had money; they had the backing of the California press. Although hundreds of performers courageously refused work during those days, many (and among them some of the biggest names) did not. Production did not stop. Worst of all, dissension developed in the union leadership. Ethel Barrymore, who had been negotiating side by side with Gillmore for the union, suddenly made an unexpected, public statement in which she said that the whole thing had been mishandled by him and left for San Francisco. Miss Barrymore bore one of the greatest names in theatrical history, and because she had been a staunch supporter of Equity in its original fight and was at the moment an officer in the union, her act had an immediate and lethal effect.

One by one, the disheartened players deserted and started accepting calls to work for the studios; then the leadership retreated to New York City, and, at last, even the Pawnees and the Blackfeet buried their hatchets.

No one mentions that abortive Equity strike any more. For many years it was too painful to talk about and now it is forgotten. A myth has grown up to explain the splintering of theatrical unions into five separate organizations—theater, screen, radio-TV, musical, and variety. The stage actors were just too snobby, any young player will tell you, to wish to associate with the "lesser" performers in the other media. That is not true. The wounds suffered in attempting organization of those disparate groups—dancers, wrestlers, stuntmen—in C. B. De Mille's citadel of conservatism never healed. Better to let each branch of the entertainment world handle its own affairs, reasoned the heartbroken Equity leaders, and at the time it was probably the wisest course.

However, now that show business has become largely a matter of electronics, that decision has become a blight. Most actors have at least three union cards, pay three sets of dues, and face afresh the threat of jurisdictional disputes with every advance in the world of science.

In 1934, when management threw up its battle standard on the wall at KFI, the combined memberships of our two little social clubs were not more than thirty-five people. We had never dreamed of tossing down the gauntlet to anybody. We were each too absorbed in the individual struggle to pay the bills. In the Women's Radio Guild one evening, however, we did solemnly promise each other that we would not work on the air unless we were paid for it. Many of the members had worked in the early days without remuneration and we were still being asked to do it. If a program had no sponsor, the actors were usually expected to perform for nothing in the hope of catching one. If an advertiser did buy the show but later dropped it, the program immediately went back on a "sustainer" basis and the actors would again donate their services.

I had been lucky enough never to have been called for a job that paid in nothing but promises and hope. On the other hand, I had done many free auditions. The difference was that the auditions were not broadcast.

We were usually as eager as the shows' owners to snare a sponsor, and we put everything we had into it. Sometimes it paid off. More often it didn't. KHJ's "Rocket to the Moon" sold to the Rocket gasoline company, and the actors, who gave their services to the free audition, had steady work for six months, adding $4.50 a week to their incomes.

Then the Lang studios created a show for the Red Lion gas company called "Red Lion Trails." The program had many assets. There was that alluring plug for the product right in the title (a favored device of the era); there were sharp scripts, packed with action and suspense; and there was a Red Lion Safari Song, crooned by Bret Morrison, who had a beautiful baritone voice. Bret also played the Great White Hunter, a couple of natives, and a French guide. Of the several roles assigned to me, the most challenging was that of a pygmy lady having labor pains. What with the specially written music and the other embellishments, we thought we had a flashy affair with a good chance of selling.

A day and a half went into preparing the audition. On the evening of the second day, the prospective sponsor, a florid, combustible-looking chap, strode through the studio on his way to the private office where he was to hear the show. Hardly had the last note of Bret's closing theme died away than he was striding out again.

"Red Lion Trails!" he snorted. "What do you mean, Red Lion Trails? We don't trail, we *lead!*"

The producer tried to comfort the group of disappointed actors. "Don't worry, kids," he said. "It's a good show, and we'll find another sponsor."

Later we learned that they did consider a number of possibilities but none of them seemed to fit in with the title. The Carnation company, for example, was in the market for a show, but neither "Carnation Trails" nor "Milk Trails" seemed to carry much wallop. They thought they had it in "Bayer Trails," and broached the idea to the aspirin company. The man in that office, however, just laughed when he heard it.

An audition that required much time from those who were involved was the elaborate production prepared to sell Louella Parsons' program "Hollywood Hotel" to the Campbell Soup Company. The director, George MacGarrett, came out from New York to hold lengthy voice tests among the local radio actors. Duane Thompson won the part of the switchboard operator of the mythical hostelry, and one of our best and busiest West Coast radio actors, Cy Kendall, was picked for the hotel manager. During the five days of rehearsal required to get the audition in shape, excitement ran high among the members of the cast. They were sure that this time they had a winner.

Campbell did buy "Hollywood Hotel" on the strength of that carefully prepared audition. Almost immediately the format was changed, a new director came out from the East, and the behind-the-scenes hotel material was dropped. In the shuffle, Cy Kendall lost his job. It was no one's fault. The part was simply eliminated. He might have felt better if he had been paid for the five days of rehearsal and audition, during which time he had to refuse several other good programs. The $20 for each of the few "Hollywood Hotel" shows he played on did not begin to make up for what he had lost. It was not even a full $20.

In those days the networks had sticky fingers. They had set up "Artists' Bureaus" and classified themselves as agents. In this way they were able to charge us 10 percent for hiring us. CBS made every affiliated station in its network a branch of its Artists' Bureau. Their main purpose was to find bookings for the dance bands that had become nationally known through exposure on the air. But as far as we were concerned the system operated in such a way that when KHJ engaged us for a sponsored local show that paid only $5, it gave us $4.50 and the Artists' Bureau pocketed fifty cents. So the supporting actors on "Hollywood

Hotel" were getting $18 for an hour-long network show with two days of rehearsal.

The new director, William Bacher, had deserted his dental practice in New Jersey to become a radio director in New York and Chicago. An intense man with a great shock of reddish-brown hair, he was already known as something of a genius. He had one quality that was important to "Hollywood Hotel"—his ability to conduct rehearsals with a very firm hand. This was necessary because a peculiar situation existed on Miss Parsons' show. While the supporting actors were paid less than on other network productions, the great film stars were not paid at all. The entire program hung on Miss Parsons' ability to induce the biggest luminaries in the movie world to contribute their services to her show for nothing. The movie columnist of the Hearst syndicate carried solid weight. Out of the entire film colony, only Ginger Rogers, it was rumored, ever had the courage to refuse her invitation to join, gratis, in the soup-selling program.

There was nothing startlingly unique in the format introduced by Bacher—a variety show with an interview and a dramatic skit tossed in —but there remained an "inside Hollywood" flavor that gave the public the zest of feeling "in the know." It supposedly took place in the Hollywood Hotel. Actually, it was first broadcast from a radio studio at KHJ and later moved to the Figueroa Playhouse to accommodate an invited audience. It invariably opened with Duane as the switchboard operator. "Hollywood Hotel—Hollywood Hotel. Good evening," Duane would say as Raymond Paige's orchestra swung into the theme. Early in the proceedings, Louella would make her appearance and greet the announcer, Ken Niles.

"Why, *hello* there, Ken," she would gush, as if she had just discovered him behind a potted palm. "This is a gala evening here in Hollywood Hotel. We are having just a *marvelous* time!" Whereupon the underpaid radio actors (they soon took to calling themselves ironically the "Gay Ad-libbers") would circle the microphone, trying to simulate people having a marvelous time. "What *fun* to be here!" they would cry. "My! Doesn't Myrna Loy look gorgeous! Whoops! There's Bette Davis!"

Some musical numbers, sung by Frances Langford and Dick Powell, would follow, and, as the climax of the program, one or two of the biggest stars in the film world would be interviewed by Louella. Afterward, they would appear in the dramatic sketch, usually a scene taken from their latest picture.

These people were accustomed to receiving enormous sums for their appearances on other network programs, and while there was always a

Typical full-stage audience show was "Hollywood Hotel." At center mike is Dick Powell, flanked, left and right, by Lurene Tuttle and Ann Jamison, a soprano. Frances Langford is at mike at left, Raymond

Paige on podium with producer Bill Bacher. At right, seated, are the Gay Ad-libbers. Duane Thompson is on left of front row, Margaret Brayton in center, and Ted Osborne in the back row, second from right.

fine display of camaraderie during the rehearsals of the soup show, the radio actors sometimes thought they detected a slight strain in the air. Occasionally a guest star would give way to bursts of temperament. Bacher was excellent at handling these situations. When a well-known film star, for example, claimed that the script was just impossible and she couldn't allow her public to hear her saying those words, he arranged that on her arrival at the next rehearsal she would find Margaret Brayton at the microphone rehearsing the scene. It worked perfectly. Margaret was an excellent actress and it was clear that if a crisis arose she could fill in beautifully. The star made peace with her artistic scruples and took back the part without further ado.

Bacher didn't always win, though. During dress rehearsal Mae West interrupted proceedings just before a song she was to sing.

"Where's the spotlight?" she asked.

The director explained that they never used that sort of lighting on the show.

"I don't sing without a spot," Miss West said.

He explained it all again in his usual "brooking-no-nonsense" manner, and the lady who was then the sex symbol of half the civilized world shrugged her milky white shoulders and sauntered off into the wings.

On the air that night, after the sketch and Miss West's interview, Paige's orchestra began the opening bars of her song. The star of "Diamond Lil" snuggled up close to the microphone and murmured through half-closed lips, "I'm supposed to sing a song here. But I—don't—think —I'm—going—to—do—it." Then, hand on hip, she undulated off the stage.

Bacher seemed always to have hedged himself about with a few precautionary measures in advance of every broadcast. On this occasion he signaled immediately to Raymond Paige and Dick Powell, the band switched to "Hesitation Waltz," and Powell joined in for the refrain.

There were accidents, however, that even Bacher's quick thinking and sturdy determination could not prevent. Just as actors are terrified of "going up" in their lines, so singers are nearly always apprehensive about remembering the lyrics of a song. But if memory does skip a beat, a clever artist can often fill in with words of his own devising. Igor Gorin had the misfortune during a "Hollywood Hotel" broadcast to "go up" while singing, of all things, "The Lord's Prayer." No improvised text could slip in here unnoticed. He had leaped from the third line of the prayer to the last one. He had hardly got started when he heard himself chanting "Amen." The band managed to follow him in a ragged sort of way. In the control booth Bacher scribbled a note that was rushed out to Ken Niles on the stage. Ken stepped to the microphone and simply and sensibly told the listeners that a mistake had been made and that Mr. Gorin would repeat the song. He did so magnificently. Never had that rich voice rolled out with more command and resonance. But, the incident took its toll. When it was all over and he was safely offstage, the great baritone burst into tears.

The supporting parts on the guest spots on the program were usually filled from among the Gay Ad-libbers. Once in a while, though, Bacher would call an outsider for a specific role. Francis Lederer requested that Barbara Luddy be called to play opposite him when it came his turn to donate his services to Louella's show. The radio people never received billing on "Hollywood Hotel." They were just nameless voices. Barbara was amazed and delighted, therefore, when during dress rehearsal she heard her name announced right after Mr. Lederer's. A gentleman in a dark blue business suit, who seemed to be connected with the program, sat down beside her and started a conversation. Barbara seized the opportunity to ask how much she could expect to receive for her part in "Hollywood Hotel."

The gentleman looked at her in astonishment. "You're not going to be *paid*," he said. "You're getting *billing*."

Barbara took a deep breath. She had a vision of twelve pairs of mascaraed eyes gazing at her over chicken-filled patty shells. "I'm sorry," she said. "I don't work on the air for nothing."

His jaw dropped. "You don't understand," he said. "Everybody does 'Hollywood Hotel' for the publicity value of it."

"I'm sorry."

"Not even Mr. Lederer is being paid."

"Mr. Lederer is a film star. I'm a radio actress," Barbara said. "I'm earning my living this way. I can't work for nothing."

Barbara's name was stricken from the list of credits given on the air and a few days later she received a check for her anonymous services —$18, after, of course, the CBS Artists' Bureau had extracted its $2.

In his wonderfully accurate articles dealing with daytime radio programs, published in *The New Yorker* magazine in 1948 under the title "Soapland," James Thurber put it very clearly: "In the days before the American Federation of Radio Artists and the Writers Guild were formed, the broadcasting industry took an easy and cynical advantage of the actors and authors . . ."

A detailed chronicle of abuses would be tedious here. They are only important because they gave birth to the union. It started early in 1937. A group, headed by a young actor named George Heller, began meeting in the New York offices of Actors' Equity Association. In Hollywood, Eddie Cantor gave his support to a similar group. On August 16, meetings were held in both cities (I attended the one in the East), the vote was unanimous, and the American Federation of Radio Artists was born.

Stars such as Cantor had nothing to gain from a union, of course. They stood only to lose the affections of networks and sponsors. It is heartwarming to remember how swift most of them were to throw in their lot with the rest of us. They brought enormous weight to the negotiating table. For a sampling of that early membership, let's take a look at the first ten cards issued by AFRA:

1. Eddie Cantor, who also served as our national president.
2. Lawrence Tibbett, Metropolitan Opera star.
3. Norman Field, actor.
4. Jascha Heifetz, the violinist.
5. Jimmy Wallingford, a top announcer.
6. Emily Holt, AFRA national executive secretary.
7. George Heller, actor, later AFRA executive secretary.
8. Lucille Wall, actress ("Portia Faces Life").
9. Ted De Corsia, actor.
10. Edgar Bergen, comedian-ventriloquist.

CHAPTER VII

The End of the Ice Age

Louella Parsons kept the cauldrons in the Campbell Soup factory bubbling overtime. A particular broth would be mentioned on her show "Hollywood Hotel," and presto!—store shelves across the nation would be swept clean of the product and distributors would be clamoring for more. At one point she forced a crisis on the cream soup division: the sponsor ran out of tomatoes.

In the normal course of things, a success such as "Hollywood Hotel" would have inspired a host of imitators, but the basic asset of the program was Louella herself. She alone, it was said, could produce such galaxies at no expense to the sponsor. This assumption was destined to be challenged—just once.

In the remoteness of Manhattan, far removed from the Hollywood scene, two young men dreamed a dream: Mary Pickford, First Lady of Hollywood. Suppose a microphone were set up in Pickfair, the magnificent home that Douglas Fairbanks had built for her before their marriage. Surely, America's Sweetheart had as much pull in the movie colony as any mere gossip columnist. (Even Madison Avenue can be naïve at times.)

The two young men, Nat Wolf and Marion Parsonette, set about finding a sponsor, and "Parties at Pickfair" was born.

There were no long, arduous auditions. Nat Wolf wrote from New York to Eric Snowdon, one of the most active of the Hollywood radio group, and asked him to assemble a few versatile players for the program-to-be. Eric selected Bret Morrison, Ted Osborne, Lou Merrill, and me and took us down to the Ambassador Hotel to meet the young producer soon after he arrived.

There, the elegantly tailored, rather hawklike easterner leaned non-chalantly against his hotel bureau and outlined for us the plan for the new show—a series of parties given by Mary in her Beverly Hills home. The music would be provided by Al Lyons' orchestra and the Paul Turner Singers. But the butler heard on the air would be Pickfair's real butler, Albert, and the glamorous guest stars would all be real friends of Mary, only too glad to appear on her program, as they did on Louella's —for nothing. The radio actors were to be the Pickford version of Parson's Gay Ad-libbers. We, however, were going to have something to be gay about. This show, Nat said, would pay us each $50 every week as long as it was on the air. We left that hotel purring like six lean cats who have just found a secret passage to the cream shed.

The following week, Ted Osborne, an old friend from the "Coronets" cast, drove me to Beverly Hills. Ted approached Pickfair as though he had reached the end of a lifelong quest for the Holy Grail. "Imagine," he was saying, "me—Ted Osborne—little boy from Grand Rapids— actually *here*—in Pickfair—*Pickfair*."

I was trying to look as if this were all old hat to me. "It's just a house like any other," I said in my jaded-woman-of-the-world way.

But it wasn't. Even I had to admit that Pickfair was beautiful. Once inside, however, I had a shock. Technicians had set up equipment all over the place. A sound-control booth had been built in the entrance hall. A good-sized orchestra had arrived and spread itself out over a large area of the living room. (I remember counting, during the days that followed, the cigarette burns that appeared, one by one, on the exquisite little white piano. I have nothing against musicians, but it is a fact that they are messy.) Ted and I stood transfixed, trying to take it all in.

"Look what they've *done* to the place!" I said.

He didn't answer. He was gazing upward. Mary Pickford was making an entrance. Her soft, rose chiffon gown settled in graceful folds as she carefully timed her pause at the head of the curved staircase. Then she cast a dazzling, if impersonal, smile around the room below and glided regally down to us. It was the sort of performance one expects of stars when they are dealing with the adoring public—not with other actors.

But Mary came right over to us with a warm greeting. "This is like old home week, isn't it?" she said and turned to Nat Wolf and Marion Parsonette, who had just entered the room. "We all worked together last year on my Royal Gelatin show," she explained.

Parsonette, in spite of a name evocative of the Folies Bergères, proved to be a tall, virile chap, turned out by a tailor almost the equal of Nat's. Together they made the most urbane pair I had ever seen—

quite a contrast to the California actors in their open-necked sports shirts and slacks.

We were given scripts and read through what amounted to a rough outline of the show. Mary, as hostess, practiced greeting; we as background practiced babbling; and Albert—well, Albert turned out to be a problem. He may have been the world's finest butler but he wasn't even its worst actor. He was just no actor at all. After struggling through his scene several times, we gave up and went on to the musical numbers and the closing. What we had was a skeleton on which to mold the glamorous flesh of the show—the interviews and sketches with the stars. They were not due until the next day, so we were dismissed and went home.

On the way back from Beverly Hills to Hollywood I was totting up the assets connected with the new job—elegant parties at Pickfair, hobnobbing with the great of filmdom, and $50 every single week.

" 'Parties at Pickfair,' " Ted said, "The poor man's Hollywood Hotel."

"It is *not!*" I snapped. "This features the glamor of Pickfair and it pays fifty dollars!"

"Well, at least," he said, "it's a better format for her than the one she did last year."

He was thinking of the Royal Gelatin series with its hour-long adaptations of stage plays. Cal Kuhl, who had sent me to the Pomona Fair with Edward Everett Horton, cast it with great care, holding lengthy auditions, and Ted and I were both among the fortunate few he had chosen to play supporting roles.

Mary Pickford was, of course, a beautiful woman. But more than that, she possessed tremendous personal magnetism—a quality she could turn on and off like a faucet. She had walked into the old NBC studios on the RKO lot, tossed us that famous smile, which left the glow of a couple of martinis, and gone to work on her part.

At the table she was relaxed and comfortable, but as soon as she approached the microphone she got nervous. During one broadcast (we were playing "Mrs. Moonlight," with Miss Pickford in the title role and me as her daughter), she dropped her script. The sixty or more pages spread out around her. To retrieve them during the scene would have been impossible. I stepped quickly to her side of the microphone and held my copy in front of her. During the music bridge between scenes, a young actor, James Eagles, gave his script to the star, and for the rest of the show he danced about, peeking over the shoulders of the other members of the cast, snatching one of his speeches here, another there. Scriptless and on the wing as he was, he managed to give a good performance; but after the broadcast Jimmy was pale, my heart was pounding, and I don't think anybody felt any too good.

Ted and I agreed that the "Parties at Pickfair" formula did seem one that would show Mary off to better advantage.

The next day, the three other radio actors were already settled at Pickfair, thumbing through magazines, when Ted and I arrived. We joined them and half an hour passed. No sign of Pickford, Parsonette, or Wolf. I was in the hall looking at a picture, when a door flew open and Nat stumbled into me. He muttered something and bolted out another door. A few minutes later he was back.

"We've hit a snag," he said. "Two of our guest stars called this morning to say they can't appear on the show tomorrow night."

It was a snag, all right. Even Mary Pickford would find it late in the day to start lining up big names now. Another door opened and Marion came in. "I haven't been able to *reach* anybody," he said with a frown.

"Nobody? Out of that long list?"

"Not a damn soul. And—brace yourself—one of next week's stars just canceled, too."

"What the hell's going on?" Nat said, tearing off his Sulka tie.

"I've been thinking," Parsonette said. "You don't suppose Louella has torpedoed this show?"

"Why, how could she?" Nat said.

"No star is going to risk the threat of a boycott by the Hearst syndicate."

"Do you think she'd do *that?*"

"I think she *has!*"

Sometime later a frantic Nat came to me and asked if I could type. When I told him I could—a little—he led me to a room where Marion was pacing the floor. "Two of our stars are unable to appear," Marion said. "We're trying to get replacements but just in case—well—we've added a few pages to one of the sketches. We still have one good big name star."

They gave me some handwritten copy and I started in my fumbling way to tap it out. The two producers stood behind me, peering over my shoulder.

"Telephone for you, Mr. Wolf," a voice said.

Nat left the room. I pecked on. I had finished my spotty copy when the door swung open and he staggered back in. His big form collapsed on the couch. "Our last star just canceled out."

Marion dropped to his side. They buried their faces in their hands. I sneaked out. No woman likes to see a man cry.

Eric joined us on the drive back to Hollywood that evening. He had had a private talk with Nat. They had tried to reach other Hollywood notables, he told us, but people were not answering the telephone. Pickfair was as isolated from the rest of the movie colony as Admiral Byrd's expedition in the South Pole.

The calm, cool radio actors in their open-necked sports shirts looked soigné beside Nat Wolf and Marion Parsonette two days later, on the day of the show. I think that pair had been catnapping in those custom-made suits.

"We're bringing in an outside writer," Nat told me. "Mary and you kids are going to have a much heavier burden than we had planned. We've managed to get Edward Everett Horton—at a good, fat fee, of course," he sighed.

"Didn't any of your original stars turn up?" I asked.

"Not one. But after you left the other day, we invited Louella herself to be on the show."

"And she accepted," Marion said. The two producers exchanged a foxy smile.

I felt a hand on my arm and looked up into a friendly Irish grin. It was Jerry Cady—one of the best and most prolific writers radio had yet produced. He had left the writing staff of KFI, where he had created the successful "Richelieu" series, to go to New York. He made an outstanding success in radio there and soon returned, the possessor of one of those fantastically profitable contracts the film studios used to hand out. Just the sight of Jerry soothed my edginess. Any author who could compose a film for Fox, write fifteen programs for the New York radio market, and at the same time turn out the five mystery shows I was currently recording for him each week, would not be fazed by the Pickfair problem.

Marion and I saw him snugly tucked in behind his Corona and tiptoed out of the room. I joined the actors. Late in the afternoon we had a rough run-through of the show—rough, because Cady was rewriting a still unfinished script. I acted as a stand-in to read Louella's part, and Eric was told to take over the role of the butler. The rest of us breathed a sigh of relief. We knew that Eric would see to it that "Parties at Pickfair" got off to a good bright start. Edward Everett Horton arrived, businesslike and ready to perform one of the typical sketches he was in the habit of doing on "Shell Show," "Kraft Music Hall," or "Camel Caravan." And Marion had somewhere unearthed and presumably paid a cherubic boy soprano to pad out the proceedings.

The gritty gears of "Parties at Pickfair" were meshing at last. But I had a feeling they'd been oiled, not by friendship, but by hard cash.

71

The orchestra began to tune up. Mary made no elaborate entrance this time. She looked stunned. I went in to the control booth to hear part of the rehearsal. There was a crackling sound.

"It's Mary's script shaking," the engineer said. "Sounds like a damned forest fire."

It did remind me of Teagarden roasting heretics for "English Coronets."

Late in the day, Jerry announced that he had completed the final version and we were told to take a half-hour's rest before starting the dress. Jerry settled down with his old friends, the radio actors.

Suddenly Marion Parsonette stood in the doorway, chewing his underlip.

"Thank God, you haven't left," he said. "I was afraid you had."

Jerry groaned. "Oh, hell," he said, getting up. "What's gone wrong *now?*"

As they left the room, Marion's voice became inaudible but Cady exploded. "You mean to say I have to throw out all that stuff I wrote for Parsons?" he bellowed.

Ted Osborne looked at me. "Louella must have waited until now and then backed out," he whispered. "So damned close to air time. What a filthy trick."

We stopped gossiping when a stocky man with gray hair wandered into the room. He peered at us through thick glasses and smiled vaguely. I had seen him several times before and had at first taken him to be one of Mary Pickford's staff, but his dark business suit and heavy gold watch chain didn't suggest domestic help or even a secretary.

"Why, that's the sponsor," Ted said in reply to my question.

"The *sponsor?* But he looks so cheerful. Doesn't he know what's going on?"

"I think he's in a world all his own," Ted said.

"What is the product?" I asked. "What are we selling?"

"Ice."

"*Ice?*"

"That's right. He's the head of the organized ice companies of America. They've banded together to fight mechanical refrigeration."

I went back to the control booth to find a copy of the commercials. It was true. We were the shaky bulkhead thrust up by the ice industry to stem the tide of Frigidaires, Kelvinators, and Westinghouses that was flooding the U.S.A. The sponsor had devised a slogan: "Cold *alone* is not enough!" I was trying to decide what that meant when Nat came in and stood looking wearily over my shoulder. I pointed to the copy.

"I don't quite understand—," I began.

CBS

Louella Parsons and Mary Pickford preparing for Louella's "Hollywood Hotel" in 1935. The following year Louella backed down from appearing on Mary's "Parties at Pickfair."

"Nobody does," he groaned. "It sounds like we're *selling* mechanical refrigeration, instead of fighting it. The sponsor insists on writing it himself." He threw an anguished glance at his watch. "Cady will *never* get that script out in time!"

Marion stuck his head in the door. "Mary says we've got to do something about Albert," he said.

"Who?"

"Albert. The butler. She's afraid she'll lose him."

"To hell with Albert," Nat exploded. "I've more important things to worry about."

"I'm not kidding, Nat. That's one mad Swiss."

"What's he got to be mad about?"

"He refuses point-blank to be impersonated by an Englishman."

I giggled hysterically. Even Nat managed a sick smile.

"What do we do—cut the part?" Marion asked.

"Yes," said Nat. "No! It's too late now. Change the butler's name to—to—."

"Alvin?" suggested Marion.

Nat began to laugh weakly. "Why the hell not?" he said. "Make it Alvin."

We never had a dress rehearsal. Jerry kept on writing frantically until air time. The rumor spread that years before Mary had once fainted from mike fright. So a table microphone was provided for her use, and the rest of us, with thumping hearts, gathered round the standing mike. The hands of the clock pushed inexorably on to zero hour. Al Lyons lifted his baton, and in the control booth Marion Parsonette closed his eyes and threw a cue. A show called "Parties at Pickfair" rose uneasily into the air like a half-filled balloon.

Most of that first program was music. There was much, much music. Eric played the butler, but under the name of Alvin. (As far as I know, this simple change pacified the anti-British sentiments of the real butler and all was serene below stairs.) Then the "guests" arrived. That is, we radio actors took turns strolling past the microphone imitating the voices of famous stars, being careful not to mention names. We had been told to ad-lib—and if someone mistook Bret's voice for that of Maurice Chevalier, or if a listener imagined he detected the nasal tones of Ned Sparks when it was really only Ted Osborne holding his nose, it was all part of the game.

Early in the program I was introduced as a protégée of Mary Pickford and I wandered out onto a make-believe balcony and gave vent to some pretty high-flown prose.

"See," I said, "how beautiful . . . the lights of the city shining there below ... a handful of precious jewels tossed on the black velvet cushion of the night."

"Ah," quoth Ted. "The moon is a goblet of blood red wine ..."

A page and a half of that sort of chat and music again. Jerry had had only about forty-five minutes to prepare the last version of a full-hour script. He had been forced to put down the first things that popped into his head. It was a tribute to the quickness of his mind that the show got on the air at all.

After the program came the big moment—the after-show party we had all been anticipating. That, at least, was all any of us had hoped for. At the end of the table was the lady of Pickfair, a beautiful and gracious hostess, and across the pink roses in front of me I could see the sponsor beaming.

As we drove along the Sunset strip on our way home, I made a sweeping gesture with my hand. "Look," I said. " 'A handful of jewels tossed on the black velvet cushion—the moon is a goblet of blood red wine—.' "

"I'm going to let you out at the corner," Ted said. "If you're as tight as that sounds, I don't want to face your mother."

We were naturally eager to see what the trade papers would have to say about the show. "Parties at Pickfair" had been given an enormous publicity campaign before it went on the air. The press boys seemed puzzled by what they heard when it did. *Billboard* said, in part:

"Entertainment proved rather peculiar in that things moved along quietly, smoothly, and while the listener was still waiting for the high spot the program came to an end ... possibly this ice show will need a little jolt to make itself felt."

(Dear Heaven, no! We needed many things but another jolt was not among them.)

Variety's critic was equally perplexed:

"A tough program to analyze on the basis of one listening ... Program has two main problems ... First the entertainment formula. Second the selling of ice and ice boxes. On the entertainment side the title is self explanatory.... As sampled by the first time at bat it has pitfalls ... It was thick with phony sentiment and became satire of the unconscious type ... Horton alone could not carry out the idea that the party was stubbed with celebs. (Louella Parsons was publicized in advance but failed to show) ... Second part of the ... problem is related to the nature of the sponsorship ... No brand names are mentioned—just the ice that's sawed off the ponds in the winter and carried into the pantry on the rubber capes of stalwart Americans ... Anachronism may be considered part of sales difficulty."

The next week when I entered Pickfair, Mary was standing near the foot of the stairs. I caught her eye and smiled but she turned her back abruptly and walked into the improvised control booth where I could see her talking to the two producers, a frown on her usually smooth brow. As she opened the door of the booth to leave, I could hear Nat's voice. "She doesn't sound like you," he was saying. "I promise you she doesn't."

Mary brushed past me. Inside the booth Nat took my hand. "Mary says your voice sounds like hers," he said.

"It's all nonsense," Marion said drily. "Jerry gave you too many lines last week. It was a mistake."

"We want to keep you on the show—so just stay in the background and mumble," Nat said. "You know, Walla-Walla, rhubarb-rhubarb. No definite phrases. That's a good girl." He gave me a pat on the shoulder.

"Now," said Marion glumly, "we have to tell the other radio actors about the party."

"You do it, Marion," said Nat.

"No, you do it, Nat."

In the end they did it together. With faces flaming above immaculate collars, and much shuffling of custom-made shoes, they explained that Miss Pickford had decided that the dinner guests thereafter should include only the stars.

"However," Marion faltered, "Miss Pickford invites you to have a drink before you go home."

The radio actors moved into a tight little knot. We stayed together through rehearsal and left together after the show. None of us availed ourselves of Mary's invitation to visit the bar.

The following week when I walked through Pickfair's door I felt as if I had entered one of the sponsor's ice chests. I could see Miss Pickford once more in the control booth with a miserable Nat Wolf and a depressed Marion Parsonette. They didn't look at me but a soft voice spoke in my ear.

"Young lady, excuse me—would you mind?"

I turned. It was the sponsor—glasses, watch chain, and all. He smiled and the air around me began to thaw.

"Would you mind reading this over for me?" he asked. "I'd like to hear how it sounds in a woman's voice."

I read a little patch of his double-talk copy for him. He took the paper and smiled again.

"Thank you," he murmured. "I'm going to have you do the commercial."

I jumped. "Do *they* know?" I pointed at the control booth.

"I'm going to tell them right now," he said, placidly.

There is nothing like having the purse strings securely in your hands to induce calm. There was no calm in the control booth. I couldn't look. I moved into the other room when I saw Parsonette approach Mary's little table.

Her voice rose. "But they'll think *I'm* doing the commercials," she said.

I can understand why Mary Pickford would not want to be caught selling ice in the era of mechanical refrigeration. Me, I didn't care. I just wanted to hang on to that $50 check.

Before we started the program the sponsor handed me the advertising copy. I looked into the control booth. Two dazed men nodded back at me. I read the opening commercial on the air.

The next day, Marion called me on the telephone. "I'm sorry, Mary Jane," he said, "but you are definitely and forever off the Pickford show. There isn't a damned thing we can do about it. I have it on good authority that if you show your curly head in that house again America's sweetheart will knock it off."

I never listened to the "Parties at Pickfair" shows. I like to cut my losses and forget them. Things could have been worse. I was still making $25 a week from Jerry's recorded mystery show. "Coronets," after beheading Mary, Queen of Scots, had dropped the "English" from its title and was now drifting slowly down the Nile with Cleopatra. I was playing Arsinoë, sister of the queen, and her little brother was impersonated by a child actor, Dickie Quine, who has grown up to become one of Hollywood's top film directors. Hugh Marlowe (later radio's Ellery Queen) was Anthony, and Gayne Whitman, who was frightening the kiddies during the week as Chandu, the Magician, was, on Sunday nights, heard as Julius Caesar. There was, too, the free-lance work on the big network shows. I wasn't getting rich but I was keeping the wolf and that disconsolate gasman away from the door.

Then out of the blue I got a call for the Pickford show.

"You'll never believe this," Nat said, "but the sponsor insists on having you for his commercial. He's a very stubborn man when he wants to be. So you just come along half an hour before we go on the air and run through the copy once—OK?"

And so it was that for the final broadcast of "Parties at Pickfair" I crossed the room where Miss Pickford sat with eyes averted, marched up to the microphone, and sounded what must have been the last appeal for the Vanishing Iceman:

"Ladies—*surely*—cold *alone* is not enough!"

Eddie Cantor with Rubinoff the violinist and the moustached Bert Gordon, the Mad Russian, in 1936.

CHAPTER VIII

Flop Sweat

In the summer of 1966 Henry Morgan was acting as emcee on NBC's "Tonight Show." His principal guest was Jerry Lewis. In the middle of an almost serious conversation, Jerry suddenly seemed to swallow his cigarette. He crossed his eyes and fell out of his chair. It brought a roar of laughter from the audience.

"Now, that's the trouble with you, Jerry," Henry said, peering down at the writhing comedian. "The show's going along fine, you have some interesting things to say, and then you start yelling. Why do you do it?"

A momentary look of dejection slipped across Jerry's mobile face.

"Flop sweat," he said.

"Flop sweat?"

"Yeah. It gets quiet out there"—indicating the audience—"and I begin to feel the flop sweat trickling down here"—touching his forehead—"and I think, 'Those people aren't interested in brain surgery or nuclear fission. They're hoping I'll take my pants down.' "

He had touched on an essential difference between comic and serious acting. A serious actor may wonder how good he was during a performance. A comedian knows exactly how good—or how bad—he was. The audience lets him know, on the spot. No other performer, with the possible exception of a bullfighter, is so quickly aware when things go wrong.

"That was no lady. That was my wife." Silence. Silence that is stiletto-sharp, instant criticism—the most hideous thing that can fall on the comic's ear. It explains why the vaudevillians came into radio trailing their audiences behind them.

TUNE IN TOMORROW

At first, all programs were sealed into airless, draped, "dead" studios. Then Ed Wynn, one of the great acts from the Keith-Albee circuit, started his Texaco radio show from the New Amsterdam roof. An audience was invited, but a soundproof glass curtain was lowered between it and the performers. Wynn's nerve promptly broke under the ominous silence. He insisted that the curtain be raised. Thus a pattern was set that Benny, Cantor, Burns and Allen, Penner, and the other variety performers were quick to follow. The lone dissenter was Fred Allen, who maintained that a radio show could best be produced in the privacy of a closed studio. He was forced, however, to yield to his sponsor in this matter and so he, too, performed to the lively sound of laughter.

On the other hand, the comedians who had their roots in radio (many of them announcers who drifted into monkeyshines while doing ad-lib shows)—Stoopnagle and Bud, Bob and Ray, Henry Morgan— were not trained to audible reaction to their quips. Lum and Abner, Vic and Sade, and the Easy Aces went along for years, serenely addressing themselves to an enormous but unheard home audience. But to the boys from the Orpheum circuit, silence was the sound of failure.

Every actor needs reassurance from time to time but the comedian's entire life seems to resolve into a search for it. I gradually learned to take the insecurity of radio comic stars for granted. They were meticulous craftsmen, those vaudeville people, used to polishing an act for months in the sticks before ever taking it to the big cities. Snatch away the old reliable trial-and-error method and they plunged into a chasm of neurotic self-doubt. When radio came along, it demanded from them an entirely new act each week.

Always following the same general pattern, the birth throes of those weekly offerings were awesome. Hardly would the last chuckle die on the air waves of one show than the sweat would start over the next. No tiny rivulet, either—a veritable Niagara.

At the first story conference, the writers would proffer possible themes for the next show, while the star would sit glumly by, rejecting them. Just before closing time he'd reluctantly and provisionally accept an idea.

"OK," he'd sigh doubtfully. "See what you can do with it."

At the next meeting a complete script would be presented and, more than likely, be promptly tossed out. At the very best, it would be met with cries of dismay.

"Oh no, fellows—that's not what we're looking for. Can't you do better than *that*. It's got to be *funny*. Now, take this line—."

Then the writers' chorus: "Look Joe, I swear it'll get a laugh . . .

You *use* this ... It's a *sure* laugh ... I *swear* it ... I *know*. I've *been* there ... I'll stake my job ... *Use* it, Joe ..."

"I don't think so."

"Trust me, Joe. If this doesn't get a laugh—."

Line by line, the script is torn apart. The experienced writer doesn't commit hara-kiri. He files the deleted gags for presentation the next week—or the next.

Once rehearsals begin, the flop sweat that has submerged the writers engulfs the supporting cast. The comic has a conviction that if by some miracle he does wring a laugh from that lousy material, somebody is sure to kill it. As a matter of fact, the situation *is* tricky. If you speak too soon you *will* stop the laugh. But if you pause—and no laugh comes—you let the show drop to its knees. The comic might disembowel you for that.

When Eddie Cantor moved to the Coast, I won the audition for the only woman's part on the first show. I was to play a cat woman, that is, a woman who spoke as a cat would if a cat spoke.

After the audition Duane Thompson gave me some advice. "I worked with Cantor last year," she said. "He'll do anything for a laugh. If he thinks the material is dying he's apt to slug you. He gave me a hard swat."

"What did you do?"

"Big Mack Sennett take," she giggled. "But hold on to your script. He hits hard."

In three days of rehearsal I never saw Cantor smile. He worried over everything—especially my exit. It was, after all, a radio show and so I moved easily away from the microphone, yowling and hissing in a long fade.

"No, no, no," Cantor said. "It's got to be *big*."

He worked out an elaborate piece of business. I shrieked, staggered, nearly fell, then limped slowly off—a purely visual effect that must have left the millions at home wondering what was going on. Cantor never seemed to think about them at all.

If he was so set on sight gags, I decided, I'd better cooperate. On the day of the show I went to the old wardrobe trunk we kept in the garage and found a frumpy hat, a pair of horn-rimmed spectacles, a dowdy coat, and a moth-eaten boa. When I appeared in my trick-or-treat outfit, Cantor circled me, nodding approval.

"Very good," he said. "Very, very *good*."

During the last rehearsal one of his writers came up with a line that made even the jaded boys in the orchestra laugh (a thing notoriously hard to do). Eddie stopped and considered.

"That's funny," he said, solemnly. "That's *funny*." He stood wrapped in thought a moment. "*Too* funny," he said at last. "Too smart for my audience. They'd never get it."

He stewed on, worrying each tiny point until air time. Then he came dancing blithely out of the wings, eyes rolling, hands clapping—the most carefree, lighthearted chap in the world. He forgot everything but those people out front. To them he made love. But when he thought they weren't responding loudly enough—Wham! I got it. Right in the seat. I threw my arms in the air and yelled like a banshee.

Cantor was tickled with the big laugh it got and later told me so. As it turned out, though, I was encouraging him in a habit that led to trouble. When the dignified and beautiful star Mary Boland got that unrehearsed swat across the fanny she went into hysterics and never did forgive him.

Much later, when Cantor was broadcasting before an audience of servicemen during the war, a scene with Ida Lupino brought the house down. The next day I asked a friend in an advertising agency what had happened.

"Eddie goosed Lupino," he replied, "and she flattened him."

I don't believe it. Not even Cantor could get *that* nervous. He was a polite, if anxious, man and I'm sure it was what I have described— a hard slap across the bottom—just good clean horseplay. And all for the benefit of a stupid studio audience. On second thought, perhaps those people were not so much stupid as tired. They spent the better part of their days trundling from one radio show to another in search of free entertainment. They would struggle into the night shows weighed down with chocolate bars, cake mixes, and peanut butter—gifts collected on their endless trek through the daytime shows. Whatever the cause, they were slow on the uptake. My estimate of them is not unique. Through the years, critics have remarked on their dullness. As early as 1931 *Variety* carried this observation under a San Francisco dateline:

"Broadcasting programs played to a studio audience draw the poorest class of customers in the country. Attendants at these shows are a motley crew. Mostly they're disappointed wives, and unemployed Santa Clauses whose I.Q. isn't much over 22 . . . they can't savvy anything newer than 'who was that lady I saw you with last night?' . . ."

The collective low intelligence of those free-ticket audiences was, I am sure, responsible for the steady decline of radio material.

Of all the ex-vaudevillians, only Fred Allen seemed to be aware of this trend and to fight shy of it. He criticized comedians who relied on props and funny hats instead of wit. He even broadcast his views on the subject.

82

Here is *Variety's* review of "The Fred Allen Show" of January 19, 1938:

"Fred Allen, who detests the radio practice of mugging for the benefit of the studio audience illustrated what he means and made it very funny . . . Allen and [Harry] Von Zell introduced a couple of purposely flat jokes that got no response whatever, then proceeded to repeat the same tepid gags but accompanied this time by horseplay, grimaces, comic props, etc. Studio audience, as expected, went into roars of laughter.

"As heard over the air the original flat jokes remained the same when repeated, although the near hysteria evidence of the studio audience indicated vividly what mad antics were presumably in progress.

"Allen punched the message by the remark, 'Isn't the radio audience supposed to be important, too?' "

Allen would occasionally use a visual prop but never so as to mystify the unseen listeners. He did have a lemon pie brought on the stage for a scene with Jack Benny, but the pie was used only to heighten the effect for the spectators and not as an entirely new element in the show. The script was so written that both the listeners and those present expected Allen to throw the pie at Benny. One of the actors, Kenny Delmar, stood by, holding the pie. It must have been the lightest confection ever baked. When Kenny shifted his weight and inadvertently gave the platter a little boost, the meringue rose like a cloud and drifted away. No one could have anticipated that effect, least of all the home listeners. It brought the house down and, I am sure, would have tickled Cantor. Allen, on the other hand, was mad. He didn't like that unexplained and unexplainable roar going into the home to make the listener feel excluded.

Allen had nothing against an unexpected laugh, however. It was only the purely visual gag he shunned. When Ken Delmar came up with a brilliant ad-lib on the air, Allen was delighted. Afterwards he wrote it into the script week after week until it worked its way into our American idiom. Kenny played Senator Claghorn—a southerner so dedicated that he refused to wear a union suit. After a quip that got a laugh from the audience but no response from the sleepy character playing opposite him, Kenny leaned forward and added, "That's a joke, son." Thus was born one of the most quoted of radio's catch lines, one that rivaled in popularity and surpassed in longevity Penner's "Wanna buy a duck?" and Baron Munchausen's "Vas you dere, Sharlie?"

The Senator himself showed signs of longevity. He was one of only two out of radio's vast dramatis personae (Mollie Goldberg was the

CBS

NBC

Ex-vaudevillian Ed Wynn, top, introduced the studio audience to radio and went in for sight gags. Here he is in 1936, but without his usual Firechief's hat. Orson Welles, bottom, meets his match in Charlie McCarthy and friend, Edgar Bergen, on "The Chase and Sanborn Hour."

At top with Fred Allen in 1948 are two residents of Allen's Alley, Minerva Pious (Mrs. Nussbaum) and Kenny Delmar (Senator Claghorn). Bottom, movie mogul Cecil B. De Mille with cast of a "Lux Radio Theater" presentation—film stars John Howard, Gary Cooper, and Helen Mack.

Two of radio's top clowns during a rehearsal break—Fred Allen and Jack Benny.

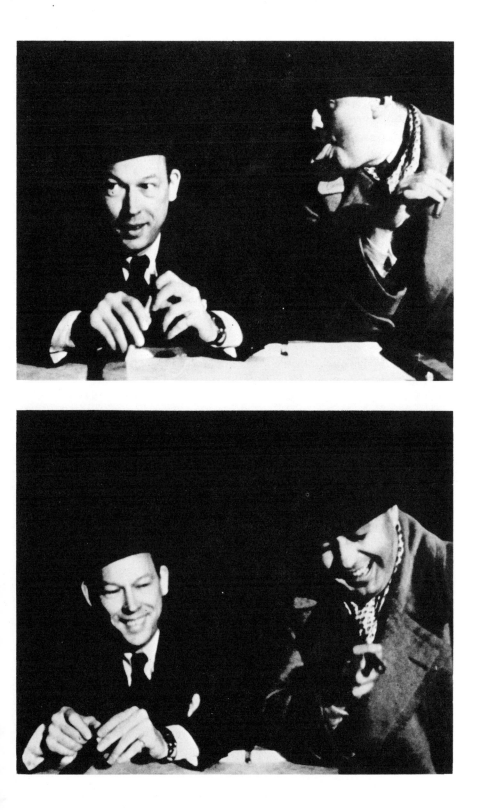

other) who made the transition from radio to the Broadway theater. Kenny starred for two years as Claghorn in the musical "Texas, Li'l Darlin'." Fred Allen gave Kenny the rights to the character of Claghorn (an Allen brainchild) with a free and open hand—just as he gave the poet, Fallstaff (sic), to another member of the famous Allen's Alley, Alan Reed.

His actors were in awe of Fred Allen. No flop sweat flowed through his rehearsals. They were calm and dignified, the reason perhaps being that although he had a writing staff (Herman Wouk, Arnold Auerbach, and Nat Hiken, among others), he wrote a good part of his material himself and he had confidence that he knew what was funny. He seems to have been completely at peace with the world within the studio but at war with the radio Establishment. His crusade against vice-presidents made history.

One of the things that griped the Irishman from Boston was radio's arbitrary time division. He resented having to cram his brainchildren into an exact allotment of time. Occasionally the Allen show would run overtime. Then it would be cut off abruptly to give place to the next offering. Fred didn't like it and once had the network picketed by midgets bearing signs that read, "This Network Unfair to the Little Man."

Allen never came to the Coast during the years I worked there. He didn't take to movie-making until later, and it was, of course, the films that brought us the radio shows of Cantor, Benny, and Burns and Allen.

I was doing well in radio by the time the great vaudevillians began to brighten up the California scene. I was playing the lead in a sketch on "Shell Chateau" each week—a saccharine tale, purporting to be the private lives of the program's two singers. Jolson would say something like, "Remember the two kids I told you about who are so much in love? Well, the other day I heard him say to her . . ." and Fred MacKaye and I would play a love scene, culminating in a duet sung by Nadine Connor (later a Metropolitan Opera star) and a baritone whose name I never knew. (None of us got billing.)

Shell's twenty-five dollars plus the twenty-five for Jerry Cady's recorded mystery shows gave me a basic minimum of $50 each week. It would have been easy to push up to a hundred, except for two things —the many days of rehearsal required by network shows and the vast distances between the radio studios. It was impossible, for example, to do both the Benny and the Cantor shows in the same week. They rehearsed at approximately the same time and miles apart. We called this situation a "conflict," and it forced some agonizing decisions on us.

When Jerry Cady set up the time for his recording session it came in direct conflict with "Camel Caravan." Jerry was offering me a steady job. Camel was in the habit of calling me about once a month. I chose Jerry. One day when Camel's producer, Robert Redd, called me and I refused, he doubled the fee to $50. I still refused.

"I'm going to make it hard for you to say no," he countered. "Seventy-five." I was amazed. We never negotiated with the agencies. Each show paid a set salary.

"No. You see, I'm playing the lead on Jerry Cady's new series and—."

"Oh, is it Jerry?" He said. "I'll get back to you."

After a day of wire-pulling, Bob got Jerry to let Barbara Luddy replace me for one recording session, and he upped my Camel salary to $100.

I had always played tragic roles on "Camel Caravan" and I was prepared for another teary interlude when I arrived at the Hollywood Music Box (by then a CBS radio studio) for the first rehearsal. The sight of a small, round-faced man standing alone on the stage shot my spirits into high gear.

"You're Harpo!" I squealed.

"No," he said, gravely. "I'm Chico." (He pronounced it Chick-o.) It was my favorite Marx brother—the one with the hilarious piano technique. We were alone in the theater and I flattered him into giving me a private concert—a rollicking recital, the pianist shooting out the high notes with thumb and forefinger. But as he played on and on, he began to look perplexed.

"I can't find the end," he said, finally. "I think I passed it."

Only the name of my character—Josephine—and one line of that Marx Brothers sketch remains in memory: "Napoleon," I had to say, "was not at Valley Forge."

The Marx Brothers seemed calm. They stayed calm until about three hours before air time on the last day. Then Chico began to brood. He called his brothers and me into a huddle and dropped his voice to a near whisper, although everyone else had left for the dinner break.

"We're doing the wrong script," he confided. "It isn't funny. It isn't *funny*," he repeated.

Oh boy, I thought—here we go.

"Oh, I don't know," said Groucho, and sat down in the front row of the auditorium. Harpo, standing on the stage beside Chico, said nothing.

"Even this one is better," insisted Chico, pulling some wrinkled pages from his pocket. Slowly and somberly he read every line of a ten-minute skit aloud, his brothers listening gravely.

"There," he said morosely when he'd ended. "Isn't that funnier?"

"Oh, I don't know," said Groucho.

Harpo said nothing.

Chico turned to me.

"What do *you* think?" he asked.

"I don't like it," I said. "There's no part for me."

"I hadn't thought of that," he replied with real concern.

Groucho cleared his throat. "I think we'll stick to the first script," he said. "We'll cut the last four lines in the first scene—and segue right into Josephine." He rolled his eyes and flipped his brows at me. "Fine talk!" he added.

"But it's not *funny*," said Chico, doggedly.

They had reached a stalemate.

"Groucho is right," said a firm voice.

Harpo had spoken. Chico immediately stuffed the papers back in his pocket and the crisis was over. The flop sweat had passed.

I started out.

"Where are you going?" asked Groucho.

"To dinner."

"You're going to have dinner with us," he said. "We've sent for it—the Brown Derby."

So I sat in my old dressing room in the Music Box, where once had flown the Wendy Bird, and dined with the Marx Brothers. Lobster Newburg, as I remember.

The atmosphere before the show was relaxed but serious. Each Marx brother knew that he was flanked by two expert laugh-getters. It made for confidence.

They were as careful craftsmen as ever came off the Orpheum circuit, and the collective Marx mind, like that of every comic since the days of Aristophanes, was on just one thing—the Audience.

Once the Camel show was on the air, Chico, Harpo, and I stood together in the wings watching Bill Goodwin make the opening announcements. When he had finished and the orchestra struck up a tune, the announcer turned and casually walked upstage.

Harpo's jaw dropped.

"Did you *see* that guy?" he whispered, incredulously.

"Yeah," said Chico, amazement in his voice. "Turned his *back* right on the *audience*."

"Radio—it's a funny business," said Harpo, and they both shook their heads.

Chico wandered away and Harpo and I stood alone in the wings, watching the show. Seconds before his entrance he turned to me.

"Think you could find a hammer?" he whispered. "A big one?"

I scurried off to a stagehand and borrowed an enormous one.

"Listen," Harpo said when I returned. "If I put it in my pocket, sit down at the harp, and then take it out—*will that be funny?*"

It was funny, all right. He sat down by the harp, touched the strings, and a look of wild consternation spread across his face. When he pulled out that lethal-looking hammer the audience convulsed.

Midway in the sketch I had to make one of those dreaded decisions. An expected laugh didn't come. I waited. When I felt dead air closing in on me, I jumped in with my next line. One of the writers dashed up when we came off the stage.

"She stepped on that laugh," he bleated.

"No, she didn't," said Groucho, firmly. "There *was* no laugh."

"Writers always blame their bad lines on the actors," said Chico.

That gallant defense won the Marx brothers a place in my heart forever. All that, and Lobster Newburg, too. It was only thirty minutes by bus, but I felt light years from Pickfair.

I was a frequent visitor to the Music Box in those days. Several CBS audience shows were broadcast from there. The most important from my point of view was "Lux Radio Theater"—because it paid $50. It had started in New York, featuring Broadway plays and players. Later it shifted to Hollywood to take advantage of the wider appeal of the motion picture names. My first appearance was on the second show from there—"Laburnum Grove," starring Frank Morgan as the genial counterfeiter. I played his daughter. After that I averaged one Lux show a month.

No devotee of the unseen drama can ever forget that portentous opening: "Lux presents—HOLLYWOOD." A musical fanfare followed. Then the announcer, Mel Ruick, continued, "Lux Radio Theater brings you . . ." Here he gave the name of the play and its stars. Then there was another flourish of music, followed by Ruick's saying, "Ladies and gentlemen—your producer—Cecil B. De Mille."

Wouldn't you have gathered from that that Mr. De Mille produced the radio epic you were about to hear? Well, he didn't. As a matter of fact, he never turned up until the last day of rehearsal, and then only to read through his brief narrations before going on the air. The producing was done by an unassuming young man named Frank Woodruff.

De Mille was agreeable to work with. He was polite enough to actors when they approached him singly. It was only when they collectivized into unions that he seemed to hate them. A few years after he became the nonproducing producer of Lux, the American Federation of Radio Artists was founded. He seems to have joined quietly enough, but when in 1944 the union levied a tax of $1 per member to fight a so-called "right-to-work" bill in California, he balked. Still flexing his muscles from his victory over Actors' Equity Association sixteen years before, De Mille forced the radio actors into a position where they had to suspend him. Then he took them to court.

Mr. De Mille voiced his views on the air. So the following week, the great Metropolitan Opera baritone Lawrence Tibbett (then president of AFRA) appeared on "The March of Time" program to give ours.

"AFRA," he said, "is out to establish that when any protective organization is threatened by proposed legislation its members have the right to assess themselves by majority vote for the education of the voters as to what issues are involved."

Judge Emmett Wilson ruled in favor of the union. Cecil B. De Mille was whisked off the air (which, according to *Broadcasting* magazine, cost him $98,500 annually) and enshrined forever as martyr-hero in the hearts of Hollywood's right wing.

J. Walter Thompson was forced to find a substitute. They settled on the film director William Keighley. Frank Woodruff went on doing the real job as before. Years later when Woodruff left, a radio actor, Fred MacKaye (my companion of "Shell Chateau" and one of "Hollywood Hotel's" Gay Ad-libbers), took over as director. Then began what was surely one of the slowest "burns" in theatrical history. Here is the record from our leading trade paper, *Variety:*

"After 8 years of directing Lux Radio Theater, Fred MacKaye has ankled because . . . he wants director billing. Cornwell Jackson v p of the J. Walter Thompson agency agrees with MacKaye that the Lux format now implies producer-host William Keighley is director but says that's the way it's been set up for 18 years and it can't be changed now."

What *Variety* apparently didn't know was that even the term "producer-host" was misleading. Just plain narrator would have been more accurate.

I sympathized with Fred's cankering dissatisfaction. It was a similar emotion that made me leave Hollywood forever—a nagging conviction that if any real plum came along it would automatically be handed over to a movie personality.

Other considerations, too, led to my decision. Father had died suddenly of a heart attack two years before (in 1934) and any joy I felt in my work seemed to go with him. Then, in 1936, Jerry Cady came back from New York with a fat film contract in his pocket.

"You're wasting your time here," he told me. "You'd make a killing in New York. Look at my case. I could hardly make seventy-five a week before I left. Now they're paying me fifteen hundred. You can't do that from Hollywood. You have to get away."

I remembered a conversation I heard as a child between my father and Clark Gable when we met him once on Hollywood Boulevard.

"Get out of here, Bill," Gable had said. "Get back to New York. It's the only place for an actor. Don't come out again till you have a contract."

Father, at the end of his life, had been reduced to bit parts to keep that gasman from the door. When a call had come through from New York, offering him a role in the Theater Guild's production of "Uncle Vanya," he couldn't get released from the insignificant thing he was doing. His death at a time when he was poor and heartbroken left me with an unreasoning resentment of my surroundings.

So Jerry Cady found a ready audience for his enthusiastic descriptions of the New York radio scene.

"Look at Hanley Stafford," he said. "He went east when I did. I know as a fact he made $100 over the first weekend. And take Jeannette Nolan. She's starring on her own show on CBS. She could never have got so far here. I promise, you'll make a killing. Look. I'm writing four shows that come from there. I'll write a part for you in each one, insist that you play it, and threaten to write it out if you don't. You'll make four hundred the first week."

He couldn't understand why I hung back.

There were three reasons for my reluctance.

The first was Mother. Rita was married and living in another city. My brother Millard had left home while I was still a child. He, too, was married. Mother and I were alone. To leave her would be cruel.

"Is it money?" Jerry asked.

It was that, too. After nearly five years in radio I didn't even have a bank account.

Jerry offered to stake me, but I was still reluctant.

The third and strongest deterrent was that I had never spent a night away from home alone in my life and the thought sent my stomach plummeting to my heels. All in all, I had strong anchorage that might have kept me moored to my hated but snug little harbor forever, had not a couple of hurricane winds, named Josephine Brown and Wauna Paul, mother and daughter, blown into port. They were old friends from pre-"Peter Pan" days. We had met five years before, at a cocktail party. I had arrived late and I heard what I took to be a "whiskey" tenor voice, hoarse but with vestiges of great beauty.

"Portugal," it announced, "was a veritable spies' nest during the war."

The speaker was a lovely woman with flaming red hair. She was holding a group of young actors spellbound.

"It was worth one's life to cross into Spain," she went on, turning enormous gray eyes on me and drawing me into the circle. "Our train was stopped at the border. I lost my head when they questioned me and couldn't answer intelligently. They held me incommunicado for most of the day—thought they had caught another Mata-Hari."

She paused for the gasp that ran through her audience. "It was terrifying, but not so bad as what happened to the English school teacher who shared my compartment. She had gone to the ladies' room, and you know how filthy those public facilities can get—well, she took a letter from her bag to cover the seat. It was closely written, as I recall, in purple ink. Later the matron who searched her noticed something unusual and reported it to her superiors. Well, my dears, they held that poor creature forty-eight hours—trying to decipher her!"

The speaker expelled a cloud of smoke. "That's why," she added, with even more startling irrelevance, "I've always said everyone should speak French. Wauna speaks beautiful French. Don't you, dear?"

She turned to a young girl in blouse, skirt, and beret, who was sitting in a window seat.

"I'd be an ass if I didn't," said the girl. (She pronounced it ah-ss.) "I went to school there eight years."

Wauna grinned, looking like one of the Campbell Kids—round face, green eyes, perfect small teeth, and deep dimples. Her mother turned back to the young man.

"It was only my knowledge of what you might call 'gutter Spanish' that kept a crowd in Madrid from tearing me limb from limb. I was playing on the same bill as the great dancer Argentina at the Teatro . . ."

I was entranced. By the time I followed the crowd of gaping juveniles to install Joey (as she was called) in her aged Chevrolet sedan, I had accepted an invitation to meet the legendary Eurasian Sadakichi Hartman, and hear a young Italian bootblack who, according to my new friend, had a voice like Caruso and the technique of "Mishoo" Elman. I asked if she didn't mean Mischa, not Mishoo. She replied that she did indeed but that she called him Mishoo because he had *asked* her to call him that.

Wauna, so Joey said, was an Indian name, given her daughter because she was born in this country and deserved something "truly American." (Joey, too, was born in this country—Bloomington, Illinois. But it was years before I unearthed that information.) Wauna, her mother told me, swam as well as she spoke French. It was a trick she had picked up at the age of eight in the mountain stream that ran through the Basque village of Itxassou and separated their house from the village bar. During parties it was often necessary to replenish the household stock of champagne, but the ferry stopped at sundown. The picture of the plucky little tike plunging into the icy torrent, festooned head to foot with bottles, was one of the more inspired bits of her mother's smoky repertoire.

The extraordinary part of these tales was that they were true. Wauna could swim like a porpoise. She really had taught herself in that turbulent Pyrenees stream. She was also a wine and champagne expert. At the age of sixteen, she could determine, by tasting, the point of origin of any French wine and, like as not, its vintage year, too. And she spoke French with the raciness of a Paris taxi driver. She had been taken to Europe at the age of six months and not returned until a few weeks before our meeting, when she was sixteen.

Joey had begun life as a child violin prodigy, playing, from all accounts, with a fiery technique and total lack of pitch. In her teens she had a brief but dazzling success in the theater (leading woman with William Gillette and John Barrymore), had run away from a dominating mother to marry an English wine importer (Feuerheerd ports and sherries), lived in Paris, been sculpted by Rodin, painted by Augustus John, and stranded in Spain and Portugal by World War I.

Josephine Brown and Wauna Paul were warm, kind, but hardly what you'd call simple people. We formed a lasting friendship that cast a bright if bewildering glow over my life.

About the time I discovered "English Coronets," my two friends moved to New York. Four years later when Joey came huffing and puffing up the stone steps of my hillside house I didn't recognize her. She had gone from a hundred and fifteen to two hundred pounds and shifted personality to suit her new size. She was now a jolly, ribald, female Falstaff. Wauna had hardly changed at all. They had both been playing in the Broadway theater and had made several trips to Europe as well.

"And what have you been up to?" Joey asked.

Radio sounded pretty drab, I thought, as I told them about it, but Joey sparked immediately.

"Why, that's what my friend Anne Seymour does," she said. "I hear she's making a fortune."

One could do better in the East, I explained, because there was more work, and fees were higher. Mother and daughter exchanged glances.

"We'll be going back pretty soon," Joey said. "Perhaps you could come with us. We'll be driving."

Mother came in then and I changed the subject. A few days later Wauna said, "You know, when we came to see you before leaving for New York, you were wearing a Russian blouse and sitting at the piano. We came back four years later and the first thing we heard was the sound of your piano, and when you opened the door there you were in the same—."

"It's not the same Russian blouse," I countered. "It's a new one."

"It's depressing," Joey said. "You must *do* something. You mustn't go on like *this*."

When they heard about Jerry Cady's offer, my friends caught fire and started a campaign to get me out of Hollywood, and when Joey and Wauna started a campaign something was bound to give. In this case it was Mother. We went through six months of tears, tempest, and re-crimination. Joey had an apartment in the Hotel Plaza. She offered to put me up there indefinitely. Wauna had a new Lincoln Zephyr. She offered free transportation.

"What will happen if she gets sick?" my mother wailed.

"We'll toss her in the hospital," Joey said.

Mother begged me to wait until she and I could amass enough capital to go together. Rita kept away and was noncommital. My brother took me out alone in his car one evening.

"You should have left home long ago," he said. "I should have seen what was happening. Go now or you never will."

Millard and I were very close, although he had been away from home most of my life. It was his voice that made the final decision.

I couldn't wait to break the news to Jerry Cady. He sat behind his big desk in the film studio and stared at me. Finally, he spoke.

"You picked a hell of a time for it," he said. "I've just given up my radio shows. The studio insisted."

Deep-seated cowardice must have shown on my face because he added quickly, "I still think you ought to go—I'll do everything I can to help you. I'll write Himan Brown. He's a producer. He can give you lots of work."

I talked it over with Nat Wolf. (At that time "Parties at Pickfair" was still on the air.) He was not encouraging. He gave me letters to twelve New York producers but he said, "It's a tougher game back there than it is here. A hard little core of people do all the radio work and some top Broadway actors have found it impossible to crack it."

I wrote to Ed Rice, the former script editor of "Shell Chateau," who had moved to J. Walter Thompson's New York office. I got back a telegram that ran right off the first blank and filled up a second. The import was that Ed thought I was a fine actress but fine actresses were

96

a dime a dozen in New York, work was scarce, and competition fierce, but that if I were fool enough to risk it, he would do everything he could to help me.

Bob Redd gave me a blanket "To whom it may concern" letter stating unequivocally that I was the best radio actress in Hollywood. It was so fulsome I was embarrassed to show it to people.

NBC's Hollywood representative, Cecil Underwood, frowned. "Aren't you picking a funny time?" he said. "So many shows are moving *here* now." But he gave me a letter to Bertha Brainard of NBC's Artists' Bureau.

There were eighteen letters in all.

The plan was to leave during the first week in January, 1937. As Christmas approached I grew steadily slimmer and so keyed up I couldn't sleep nights. Mother started crying along about Thanksgiving and kept it up through New Year's.

Finally the day came, and I skulked down the front steps—feeling like Cain, Judas, and Benedict Arnold rolled into one. The last thing I saw as we drove away in the cream-colored Lincoln was my brother standing on the porch, holding my hysterical mother in his arms. I was nearly as miserable as she was. Hardly was the house out of sight, however, than my spirits shot up like a rocket and I was ashamed to find that I was happy—happier than I had ever been in my life.

I had $50 in my pocket and free board and lodging in the Land of Promise. I felt lightheaded, daring, and reckless. The world was my oyster, and 1937 was my year!

How could I know that ninety percent of the nighttime shows were even then moving west, and that I would soon be up to my chin in a type of flop sweat entirely my own? It was not until almost thirty years later, while doing research for this book, that I learned what went wrong.

My year—1937! Why, that was the year they learned to reverse the Round Robin!

CHAPTER IX

The Black Hole of Calcutta

We skimmed the miles from Hollywood to New York in Wauna's cream-colored Lincoln and drove up before the luxurious Hotel Plaza, where Joey had an apartment in the annex. Once inside, I stood at the window, marveling at the sweeping view of Central Park, while Joey and Wauna busied themselves prying open a recently delivered case of champagne, which bore the card of a French nobleman they knew. Joey suggested a hot bath and scented it with jasmine oil, then placed a glass of champagne on a small table beside the tub. As I slid rapturously, glass in hand, into the steaming, perfumed water, something told me I was going to like New York.

Nineteen thirty-seven was one of the warmest winters in the history of the Eastern Seaboard, but I didn't know that. I had been brought up in a semitropical climate and expected chilblains to appear the moment I put foot out-of-doors. So the following morning I wriggled into heavy woolen underwear, two of the seven sweaters I had brought, a wool skirt, wool jacket, fur hat, and a muffler. Over this I squeezed the old leopard coat.

With three of the letters of introduction I had brought from the Coast, I made for Madison Avenue and the Columbia Broadcasting System building. Soon I was in the office of one of the executives, peeping out at him from my furry cocoon, and shoving my letter of introduction across his desk. He took me in to meet Marge Morrow, the casting director of the network, and Earl McGill, one of the producers, and between them they arranged for me to play a part on the "Columbia School of the Air" the next day, which was a Tuesday.

"School of the Air" was an educational feature, carried as a public

98

service by the network, and it was a "sustainer." The actors called these half-hour network sustainers "slow twenty-ones" because they paid $21 and were rehearsed for what seemed an interminable length of time.

In a spurt of confidence I crossed the street to the advertising agency of Benton & Bowles and talked my way in to see a taciturn Scot, Ken MacGregor, who gave me an immediate audition and cast me for the lead opposite Lanny Ross on "Show Boat." This was an hour-long program, sponsored by Maxwell House Coffee. It paid $30. So far, so good.

I was reassured at the "School of the Air" rehearsal next day. Everything seemed to be about the same as in Hollywood. I did think the announcer was exceptional. I was right. It was Robert Trout. Thursday brought "Show Boat" and my spirits soared. I had marvelous billing, coast to coast—my name coming right after that of Lanny Ross.

That night when I returned, tired but happy, to the Plaza Hotel, I thought pityingly of the struggling radio actors at home in Hollywood who must have heard me and my billing. I slipped into another jasmine scented bath, another glass of champagne in my hand. Oh boy, if they could see me now.

We were thrown out of the Plaza six months later. Not bodily. We got a letter.

The stiff, formal note demanded that we leave within a week. I read it and went into shock.

"Oh, she's upset," Joey said. "You mustn't take it to heart, silly one. I'll send down for some champagne and—." She broke off and laughed again. "Oh dear. I suppose I can't any more, can I?"

"Good Lord, no, Mother." Wauna never called Joey "Mother" except in times of stress. "That's been the trouble." They looked at each other and giggled.

In a flash the whole situation became clear to me. I had been contributing what I thought was an adequate sum to the running of the Plaza apartment, and Joey had converted into cash a good-sized insurance policy left by her late husband. But for each radio job I had landed we had held a celebration; for each tiny disappointment we had held a consolation party; for every old friend who dropped in to say hello we had tossed a minor reception. On each of these occasions, Joey had called Room Service for a bottle of champagne and a platter of caviar. In a luxury hotel—and anywhere else, for that matter—this has a tendency to mount up. It had taken us six months to guzzle our way through Joey's capital.

Wauna lit a cigarette, stretched out on the couch, and said, "Well, I think we ought to take a vacation. We've been working too hard looking for work, and now we need a rest. All work and no play, you know—."

"But we haven't had any all work," I countered. "At least none to speak of."

It was true. In spite of my auspicious start, New York radio had not been consumed in the blaze of my glory. I was working on a job-to-job basis and making about $100 a week. With fantastically bad timing, I had arrived when most of the big radio shows were moving out to the Coast (that damned Round Robin, of course) and some of my letters had remained undelivered because the addresses were already in Hollywood.

Meanwhile, according to Mother, my stock had risen so high on the Coast that I could have incorporated and sold shares. "Benny called you again last week," she wrote, "so did Cantor. Bob Redd called to ask if you were coming home soon. There was a good part on Lux, too . . ." It was discouraging.

"Mm, I see what Wauna means and I think she's right," Joey said. "I have a few bonds I can sell. If we can find a cheap enough place in the country we ought to be able to squeak by for the summer. Then we'll come back full of pep and take New York by storm."

The next morning we drove to Woodstock, New York, and rented a primitive cottage in a wood—$200 for the season.

That summer in Woodstock was one of the best vacations I have ever had. I had put in five years in Hollywood trying to make ends meet, and six months of knocking on doors in New York. Lolling about in the sun, doing nothing, had a wonderful effect. I was brown, healthy, and relaxed at the end of it.

Wauna and I went down to New York a week before we had to give up the cottage in order to find winter quarters. This tiresome duty was complicated by the fact that we were hardly in a financial position to sign a lease. So we dragged from one furnished rooming house to another, all horribly dingy. My depression was augmented by the fact that my singing voice was the major obstacle to our finding accommodations.

"I know what's wrong," Wauna finally said. "We haven't been looking in the right neighborhood. The West Side. That's where we have to go. The West Side." We had been tramping Greenwich Village in our dismal search.

"What makes you think the West Side will be any easier?" I asked.

"That's where all the opera people live," she explained.

We took the subway, got out at Seventy-second Street, and started marching up and down the streets off West End Avenue. On Seventy-fourth Street we saw a sign in the window of a pretty brownstone building, "Furnished Rooms." We went in and were met by a tall, fleshy woman, upholstered in plum velvet. She was Alice Watson, landlady and owner of the house, a former Metropolitan Opera singer.

"Ah, yes," she said in even, oval tones. "The second-floor front is empty."

We followed her up the carpeted stair. The place was cheerful. I decided at once that we couldn't afford it. Everything we had seen within our price range had included peeling paint and male tenants hanging about in their undershirts in fetid hallways. Here, in the second-floor front, sunlight poured through a beautiful casement window. The room was enormous—obviously the converted upstairs parlor of an old townhouse. A bath had been added to it. There was a large clothes closet and a small open alcove beside it. The furniture was sparse, but a concert grand Steinway stood in the middle of the room.

"Will you leave the piano?" I asked.

"Oh, yes, most of our apartments have pianos."

From the second-floor rear came the sound of a Chopin etude. Wauna gave me her "I told you so" look.

"You have musicians in the house?" she asked.

"Ah, yes. Nearly everyone here is an artist of some sort or other." The etude came to an end and we could hear from another floor the quavering sound of a breathy coloratura, perilously ascending a staccato scale. The room, Miss Watson informed us, was only $60.

"The trouble is," Wauna was saying, "we need more space. There are three of us. You haven't a larger apartment, I suppose?"

"No." Miss Watson reflected. "I have another smaller room and bath. Very nice and it's only forty dollars. It's in the building next door."

Wauna took a last happy look at the second-floor front. She stood in the alcove near the clothes closet, noticed with a smile that there was a light in it, and started measuring the empty walls with her eye. Miss Watson showed long experience as a landlady.

"There is only one thing," she said. "Absolutely no cooking."

There it was—the catch I'd been expecting. We had to have a kitchen. I was starting for the door when I heard Wauna saying, "Of course not. We don't eat at home." She smiled. "Let's have a look at the other room," she said.

It turned out to be first-floor rear, dark, but with chintz curtains and slip covers. Wauna closed the deal for both rooms and left a $20 deposit. In the hall on our way out we encountered an old colored man.

"This is Lewis," said Miss Watson, majestically. "He will take care of your rooms."

Josephine (Joey) Brown, actress and Mary Jane Higby's long-time friend, in 1959.

Announcer Frank Gallop and Minerva Pious (Mrs. Nussbaum of Allen's Alley) at an actors' union ball.

Wauna glowed with pleasure. "A manservant," she whispered to me. I could tell that she saw in him the dignified old family retainer on a magnolia-covered estate. To me, Lewis was the prototype of the image the NAACP is trying to erase from the public mind: Uncle Tom, with overtones of Old Black Joe. (Later I learned that there were undertones of Caliban. He was stooped and gnarled, his head covered with a white frizz. He was toothless and his jutting jaw almost met his low, beetling brow. He would shuffle by, muttering to himself like an old scottie dog in indistinguishable growls.)

"What have you done?" I demanded of Wauna as soon as we were out in the street. "We can't afford to eat out all the time. You're as bad as Joey with her caviar and champagne."

"Oh, hush," she said. "You don't know anything about New York. I lived in an apartment in Greenwich Village once where they had strict rules about no cooking and I used to give spaghetti parties and invite the landlord. Everybody always cooks in these furnished digs." (She used English words like "digs" when she wanted to win an argument with me.) "It's common practice in New York. Miss Watson has to *say* no cooking on account of city regulations or something. All we need is a two-burner hot plate. What do you suppose that alcove is there for?"

Moving day was strenuous. We had to make the long drive from Woodstock in the Lincoln with all our belongings piled on the back seat. And every last one of them had to be lugged up a flight of stairs into the second-floor front or the first-floor rear. Midway in this operation, I went to the corner drugstore for sandwiches and a bottle of milk. We sat around, dazed and weary, and took turns drinking milk out of the one glass we had unpacked. There was a little left after we finished.

"Save it," Wauna said. "We'll use it for coffee in the morning."

"We can't save it," I griped. "We've no refrigerator."

Joey took up the bottle with a flourish, opened a window, and set it on the outside ledge. Two minutes later Miss Watson knocked on the door and told us in frigid tones to take it off and never to leave anything on the sill again.

"It's the front of the house," she said. "I can't have bottles sitting out there."

I was embarrassed to the point of tears, but Joey just laughed. "Of course not, my dear," she said blandly, "I put it there temporarily while we were straightening out and tidying up. It was our luncheon, you know." The elegant accent prevailed. Miss Watson melted and retired, deeply impressed.

"We'll have to leave the food on my windowsill," Joey muttered when the landlady had gone. "She'll never see it there."

I had written Himan Brown from Woodstock to tell him when I would be back in New York and he had three shows for me the day after we moved into Seventy-fourth street. The first was a series of recordings called "Doctor Friendly" in which I was to play the lovable old doc's daughter. The next was to start a running part on a live series, "Joyce Jordan, Girl Interne," and the third was a rehearsal of a new program, "Grand Central Station." Agnes Moorehead played the lead and I played her grandmother. I was in my early twenties. That was one of the rewards of radio work. We could play characters that no one would ever allow us to attempt in a visual medium.

That whole day was fun, exciting but tiring, and when I fought my way onto the West Side "El" during the rush hour I was looking forward to that cheerful room on the second-floor front.

I found Wauna in high excitement. She had tried out for a part on a children's show and was sure she was going to get it. Joey had left word that she, too, had got a call and wouldn't be home for dinner. Earlier in the day we had strung up a curtain across the alcove and had put there as a temporary table one of the barrels in which we had moved our belongings. On it Wauna placed Joey's double electric burner. The percolator was on the floor.

"Will bacon and eggs be all right for tonight?" she asked. "I was too tired to bother doing any regular shopping."

The feathery notes of "Si J'étais Oiseau" were fluttering down the hall from the piano studio in the second-floor rear. I opened the keyboard of our enormous Steinway and attempted an arpeggio. What I got was a series of clanks. I raised the top of the piano. The soundboard was cracked and buckled. Some of the strings were hanging loose. I closed it again. As I lit the two lamps in the room, I noticed that there were no draperies at the window, only cracked green blinds. I saw for the first time the threadbare carpet—all warp, no woof.

Wauna trotted out of the bathroom carrying a pan of water. She knelt down in the alcove, found the electric plug—and the lights blew.

The pianist faltered and stopped. I groped my way to the door. Inky blackness filled the house. The professor of piano, who occupied the second-floor rear, appeared in the gloom, his square Prussian face lit by a candle.

I started down to the street to get the flashlight from the car and groped into Lewis, who was grumbling his way up the stairs.

"Somebody put too heavy a load on the wiring," he growled.

When I returned upstairs Lewis had come and gone and Wauna had borrowed a candle from the music professor. The lights came on and the music lesson began again.

"Thank goodness," said Wauna, "I'm starving. Now I can really get cracking."

She did. Ten seconds later we were again in darkness.

There was a knock at the door. "What are you girls doing?" It was Miss Watson.

"The lights keep going off," said Wauna in an accusing tone. "We can't do anything."

Miss Watson underscored each word. "You cannot use electric appliances in this apartment. That's final."

We heard her summon Lewis and the answering growl from our manservant. In a short time the lights went on.

I went to the closet and got my coat.

"What are you doing?" Wauna was indignant.

"Be sensible, Wauna. We've got to go out to eat."

"Nonsense. We have all this food. It'll spoil. I know what I did wrong. I put two appliances on at once. I'll just cook the bacon first—."

"No! I refuse to face Miss Watson again."

"Relax. I'm not going to put any load on the wiring. You'll see."

I stood wringing my hands nervously while the bacon sizzled away, filling the room with its tantalizing odor. I had decided not to wait for the eggs but to go at the bacon first—when the lights went out. This time the pupil in the professor's studio didn't miss a note. I peeked out. The teacher had left his door open and placed candelabra on either side of the piano. He was beating time sternly. He turned when I opened my door and sniffed. Then he stalked to the stairwell and called down in a heavy guttural accent, "Someone is cooking."

I closed the door and crouched in the corner like the coward I was, while Wauna flew around disposing of evidence.

Miss Watson seemed to have grown a foot since I had last seen her. She towered at our door like an outraged Lady Macbeth, candle in hand.

"Now, girls, I told you no cooking. There is just not enough electricity. I told you that when you took the room."

"Cooking?" Wauna was all innocence.

Miss Watson gave a sniff that could have been heard in the top reaches of the Met's gallery. "Bacon!" she boomed. "Really!"

Wauna giggled and Miss Watson laughed a little, too. Then she named an Italian restaurant where we could get a good meal cheap.

"It's a private apartment. Knock on the door and tell them I sent you. They have no license to run a restaurant."

After she left I took a stand. "I'm not going to any crooked restaurant," I said.

"Don't be silly," Wauna said. "You see, in New York lots of cafes—." I didn't bother to listen to the explanation. I knew we would wind up in the illegal restaurant and, of course, we did.

The next day Miss Watson turned up with a proposition. She had one room where we could cook, a garden apartment for only $45.

"Marvelous," said Wauna. "Joey has a green thumb."

The apartment was in the garden, all right—under it, in fact. The only window was at chest level and flush with the ground outside, which was filled with ashcans and bottles. It was a square box with a low ceiling and illuminated by the half-window. Off it was the bathroom-kitchen area, a unique arrangement, in which a two-burner gas stove was perched conveniently on the top of the toilet tank, and a chopping board straddled the bath. The washbowl served as kitchen sink. The furniture was dilapidated.

Joey came along from her room to take a look and collapsed in laughter. "Not much like the Plaza, is it?" she said.

Whenever Wauna and Joey met a disaster that would stun the average person, they laughed and they meant it. They treated any problem short of death that way. They promptly christened our new home "the Black Hole Of Calcutta."

Lewis continued to do our rooms for us. That is, he used to come in and wave a dirty rag around once a day. We couldn't blame him for the grimy condition, however. The dirt from the garden blew in steadily. Later in the winter we woke to find that a pile of snow about a foot deep had sifted in through the window. We could tell that Lewis had been through all this before. He seemed to take it for granted that part of his chores was to shovel snow from the garden apartment, and he turned up fully prepared.

As the days passed, we would hear Miss Watson's musical voice ringing through the halls. "Lewis! Bring that trunk down from the attic. Lewis! Take care of the third-floor front. Lewis! There's a bulb out in the top floor hall."

Lewis always responded with his unintelligible grunt, a sort of animal complaint.

One night I woke with the conviction that there was an intruder in the room. I lay for awhile, holding my breath in terror and listening. But when I distinctly heard a man's voice, I switched on the lamp. There was no one there, but a sepulchral voice rose from the floor. "And Miss Watson, lemme tell you somep'n," it said. Then followed a string of curses.

It was Lewis. His lair was evidently even deeper in the ground than ours—under ours, in fact—a windowless, black cellar in the bowels of the earth. As time wore on, we got used to his expressing his rancor toward his employer in the dead of night.

One day, a few months after our descent into the Black Hole of Calcutta, Joey came home in a state of jubilation. The Shuberts had signed her for a part in "A Bachelor Born," a play they were importing from England. Joey, who had once been William Gillette's leading woman and who had co-starred briefly with John Barrymore, had the smallest part in the piece. It didn't bother her a bit. She was starting all over again at the very bottom of the ladder and she took it as a game.

Luckily, "Bachelor Born" was a hit and she got a full year's work out of it. The leading lady was a Canadian actress, Helen Trenholm. Helen had a dainty elegance that set her apart—always perfectly groomed, not a hair out of place, not a crease in her exquisitely tailored English suits.

On the strength of a few drinks after the show one night, Joey invited her the next day for tea. Wauna was shaken when she heard about it.

"Joey must have been drunk to invite that girl *here*," she said.

In the sober light of day Joey was still optimistic. "Oh, we can bring it off. Gay bohemian sort of thing, you know. It's not where you live——it's what you are that counts."

Helen arrived early. Wauna was still making cucumber sandwiches in the bathtub and Joey was hovering over the toilet, brewing tea, so I let her in. Our guest settled as comfortably as she could into our over-stuffed chair. The springs had given way and the chair had a tendency to shoot your knees toward your chin when you sat down. Helen smoothed the beautiful silk print dress she was wearing (something by Patou or Lanvin), and remarked that it was a truly lovely day. A good sport, she never batted an eyelid at the surroundings in which she found herself but drank her tea out of the Hotel Plaza cup just like a perfect lady.

Then she reached for her cigarettes on the table near the window, fumbling around a little before her hand came to rest on the package. After she lit her cigarette, she brushed her hand over her cheek. It left a broad, black streak.

"Oh, Helen, dear," Joey said. "I'm afraid you have a tiny bit of soot on your face." She led her into the bathroom so she could see. Helen let out a scream when she saw herself in the mirror, and Joey hastily cleared the dishes out of the washbowl so she could clean up. Finally, we had settled cosily with the tea things once more and Joey in her best English accent had worked the conversation around to her cousin, Lord Henry Something-or-other, Earl of Somethingshire, when a male voice came roaring up through the floorboards. "Miss Watson, you can kiss my ass."

That was the last social event of the season.

Wauna's kid show finally came through. She became the leading lady of a radio program sponsored by Tootsie Rolls. I was peeved and I showed it. I had come all the way from California and had been knocking my brains out trying to land a lead on a daytime serial, and Wauna, who had had very little radio experience, had walked right in and snatched one up under my very nose. She paid no attention to my surliness but there was a grim determination about her during the first week the show was on the air.

The second week she came home and waved a lease under our noses.

"We're moving," she said. Joey and I were too abashed even to ask where.

We dragged everything we owned out of the Black Hole of Calcutta and stuffed it into the Lincoln. That is, half was stuffed in, then fat little Joey was stuffed in, and the rest was pushed in on top of her. Our possessions had grown in the months we had lived at the Seventy-fourth Street address, as household equipment is wont to do. There was no longer room for me in the car. I watched the elegant Lincoln as it whipped into Riverside Drive and turned south, a huge bundle of last-minute things teetering in a red checked tablecloth tied on its top.

Bruno of Ho[l

Mary Jane Higby when she took over starring role in "When a Girl Marries" in 1938.

CHAPTER X

'Tis a Pity She's a Bore

The thing that impressed me most on my arrival in New York was not the fabled skyline, nor the Empire State Building, nor even the cluster of mammoth temples known as Radio City. It was the parade of mink that mobilized at the networks on the first chilly day. Hollywood-bred though I was, and used to the costly whims of movie stars (Rudolph Valentino's famous Eagle's Nest was less than two blocks from my childhood home, and I passed Charles Ray's pleasure dome, with its solid gold bathroom fixtures, on my way to school), still I was left slack-jawed by my initial visit to the lunch counter in the CBS Building. There luxurious fur cuffs brushed lightly across the pickle relish, and crumbs from hamburger buns sifted through the extra-long top-hairs of the wild mink collars.

"That's Valiant Lady," someone whispered, as a particularly fine Labrador coat whirled about on its stool. "She gets $1,400 for that one show."

"There goes Aunt Jenny," and not only coat, but mink hat, muff, and mink-topped galoshes sauntered by.

Mink, it seemed, was the uniform of the soap opera stars.

Come hell or high water, I intended to join that furry lineup at the lunch counter.

Audition after audition came and went. I would arrive at those studios rigid with determination, seething with the will to win. And I nearly always did achieve something, but never that glorious first place. I would wind up in the supporting cast—the ingénue trapped in the burning barn; the rich little troublemaker from the right side of the tracks; the wayward, unwed mother from the wrong side of those definitive railroad ties, or some other case of social maladjustment. After a year of such near misses I was becoming as neurotic as any of my soap opera characters. My fixation was deep-seated, and it was mink.

Spring and fall in prewar New York were enhanced by those wonderful open-topped, double-decker buses that cruised Fifth Avenue from Washington Square to Washington Heights. One sparkling day I worked my uneasy way up the narrow, twisting steps to a good seat on top, when a dark ranch mink came padding up stairs to join me. It was Barbara Weeks—star of not just one soap opera, but of *two*.

"I heard your audition for Ruthrauff & Ryan the other day," she said after we had exchanged a few polite remarks. "You want to get a daytime lead, don't you? Well, you'll never get it with the kind of audition you gave the other day." She hesitated. "It's hard to explain . . . You sound too *intelligent*—as if you couldn't possibly get into all that soap opera trouble. You can't play a daytime lead *honestly*, you see. No matter what the situation, she must always sound like a nice, *nice* girl. In real life she'd be a godawful bore."

She advised me to listen to the serials for a few days.

"Some of the stars are good actresses, some are bad," she said. "But they all have one thing in common—that nice, *nice* sound."

I sat hunched over my radio set for a week. The next time I competed for the starring role on a Soap I won it, hands down. Unfortunately, the program, which was intended as a replacement for an old standby of radio, "Myrt and Marge," never went on the air. After playing footsie with the new idea for a few weeks, the sponsor decided that old loves were the best and renewed the contract with "Myrt and Marge."

I was playing a part on the older show, and during the client's flirtation period I was sworn to secrecy about the new one in preparation. I hated the situation. I felt mean and sneaky every time I saw Myrtle Vail, the star and author of "Myrt and Marge."

When my next opportunity arose, it involved a show already running on CBS. "When a Girl Marries," a serial written by Elaine Sterne Carrington (author of the successful "Pepper Young's Family"), had, after six months, failed to achieve an adequate audience rating. (The audience measuring system employed by the industry in those days was known as the Crossley Rating.) Ken MacGregor, the director, had one of the keenest ears in the business. Among the many programs he was responsible for were "Show Boat," "Palmolive Beauty Box," "Cities Service," Ripley's "Believe It or Not," "Doctor Doolittle" (scripts by its creator, Hugh Lofting), "The Rudy Vallee Hour," and "The Joe Penner Show." He decided that the new show's rating problems lay in the casting, and, despite opposition from higher up in the advertising agency that produced the program, he set about replacing the leading lady.

Auditions were held, over and over, for a period of weeks. At the outset Ken decided he wanted me for the part, but strong resistance to the change kept coming from somewhere within Benton & Bowles, the agency. In the meantime, all the contestants were again sworn to secrecy about the pending replacement and again, unreasonably perhaps, I felt mean and sneaky about the situation and would walk around the block or duck into a doorway to avoid meeting the unwary girl who was about to be replaced. A scene was chosen to be recorded on acetate and the agency engaged my old friend from the Coast, Michael Fitzmaurice, to read it with each aspiring actress. When my turn came, Mike drew me out of range of the microphone. "Now, don't worry," he whispered. "You've got them outclassed. Go in there and [here he feinted with a left jab] give 'em the works."

Ken's advice was, "Make her different. Don't give us the average daytime lead."

Give 'em the works. . . . Make her different. . . . I wavered for a second but a vision of dark ranch mink rose before my eyes. *A nice girl. A nice, nice girl.* With a prayer to the spirit of Elsie Dinsmore, I opened my lips and spoke.

Two days later I was asked to come to the offices of Benton & Bowles to sign a contract as star of "When a Girl Marries." At last! A contract! After six years of back-breaking free-lance struggle I had reached the Promised Land.

I raced down Madison Avenue and into the agency's legal department. When the gentleman behind the wide expanse of mahogany brought out a slim sheaf of papers and a fountain pen, I could hardly refrain from crawling right up on his desk and kissing him. As I gazed through tears of joy at the neatly typed pages, he started a murmuring monologue. "We are giving you the same contract your predecessor had—."

I scanned the pages. When I found what I was seeking it brought me up with a jolt. Union minimum—at that time, $105 a week. I knew that Ken had put up a battle with a powerful ogre in this agency to get me the part. Here was security of a sort—a thirteen-week guarantee. I reached for the pen and signed. As I did, mink coat, muff, and galoshes walked slowly off into the sunset. Fadeout.

Later that afternoon I hauled the old leopard off to the furrier to be remodeled. There were enough good pieces, the man said, to trim a nice cloth coat.

Monday morning I took over the part at the CBS studios on Madison Avenue. The script consisted of one long scene between the two principal characters, Joan and Harry. The leading man was a newcomer to radio from the theater, John Raby. The voice of our announcer, Frank Gallop, was being heard weekly on "Symphony of the Air." He had undoubtedly been selected for this particular serial because of his innate dignity. Our client was the staid old firm of Prudential Life Insurance. The soundman, David Gaines, and the organist, John Winters, were both old friends of mine, but in spite of the warm atmosphere in the studio I felt shaky.

We rehearsed that soap opera with the care we would have given "Macbeth." As air time approached Ken gave us a few minutes in which to relax, but although I sat down in a folding metal chair and opened my suit jacket to let it hang loose, I kept my nose to my script and concentrated on keeping the mood we had set. During the commercial I took a few deep breaths as Father had taught me to do when I felt an attack of nerves coming on, and my diaphragm felt steady by the time Frank started the lead-in for the scene.

"Joan and Harry are standing side by side at the gate of the great white house on the hill where Joan was born. . . ."

Hoping for a sign of encouragement before the big ordeal, I glanced up at Ken MacGregor in the control booth. There behind him, her eyes swollen and red, tears streaming down her cheeks, stood the former star of "When a Girl Marries." I started casting about for something sizable to crawl under but my cue was coming up. John was already at the microphone. I tried to rise to my feet. I couldn't. The belt buckle of my jacket was wedged between the seat and the back of the folding metal chair.

With shaking hands, I struggled to free myself. David Gaines glanced up and raced to my side. Now Dave and I were both fumbling with the buckle, my icy fingers tangled in his. Frank loped across to us and tugged at my chair. "Get up, for God's sake!" he whispered. I obeyed. With the tall dignified announcer holding the chair pressed to my buttocks and Dave still fumbling with the belt, the three of us shuffled across the highly waxed floor to the microphone.

As far as I was concerned, the mood Ken had worked so carefully to create had vanished. In its place was a rabid desire to be someplace else. Then my script nearly flew out of my hand. My escorts had pinned both my elbows into the small of my back and were prying off the jacket. Pigeon-breasted and squirming like a girl with a bad case of the itch, I managed to bleat out the first few lines of Mrs. Carrington's carefully written love scene. I don't know how I got through it. Midway I was somehow wrenched free of the jacket, but I was still miserably aware of those bleary blue eyes staring reproachfully down at me from behind the plate-glass window.

When I finally reached the last line and looked up, the soggy apparition had left the control booth, the chair was back against the wall, and the jacket was folded neatly across it. I had come to the end of what remains in memory as the longest broadcast of my life.

During the following weeks I kept my ear to the grapevine, certain that auditions were being held to find yet another star for "When a Girl Marries." Nothing happened. About six months later there was a call waiting for me when I came off the air. It was from an executive at Benton & Bowles named Steel, a man I had never met.

"I thought you'd like to know that the rating on your show has gone up satisfactorily," he said. "Better than we had hoped."

"That's nice," I replied.

There was a pause. "The feeling in the agency is that it's largely because of *you*," he said.

"Thanks very much," I said.

Another pause. "I thought you'd like to know."

"Oh, yes indeed. Thank you."

We hung up.

I had a nagging sense that something had been implied but not said. Short of an engraved invitation, I don't see how he could have told me more clearly to get into that legal department and renegotiate my contract.

The rating of "When a Girl Marries" continued to edge its way up. In the spring it made a sudden spurt and shot over 5. There was jubilation among the cast.

"Now we're safe," Ken MacGregor said. "When a show passes a 5 it's sure to stay on the air."

"Let's have a drink on it," John Raby suggested. "Let's go to Louis and Armand's."

Actors who wanted to spend less than a dollar for lunch went to Colbee's in the CBS Building, but those who were getting rich, or wanted people to think they were, went a few doors down 52nd street to Louis and Armand's. There, bowing waiters led you across the ruby-colored carpet, past tables ringed by CBS executives, to leather-covered divans from which you could survey the room and wave casually to other actors who had come to breathe the heady fumes of success. I once saw a writer and an actress celebrate a personal triumph there by lighting cigarettes with dollar bills. The cast of "When a Girl Marries" was more modest. We toasted our 5-plus Crossley with daiquiris and gorged ourselves on veal scallopini. I left Louis and Armand's in a warm glow of well-being and quite unprepared for the sharp chill that was to descend two weeks later.

In the face of that beautiful 5-plus Crossley, Prudential suddenly canceled. The slight faith I might have had in the stability of any form of show business withered in that hour. As it turned out, I was to be under contract for twenty years. But I never felt I had a steady job. This, coupled with a certain embarrassment, caused me to miss most of the fun of being a soap opera star. The serials were in such bad repute, not only among the intelligentsia, but also among the merely civic-minded (the women's clubs of Westchester County once started an "I am not listening" campaign), that I felt reluctant to say what it was I did for a living. Some of the other stars seemed to feel rich and famous. I felt hand-to-mouth and sheepish.

The day "When a Girl Marries" went off the air I wandered forlornly into Colbee's and found a place at the counter. At the first sign of spring the minks had vanished and the place was less flossy-looking. It was a good thing I chose Colbee's instead of the more opulent spot down the street. Otherwise I would not have bumped into Himan Brown. That young magnate never wasted a dime or a minute impressing anybody. He was too busy to spend time toasting his success, and he would have shared my horror at the idea of burning a dollar bill. He owned and produced a large number of radio shows and was unpretentiously acquiring a fortune.

I consumed a nourishing bowl of black bean soup and told him my troubles. He promised to give me work, and he did. A rush of calls from him, plus the parts I already had on other programs, kept me in a sound financial state all summer.

The relationship between the radio actor and his many employers was always as simple and direct as that. No middleman intervened. We simply got in touch with the directors by phone or in person. Most actors made routine calls to the advertising agencies and networks every few weeks. Some of the less successful performers had their names printed on pencils, match folders, calling cards, and blotters, and distributed them through the offices. One elderly gentleman used to send out a postcard with the plea, "Call me anything—but call me!" In Hollywood, when Herb Polesie was directing "Shell Chateau," he once showed me some postcards he had been receiving week after week, which had finally won the sender a part on the show. Pictures clipped from the *National Geographic* were pasted on them and a caption typed beneath. A rear view of a coolie, planting rice in a paddy, was titled, "Joe _____ looking for a job in Hollywood." An African native riding a donkey bore the legend, "Joe _____ on his ass in Hollywood."

116

New York is a more overtly aggressive town than Hollywood, and the determination of New York actors set up a panic reaction among the directors. The third floor at NBC was an ambush. When a studio door opened after a performance, the cast would file out, chatting easily with each other, but the director would hang back, peeking out like a frightened elf, then bolt for the elevator.

He never made it. Unemployed actors would spring from every side. One young woman developed a reputation for pure adhesiveness that became a legend. She tackled Ken MacGregor on the third floor of NBC, followed him into the elevator, out into the street, across town to CBS, and up to the twenty-second floor, talking steadily all the way. Although Ken never once replied or looked in her direction, she kept the sales pitch going till the closing door of the studio cut her off. I am less certain of the story that she clung to a fleeing director all the way into the third-floor men's room. That was not an unusual thing for male actors to do, though, and the directors unwilling to be caught there usually preferred to suffer until they could get back to the locked doors of the advertising agencies.

Not many of us went so far, but the fact remains that none of the dramatic radio shows was cast through agents. This explains why, when word came in the fall that "When a Girl Marries" was going back on the air, I once more trudged my lone and ignorant way to Benton & Bowles' legal department. This was surely the time to get an agent or a lawyer, but it never crossed my mind.

The man I had dealt with before was gone. In his place was a squat, middle-aged man, whom I'll call Darland here. He pushed the new contract toward me. The fee was a bit higher because the union had got a small raise in the minimum wage, but there was a clause that prohibited my working for any company whose products conflicted with any of the sponsor's products.

"Who is the new client?" I asked.

"Baker's Chocolate."

That wasn't too restrictive. I couldn't think of many chocolate companies. Mr. Darland leaned forward to press a pen into my hand, but he didn't look at me. A warning signal flashed in the back of my mind.

"Baker's Chocolate?" I repeated.

"That's right."

"That wouldn't by any chance be Standard Brands, would it?"

"Oh, no."

"General Foods?"

At last he looked at me. "Well—yes," he confessed.

This contract would have barred me from nearly half the programs on the air.

"I'll have to think this over," I said.

To my amazement he flew into a rage. "Do what you please! There are lots of girls who would like this job," he snapped.

Years later, when I was more experienced in these matters, I might have recognized the flare-up as evidence of a man arguing from a weak position. That day it intimidated me, as it was meant to do. But I left without signing. After a restless night I decided to go to the union and ask the advice of George Heller, the executive secretary and one of the founders of AFRA.

As he read the document his face darkened and his eyes flashed. "This is outrageous," he said, and reached for the telephone.

"Don't call them, George," I begged. "Let me handle this myself. I don't want to lose the job."

"But this is filled with violations of our code, which they've just signed," he said. "Look at this. They have the right to cancel at a moment's notice. You can't cancel it at all." He went on to point out other objections to the document. Then he called an associate on the phone. "I have a contract on my desk which is a complete violation of every principle we've fought for," he said. "We've got to do something about it."

"Don't do anything now," I pleaded. "Let me get this thing settled first. I don't want them to think I'm a troublemaker. All I wanted was advice."

George lowered his head like a bull about to charge into the ring. "Just tell them you don't want a contract—that you'll abide by the AFRA Code of Fair Practices," he said. "That's all you need."

"Please wait, George," I said.

"Don't worry," he said. "We won't involve you."

When I returned home there was a message from Benton & Bowles' casting department, advising me of the time and place (5 P.M. at NBC) of the first broadcast under the new sponsor. The following Monday I went on the air. I still had no contract but I had an appointment to see Mr. Darland the next day.

At that interview he smiled and chatted in what appeared to be a friendly manner for a few minutes, then without warning, turned on me, his face twisted with fury. He pushed his appointment calendar toward me.

"See where I've been," he said. On the page was written, "AFRA—10 A.M."

I should have told him that I had been to the union to ask for advice, but I was stunned into silence. A new contract was slapped on the desk in front of me.

"Here! I think you'll find that all your *violations* [he spat the word at me] have been corrected."

I glanced at the pages. The obnoxious paragraph was still there.

"I can't accept this clause—it's too exclusive," I said. "I'd be losing money."

"You can't go on the air without a contract!"

"I am on the air," I pointed out. "I did the first show yesterday."

I was close to tears but succeeded in holding them back. Another man was now standing in the door of the office.

"Do you want this job or not?" Darland's face was contorted.

The newcomer intervened. "Perhaps the statement could be changed to read 'any product advertised on this program,'" he said quietly. "Would that be acceptable, Miss Higby?"

It was a calm, not unkind voice, and it offered a way out. I agreed. They changed the clause and once again I signed a miserably inadequate contract. I left, swearing that I would never again have anything to do with Mr. Darland.

I decided to put him out of my mind. After all, I was working regularly on all four networks and my income was more than enough to meet my needs.

Pearl Harbor came at the end of that season. A year later we lost our cheerful Irish leading man to the Army. I had bought a houseboat moored in Long Island Sound and I gave John Raby a farewell party on it that slipped out of control and lasted all night. Earlier in the day someone produced a bottle of exotic nail polish and painted Johnny's toenails a bright green. Our hero sat in his bathing trunks, wriggling his toes, and laughed. The next morning we took him to the station and saw him off to war. We forgot about his toenails. John forgot, too, until a sergeant ordered him to strip. The noncom stared at the spot on the floor where Johnny stood, curling his toes.

"Very colorful," he said.

"Well, you see," Johnny explained, "I've been to a party."

His replacement on the program was a handsome, blond six-footer named Robert Haag. Soon after Bob joined the company I learned that he was getting more money than I was. All the bitterness and indignation I had suppressed for a year went off like Krakatoa. I couldn't sleep that night, but went prowling through the apartment, fighting the urge to kick the sofa, the piano, or anything else that couldn't strike back. In the morning I was worn and spent but still burning with the injustice of it all.

Lyle Sudrow, the author, and Georgia Burke, top, rehearse "When a Girl Marries." The author, in mink at last, bottom, after taking over role of Cynthia in "The Romance of Helen Trent" in 1946. Actors David Gothard and Lauren Gilbert flank Julie Stevens, who played Helen.

Joey grew tired of my complaints. "It's all your own silly fault," she said. "If you wanted a raise why didn't you ask for it?"

"I'm going to quit the damned show!" I bellowed.

"It's a good, steady job and they're hard to come by," Wauna said, dryly. "Don't be in such a hurry. Think it over a few days."

She was playing in the Broadway run of "Uncle Harry" with Eva Le Gallienne at the time. During the matinee she told Miss Le Gallienne about my problem. Her advice was prompt and surprising.

"Tell her to cry," she said.

"Cry?"

"She's an actress, isn't she? Tell her not to say much—just sit in the office and cry." She smiled brightly at Wauna. "They'll hate that."

I called the advertising agency the following Monday and learned to my relief that Mr. Darland was no longer there. The man who had taken his place was cold and unresponsive on the telephone. He assured me that he could not make any changes in my contract, but he finally agreed to see me.

He let me cool my heels a good forty-five minutes outside, however, before I was ushered into his private office. I spent the time staring at the anteroom carpet, and, like those nasty children who throw tantrums, holding my breath as long as I could. By the time he decided to see me I was struggling to keep the tears back.

"My show has a very high rating," I began, as calmly as I could.

"It also uses up a very high budget," he said icily. "Mrs. Carrington is the most expensive writer in the business, and —."

I stopped breathing and let my face crumple up like a kid whose diaper needs changing. I saw a look of consternation cross his face.

"There's nothing I can do just now," he faltered. "Perhaps at the end of the next thirteen-week cycle—."

I pulled out all the stops and bawled. He jumped to his feet, skirted around me and out the door. Soon he was back with two other frightened-looking gentlemen at his side. By now I was a fountain of tears—a scene from one of the rougher spots in the life of Niobe or Lucrece.

Before I dried up and departed, five uncomfortable men had gathered in the office and unanimously agreed to a $100-a-week raise to start immediately, with an escalator clause that would lift the fee by $50 every year that followed.

The contract I won that day was not the greatest in the soap opera field. Bess Johnson was said to have made $1,400 on the original "Hilltop House" in Chicago, and Joan Blaine got at least that much for "Valiant Lady." "When a Girl Marries" lasted longer than those shows, however, and, as the years slipped by, the escalator clause slid up until finally I burst forth from my old leopard cocoon and appeared at Colbee's lunch counter, wrapped to the eyes in minky splendor. I found an empty stool and twirled regally into place between Ma Perkins and Big Sister.

"Make mine corned beef on rye," I commanded. "And don't hold back on the mustard!"

CHAPTER XI

The Show Must Go On— and On and On

Soap opera may well have been the lowest point ever reached by dramatic art, plumbing down deep beneath "Nellie, the Beautiful Cloak Model" and "The Perils of Pauline," but make no mistake about it, as *advertising* it was just plain great. It developed a fanatically loyal audience of many millions; it was habit-forming (the polls showed that 54 percent of the nation's housewives listened regularly); and it was cheap (two fifteen-minute serials could be put on for one-third the cost of a half-hour with a name band—Fred Waring, for example). Dollar for dollar, it may well have been the greatest value the advertiser ever got for his money.

If soap opera was a boon to its sponsors, it was a bonanza to its writers—at least to those who were lucky enough to get in on the ground floor. Elaine Carrington, the author of "When a Girl Marries," was one of them. She sold her first serial to NBC in 1932. It was called "Red Adams." (When it found a sponsor in the Beechnut chewing gum company the name was changed to "Red Davis" to avoid conflict with the name of a rival company. Sponsors are funny that way.) Later still, it became "Pepper Young's Family," one of the most enduring of all the daytime serials.

Mrs. Carrington had found success as a writer long before she wrote that first radio script. Her play "Nightstick" had a good run on Broadway and was twice made into films under the title "Alibi." She had written vaudeville sketches, and some of her short stories had appeared in *The Saturday Evening Post* and *Ladies' Home Journal*. Seven years after giving birth to Red Adams, alias Pepper Young, she created "When a Girl Marries," and in the early forties a third serial called "Rosemary."

TUNE IN TOMORROW

The three ran simultaneously for years. Her income was said to be close to $5,000 a week. She maintained a penthouse apartment in midtown Manhattan, a waterfront estate on Long Island, and another in Florida.

She was a silver-haired, full-bosomed woman with a radiant personality. She was impish, loved to tell risqué stories, and larded her scripts with double entendres just to see if she could slip them by unnoticed. Elaine was the only woman I have ever known who would sweep into a drawing room, the Plaza, or NBC, clad in lace, swathed in fur, and shod in—well, not sneakers, exactly, but a sort of gum-soled brogue. I don't think her feet hurt. I think she just didn't give a damn.

If the radio world had a First Commandment, it was "Thou shalt make no noise while we are on the air." It was not unusual for Elaine to stride past the electric sign that flashed the warning "ON THE AIR," throw wide the studio door, and boom out, "Are you on the air?" It wasn't that she didn't see. She didn't care.

This gay insouciance was valuable in dealing with agency and network officials. Fred Allen, in his autobiography, "Treadmill to Oblivion," reveals the frustration a writer can feel when subjected to pettifogging interference from Madison Avenue. He defined an advertising agency as "85% confusion and 15% commission," and described a typical encounter with agency thinking:

"The president of the new agency had been a famous quarter-back in college football. . . . [He] started sending turtle-necked memos which intimated that, as the mink said when it backed into the electric fan, 'The fur is going to fly.' The show was going to receive 'all of the agency's thinking,' which meant that everything we were doing was going to be overhauled completely. We were told that the Town Hall idea was corny. . . .

"I tried to explain the value of the Town Hall title and the appeal the locale had to small town listeners. . . . It was as futile as trying to convince a Russian delegate at the U.N. Nothing helped. The Town Hall title disappeared. We became just another group of actors gathered around a microphone in a radio studio. The colorful illusion had been completely stripped from the program."

Anyone who is old enough to remember the sheer comedic brilliance of that Town Hall opening will understand the helpless fury Allen must have felt as his brainchild was decapitated before his eyes.

When tilting with Mrs. Carrington, however, the agency people were likely to find the frustration and broken lances all on their side of the field. They had bought a quiet "family" show in "When a Girl Marries," but they kept calling for "action" and demanded frequent story conferences. Elaine became nimble at avoiding such crises. On one occasion, she agreed to meet with them and suggested lunch at "21." Elaine turned up accompanied by two executives from a soap manufacturing concern. Now, this particular agency had been angling for that particular soap account for some time. It was unthinkable, in the circumstances, to spend the hour nagging the gay, bantering, wicked author about her plot line. Instead, they spent it wooing the hoped-for clients and in the end were left with nothing but a large check to pay.

Then there was the incident of the Model Village. The agency built a complete papier-mâché model of Stanwood, the imaginary town of "When a Girl Marries." It was a large and expensive construction job. They invited Mrs. Carrington to view it and explained that, with this model on hand, any geographical errors in her scripts could be quickly detected. She admired it and went her way. A few weeks later she had Harry say to Joan, "Darling, I'm not getting ahead here in Stanwood. Let's move." And move they did, out of the mythical town of Stanwood to the equally mythical, but uncharted, town of Beechwood.

Under her frivolity, however, was hidden a very shrewd business sense. One day I happened to be in the agency office just as she was leaving a meeting. The man I had come to see mopped his brow as he glanced toward the elevator that Elaine, all silver fox and rippling laughter, had entered. "If that woman hadn't wasted her time with radio," he muttered, "she'd be president of an international bank."

Business acumen and an ability to market their own wares seem to have been characteristics of the early soap opera authors. In 1931, Myrtle Vail, then an unemployed actress, marched into the Wrigley Building in Chicago, talked her way in to see Mr. Wrigley himself, and walked out with a contract for a show called "Myrt and Marge," which kept her and her daughter, Donna Dammerell, in mink for many a day. Myrt baited her hook more slyly than Elaine. Her chewing gum king had no fault to find with the names of *her* leading characters—Myrtle *Spear* and Marjorie *Minter*.

No discussion of soap opera would be complete without mention of Jane Crusinberry and Irna Phillips. They both started in Chicago in the early thirties. There was a rumor that Jane Crusinberry wrote "Mary Marlin" from autobiographical material, but she must have drifted into fiction toward the end, because Mary wound up in the Senate.

Irna Phillips was an Ohio school teacher who wandered into radio somewhere around 1931. Within a few years she had so many programs on both networks that she had to hire a stable of writers to help her turn them out. Like most of those early comers, she managed to

"Myrt and Marge" with Donna Dammerell, Ray Hedge, and Myrtle Vail in 1938.

"Stella Dallas," top, in early '40's with Vivian Smolen (Laurel), Macdonald Carey (Dick Grosvenor), and Ann Elstner (Stella); at left, announcers George Ansbro, Jack Costello. Edward Pauley, bottom, was Steve Wilson, Fran Carlon was Lorelei Kilbourne in "Big Town," 1945.

retain ownership of her programs and later sold "Road of Life," "The Guiding Light," and "The Right to Happiness" to the makers of Ivory Soap for $175,000. With the arrival of TV she swung easily into the new medium. Her serial, "As the World Turns," passed its tenth year on CBS, and in May of 1964 NBC televised her latest effort, "Another World."

To my ear, the best of them all was a young free-lance writer from Mexico, Missouri, named Martha Alexander. When she took over the scripts of "Helen Trent" the dialogue suddenly brightened. Even my malevolent character, Cynthia, developed a subtle humor. Martha left us for "The Second Mrs. Burton" and soon ran into trouble. She had her hero ask the heroine to say an open-mouthed "ah" instead of a puckered "prunes" when he kissed her. Such depravity was too much for radio's prissy standards, and Martha and Mrs. Burton parted company.

I hesitate to include Gertrude Berg here because her comedy show, "The Goldbergs," hardly seems to fit into the communal tear duct where flowed the soaps. Her dark-as-night wild mink was the envy of us all, however, until it was swiped one day from the ladies' rest room at CBS.

Mrs. Berg was esteemed, not only for the excellence of her writing, but also for her adroit use of sound effects. She insisted that, whenever possible, the actors make the noises themselves. I met Cliff Carpenter, a friend from the Coast, on Fifty-second Street one day. His hair was rumpled, his tie askew, and, in spite of the snappy weather, he carried his coat over his arm.

"What in the world have you been doing?" I asked.

"Mrs. Berg is producing a new show," he replied. "We've just made the audition record."

The action-packed script had called for him to run across town bearing an urgent message. Sand was sprinkled around the microphone and run he did—round and round and round—through two rehearsals and the "take."

"The Goldbergs" was considered by many to be the best of the serials, and Georgia Burke was proud when she won a part on it. Georgia is one of the finest Negro actresses in the nation. I've always thought that the sustained popularity of "When a Girl Marries" was in no small part due to the warmth and love she brought to the part of Lily. As Lily, Georgia was all heart. Offstage, she was a sophisticated and witty woman. Shortly after she started her new job, she came into the studio of "When a Girl Marries," sank heavily into a chair, and started fanning herself.

"How are things going on 'The Goldbergs'?" I asked.

Her lively black eyes glinted as she leaned toward me to whisper, "You know, honey, I think I'm doing that woman's laundry!"

Carrington, Vail, Crusinberry, Berg, Phillips—these were great names in the world of Soap. But the greatest of all was Hummert. During the heyday of the medium, more than half the daytime programming of both NBC and CBS was supplied by Frank and Anne Hummert. In 1938 they bought nearly one-eighth of *all* radio time. It was in Chicago, in 1932, when they were part of the advertising firm of Blackett, Sample & Hummert, that they brought out the first hardy perennial among their serials, "Just Plain Bill."

In 1938, the Hummerts moved to New York, severed their connection with Blackett, Sample & Hummert, and opened their own production company, Air Features, Inc. This organization was a soap opera factory. In addition to "Bill," its products included "John's Other Wife," "Second Husband," "Our Gal Sunday," "Orphans of Divorce," "Mrs. Wiggs of the Cabbage Patch," "Backstage Wife," "The Romance of Helen Trent," "Wife Versus Secretary," "David Harum," "Stella Dallas," "Young Widder Brown," "Front Page Farrell," "Lorenzo Jones," "Nona From Nowhere," "Hamburger Katie," "Lora Lawton," and "Evelyn Winters." Air Features also provided a number of shows for children, among them "Skippy," "Penrod and Sam," and "Happy Landing,"as well as a clutch of mystery programs, "Alias Jimmy Valentine," "Mystery Theater," "Mr. Chameleon," and "Mr. Keen, Tracer of Lost Persons." (Incidentally, the "kindly old tracer," as he was insistently referred to in the scripts, had the longest life of any of radio's numerous detectives—from 1938 to 1955.)

A few of these titles came from popular novels, but most were the creations of Frank and Anne Hummert. They supplied the long-range plot line and hired writers to fill in the dialogue.

In those early days I had no contact with the Hummerts except for an occasional glimpse through the plate glass of the control booth during an audition. He was tall, thin, solemn-looking, and he stooped slightly. She was small, slim, cheerful-looking, with light brown hair. She wore no make-up except a light trace of lipstick. It was clear to any of us who thought about it that if Irna Phillips and Elaine Carrington were taking hundreds of thousands of dollars out of soap opera, the Hummerts were taking millions. But there was no mink about Anne Hummert. She wore a cloth coat of fine quality. Her shoes were likely to be Cuban-heeled pumps, her hats small, dark, and unadorned. She looked like a well-to-do Quaker lady.

To the eye, most soap opera scripts were alike. Mimeographed in clear black lettering, they all had a cover page that included only the title, the author's name, and the cast list. A radio actor could spot an Air Features script from across the room. Pale lavender ink covered the title page. In addition to the usual information, we were reminded that this was a "Hummert Radio Feature," that the "authors of title and original story line" were Frank and Anne Hummert, that the "general supervisors of script and production" were Frank and Anne Hummert, and that "this unpublished drama or radio adaptation is the property of Frank and Anne Hummert and is being used under special license to Air Features, Inc. . . . [As far as I could see, Air Features was Frank and Anne Hummert, too] . . . It is fully protected under common law copyright law. Damages will be demanded for unauthorized perform-ances thereof or for the making of unauthorized copies thereof either for publication, radio, or motion pictures. It may not be broadcast, pub-lished, or made into motion pictures without specific individual authori-zation in each performance thereof." The Hummerts took soap opera seriously.

All this was in contrast to the young men from the advertising agencies along Madison Avenue, who seemed to be embarrassed about the serials. Their attitude was that of a sophisticated but kindly father, who, dressed in dinner jacket and ready for a night on the town, has been asked to change the baby's diapers. They tried to be nonchalant. They were indulgent with actors who, rushing from show to show all day and part of the night, were often late to rehearsal. The agency men would sometimes wait for them as long as twenty minutes before they began to worry. Any actor who was five minutes late to an Air Features rehearsal was in trouble. There would be a message to "call the office as soon as you get off the air." When he did, the receiver would burn his ear. If it happened again, he could start looking for another source of employment.

Air Features was equally rigid in the rules set up to govern actual production. The directors were not allowed to introduce "art" effects—unessential sound, background music—that might obscure one word of the dialogue.

An actor needed a formidable technique to play a hysterical scene to suit the Hummerts. They demanded excitement and pace, but each vowel and consonant had to be enunciated with painful precision. For two characters to overlap speeches was absolutely forbidden.

As for the writer, he had a typed list of regulations to guide him—all aimed at insuring that the listener knew at every moment who was talking to whom and about what. This meant frequent character identi-fication and plot "recap." Most writers fell into the habit of using a tag permanently attached to the character's name. So we had Elderly Agatha

Anthony, the Kindly Old Tracer, and Mad Ada Dexter. No confusion here. The listener knew just what to expect of them.

The other production companies had no such hard-and-fast policies. Writers were selected for their competence and then more or less left alone. They were left alone, that is, unless the rating began to drop. Then all hell would break loose. A swift rating change could start ulcers churning the full length of Madison Avenue.

Fate dealt the industry a sharp lesson on this rating psychosis in the early thirties, but the advertising agencies never seemed to get the message. The incident concerned the most prevalent of soap opera diseases—amnesia. The first case ever to attack a citizen of the soaps struck Joe, the hero of "Mary Marlin." Soon after he started saying, "Where am I? What's my name? What town is this?" the rating showed "Mary Marlin" leading the daytime field by more than a full point. Where the other shows had reached, let us say, 4.4, 4.5, and 4.6, "Mary" came sailing by at 6.2. Havoc broke loose in the networks and agencies. Plot lines were abandoned, characters were dropped, writers were changed, and in a trice half the leading men on the air were saying, "Where am I? What's my name? What town is this?"

The next rating showed that the gap had been closed. None of the entries hit that stunning 6.2, but "Mary" had dropped back to 4.8. It was some time before the truth came out. In computing the size of the audience, a mistake had been made in the number of stations that carried "Mary Marlin." The wrong figure had given the estimate an enormous but erroneous boost. "Mary" was, in fact, leading—but only by a nose.

The legend persisted, however, that there was no cure for a falling rating like a healthy case of amnesia, and as late as 1953 the leading man of "When a Girl Marries" woke one morning saying, "Where am I? . . . What's my name? . . . What town is this?"

The Hummert preoccupation with clarity was based on the special nature of the soap opera audience. The evening listeners, it could be assumed, gathered around the radio and listened. During the day, the busy housewife manifested all the repose of a hockey team—up the stairs to make the beds, down again to vacuum the living room, head into hamper to collect the laundry, down to the basement to start the washing machine—and so on and on.

The first device employed to attract this itinerant's attention was the theme song. Usually it was belted out on the Hammond organ, but "Mary Marlin's" identifying mark was a piano rendition of Debussy's "Clair de Lune," "Helen Trent" came on to the sound of a ukulele, and "Just Plain Bill" had a just plain mouth organ.

131

Virginia Payne, the Ma of "Ma Perkins," with Al Hodge, who also played The Green Hornet, in 1959.

Another device—and I think it was a Hummert invention, although it spread to other parts of the field—was the capsuled thesis that followed the title and was designed to acquaint the new listener with the premise of the story.

"And now—Our Gal Sunday—the story of an orphan girl, named Sunday, from the little mining town of Silver Creek, Colorado, who in young womanhood married England's richest, most handsome lord, Lord Henry Brinthrope. The story that asks the question—Can this girl from a mining town in the West find happiness as the wife of a wealthy and titled Englishman?"

Or, "The Romance of Helen Trent—the story of a woman who sets out to prove what so many other women long to prove in their own lives, that romance can live on at thirty-five and even beyond."

Or (and the startling simplicity of this proposition made it my favorite), "Amanda of Honeymoon Hill—the story of a young girl—laid against a tapestry of the Deep South."

After these promising statements, it was considered safe to pause —for the sponsor's message.

Commercials have always given me a sense of security. There was never sound so sweet to a radio actor's ear as the babble of a commercial flowing smoothly by. But even as spectator I find them reassuring. I stare in numbed fascination at the bad guy, writhing in my TV set, a bullet in his stomach, or the good guy, spitting his teeth out on the barroom floor, when, without warning, the sun comes streaming through little organdy curtains and a group of happy people, every tooth in place, giggle and chew and marvel over their morning gruel. The effect is tranquilizing.

In much the same way, the lugubrious gloom that permeated the soap operas was rhythmically relieved every twelve and a half minutes by the jollity of the sales plug. The one exception was "When a Girl Marries." In this case, the hero and I burbled over with young love and faith in the future, but Frank Gallop followed us about like a Greek chorus, richly dispensing gloom. He engaged in Hamlet-like soliloquies, wondering aloud what would happen to the happy family group if the Wage Earner were suddenly snatched from their midst.

All this changed when we moved to NBC. Frank stayed on with CBS and Prudential, and Charles Stark took over our announcements for General Foods. Then the gloomy reminders of human mortality gave place to Chocolate Chip Cookery (a phrase that is the sponsor's, not mine, and which was heard at least once during the years as Chocolate Kip Chookery).

David Harum's announcer, Ford Bond, used to open that show

brusquely with the unadorned advice, "Sweeten the swill!" The product in this case was some kind of farm feed.

Helen Trent had American Stomach. At any rate Fielden Farrington, her announcer, was pushing some product guaranteed to correct this widespread condition. He seemed intent not on removing the organ, but only on changing its nationality. He never clarified what the choice was.

All the announcers were constantly plagued by copywriters who came from other media and wrote for the eye instead of the ear. I seemed to have had a purely personal shock at hearing, "Your Bayer Aspirin program is on the air!" but the whole industry was rocked by "Give your wife a gorgeous Gruen." I remember one announcer pitifully begging the director to change the last line of a commercial. No, he was told sternly, it had been passed by the client, the agency—everybody. Not one word could be changed. So, through gritted teeth, he went on the air and announced a nationwide sale, ending with the words, "And remember, ladies, J. C. Penney is the biggest sheet house in the country."

Once safely past these hurdles, we got to the blurb that led in to the story. As year piled on year, and the show went on and on and on, the lead-in would sag under accumulated plot.

Some agencies demanded a thorough daily summing up and the conscientious authors tried to oblige. Here is a lead-in from "Mary Marlin" that I have treasured in memory over the years:

"In Cedar Falls, Mary Marlin is pondering the strange fate which has revealed to her the fact that Joe may still be alive, while Joe, himself, in Freedom Outpost, is reminded by Simone of the love he once had for Mary; of how he could love her still if he had not put her out of his life; or of how he could love someone like her—like Simone, while up on the hill, Mr. Crayley looks upon the whole thing as an invasion of his privacy."

There were two ways of constructing the long-range plot line, the "Meanwhile, back at the ranch" technique and the "sequence" system. Mrs. Carrington used the first method. At the start of "When a Girl Marries" she planted the seeds of at least five major conflicts—all based on Joan's marriage to Harry Davis. Any of them could be made to sprout at the writer's convenience, and she frequently had three or four subplots going along with the current central problem. She never wrote "finis" at the end of a chapter and started a new one. I am sure that this is one of the reasons we sustained a high rating for so long. A few years after I joined the show we climbed to first place among the daytime serials and we held the spot for five consecutive years—a stunning achievement that was never, to my knowledge, equaled.

The "Meanwhile, back at the ranch" construction had its disadvantages, however. The sluggish time factor for which soap opera was famous had its roots in this technique. "Pretty Kitty Kelly" was an action-packed story, written by a hard-punching writer, Frank Daum. Yet a character, played by Luis Van Rooten, entered an elevator on Tuesday afternoon and didn't reach the sixth floor until a week after the following Friday. He was trapped not by a stuck elevator, but by a tangential plot. ("Meanwhile, in a dark cellar near the warehouse . . ." or "Meanwhile, at police headquarters . . ." but *meanwhile* back in the elevator Luis was making what was surely the slowest unobstructed six-story climb in history.)

While her plot line shot off around her like a pinwheel, Ma Perkins (in the show of that name written by Orin Toveroh) stood by her kitchen table for two weeks and a day, deciding whether to open an ominously long and thin package. Sent by someone not an admirer of Ma, it contained a venomous serpent, the touch of whose fang meant instant death. This surely entitles the episode to a high place in the long-drawn-out, cliff-hanger sweepstakes. If Ma was immobilized, though, the rest of the story wasn't. "Meanwhile, in an ambulance rushing through the night . . ."

The critics of the serials fretted more over this dragging time factor than any other thing. "Why, I tuned in ten days later and that man was still in the elevator! . . . Ma was still at the table! . . . Not a thing had happened!" You couldn't be too sure about that. *Meanwhile*, the warehouse may have blown up and the ambulance skidded into the china factory at the edge of town.

In "When a Girl Marries," the times were also out of joint. When I, as Joan, was pregnant for the first time, Charles Stark entered the studio one day and offered me his hand. "Congratulations," he said. "You've just passed the gestation period of the elephant."

The sequence-plotted shows usually moved at a livelier pace, and there were other differences in the two formulas—in the motivation of plot, for example. Mrs. Carrington drew endlessly on her originally established conflicts between characters—Harry's poverty in contrast to Joan's family and friends, his resulting inferiority complex, his secretary's love for him, the jealousy of Joan's ex-fiancé, the jealousy of Joan's best friend (in love with the ex-fiancé), the wildness of a girl (a high-school dropout) who had won the affection of Harry's young brother, and so on. In a sequence-plotted serial, a small group of permanent characters was subject to harassment from the outside. At the end of each sequence all the evil-doers would vanish forever and a new set of malefactors would enter. The drawback here was that as each sequence ended, a rating sag would occur. As a story approached its climax, the writer would try to avoid this by wrapping it all up in a hurry and plunging right into the new situation.

As a rule, the Air Features programs were written in sequences. Their individual scripts followed a stricter format than most, too. After the plot-heavy lead-in, the first scene was often devoted to "recap," the second to "action." A typical Hummert show was "Stella Dallas." Its billboard went like this:

"We give you now—Stella Dallas!—a continuation on the air of the true-to-life story of mother-love and sacrifice in which Stella Dallas saw her beloved daughter, Laurel, marry into wealth and Society and, realizing the difference in their tastes and worlds, went out of Laurel's life. These episodes in the later life of Stella Dallas are based on the famous novel of that name by Olive Higgins Prouty and are written by Frank and Anne Hummert."

In the novel, Stella Dallas bowed gently before an unkind fate. As heard on the air, Stella was a tough-minded individual who wouldn't have bowed before Genghis Khan.

Here is the outline, taken from memory, of two days in the radio life of Stella Dallas.

First day. *Scene 1* (Recap): Stella tells Minnie, her perennial confidante, that she has learned that Mad Ada Dexter is gunning for Stella's son-in-law, Dick Grosvenor. *Scene 2* (Action—between Mad Ada and her chauffeur, Rolfe): "I'd have got him last time," Ada snarls, "if you had let me use my elephant gun." She says she has learned that her victim is on his way to the country club. And she and Rolfe jump into their high-powered auto and whiz off.

Second day. *Scene 1:* Minnie tells Laurel what Stella told her the day before and adds that Stella has gone to the club to head Mad Ada off. *Scene 2:* Stella hires a sound truck and tours the golf links, shouting through the loudspeaker, "Dick Grosvenor, take over! Dick Grosvenor, take cover! Dick Grosvenor, take cover."

Stella met all such emergencies with the same astounding ingenuity. There was the time when Lollie-baby (Stella's pet name for her daughter), while out for a stroll in the Sahara, was abducted by a sheik. Only Stella Dallas would have thought of effecting a rescue by sea. She came along the bottom of the Suez Canal in a submarine. Lollie-baby managed to hold the lusting Ahmed Ben Akbar at bay. In fact, she went on holding him at bay for three solid weeks.

The rigor mortis that struck the plot that time was caused by a "giveaway," a device borrowed from the kid shows. ("Don't forget, boys and girls, to send in that box top and get your copy of the

Ann Thomas with Bennett Kilpack on "Mr. Keen, Tracer of Lost Persons." Theme song of the show, which ran almost 20 years, was "Someday I'll Find You."

G-Men's secret code!") Soap opera listeners were asked to send a quarter. In return they were promised a piece of costume jewelry "worth many times that amount." Lollie-baby struck off across the desert to give Air Features a chance to offer an exact copy of the necklace of Egypt's Queen Sit-Hat-Nor-U-Net. Stella got into the submarine, Lollie-baby into the sheik's harem, and the dialogue writer into a tight corner. *Meanwhile*, at a small factory commissioned to turn out Sit-Hat-Nor-U-Net's bauble, production hit a snag and stopped. Three weeks later, when the trinkets finally did come off the assembly line, valiant Stella strode into the harem to catch the swooning Lollie-baby in her arms, and the sweating writer quit his job.

The sequence-plotted "Stella Dallas" then went right back to its usual brisk pace. The following day the heroine opened the show. "Golly, Minnie," she said, "it sure is good to be back in Boston."

The "giveaways" were supposed to determine how many women were listening. It seemed to me that what they really determined was how many could easily be induced to part with a quarter. They were injected right into the plot and most actors would gag on the gooey dialogue that introduced them. I rather enjoyed them. "Helen Trent," for example, offered a Love Bird Pin "with real simulated-gold flashing" —an oft-repeated phrase that even now I find intriguing.

The writers might have introduced the "giveaways" more subtly, but the hectic rush of turning out five scripts a week (and many turned out more than that) left little time for finesse. When the strain got too great and the author, like a winded runner, wanted to pause for breath, he would fall back on fill-in material. A favorite was the wedding ceremony. An elderly actor would be called upon to intone, "Beloved, we are gathered together . . ." and he was good for half a script. Another trick was the "dream sequence." You can write just about anything for a dream. In "Young Doctor Malone" I once spent three days in bed, muttering about balloons, while the organ droned on in the background.

Whether plotted in sequence or with the "Meanwhile" method, as the show went on and on, its soggy lead-in would finally ooze off the allotted one page. Then a soliloquy might be introduced to absorb the drip from the recap. For this effect, the actor moved in close to the microphone and whispered while the organist noodled around in the background, tossing in an occasional "sting" (a sudden, treble "boing-ng-ng"—a radio convention that told even the dullest listener that all was not well, that trouble lay just around the bend). The following example is culled from "Lora Lawton":

"Here am I, Adam Collingwood, a discredited diplomat, walking up and down outside the country club—while inside, Lora is having lunch with Lester Coleman. What is Lora saying to Lester? What is Lester saying to Lora? . . . Hmm . . . this is a contingency I had not foreseen."

I doubt if a soliloquy quite like that would have been heard on any but an Air Features serial. The Hummerts were more unabashed in their dime-novel approach to the soaps than the rest of the field. They differed in other ways, too. A basic difference came to light when the industry faced its first great crisis—The Blacklist. Agencies, sponsors, even the networks, panicked. Any actor suspected of having been identified with a leftist cause abruptly found himself out of work. No overt accusations were made, so no defense was possible. Doors just banged shut. Names were being fed to The Blacklist by other actors, members of AFRA, for whom the kindest description I can devise is "misguided."

Through all this turmoil, heartbreak, and hatred, Air Features went serenely and courageously about its business. There is no typeface large or emphatic enough to print this statement as I would like to see it: the Hummerts paid *absolutely no attention* to The Blacklist. Out of the entire industry, they alone, it seemed, were completely uninfected by the dirty business, so much so that I used to tremble at the sight of a cast assembled for an Air Features show. There would sit the hunter and the quarry, the murderous Right and the cornered Left, each with fangs and claws bared, ready to spring. There was a surrealist quality about the scene as they glared at one another across the microphone while mouthing innocuous platitudes from "Young Widder Brown" or "Backstage Wife."

In the late forties, the Hummerts put on two new evening shows and held the auditions each week themselves. For the first time we got to know these hitherto remote, but, as it developed, pleasant people. Their programs had led us to think of them as a somewhat naïve pair from the Midwest. Now we learned that he had been one of the top copywriters in the nation, and that she had been a reporter on *The Paris Herald*. Hardly an unsophisticated background. We began to wonder if the naïveté had not been on our side of the control-booth window.

Unquestionably, they had a profound influence on the whole literature of soap opera. They, more than anyone else, determined the shape it took. Their preoccupation with clarity gave rise to soul-searching throughout the field. No one could have made Mrs. Carrington go in for identification and recap on every page, lines such as "Good evening, Mrs. Butterworth. May I present my cousin, Joe Smiley, the engineer from Detroit whose factory just burned down?" "When a Girl Marries" would contain a good dramatic scene or two each day, but as far as the long-range story was concerned, the new listener had to jump aboard and ride awhile before that larger landscape would come into view.

It was inevitable, I suppose, that at last the agency would get restive about this vagueness. Unwilling, perhaps, to risk the quicksands of a Carrington story conference, they sought reassurance from outside. They found it in a system invented at New York University by Dr. Rudolph Flesch. This gentleman said he could determine mathematically the comparative clarity of various pieces of prose.

The agency couldn't hold "When a Girl Marries" right up against "Our Gal Sunday," the top-rated Air Features show, for analysis, although I suspect that's what they were dying to do. They selected, instead, one of the Psalms of David. The findings were gratifying. "When a Girl Marries," they learned, was just as easy to grasp as the Twenty-third Psalm and a good deal more so than the Gettysburg Address.

James Thurber noted these facts in his *New Yorker* articles on the daytime serials. "I don't know about you," he observed, "but when the final delirium descends upon my mind, it is my fervent hope that I will not trouble the loved ones gathered at my bedside by an endless and incoherent recital of the plot of 'When a Girl Marries.' It will be better for everyone if my consciousness selects that other clear and famous piece of English prose, and I babble of green fields."

The kindly old humorist was joking, of course, but his statement has caused me some personal discomfort. There was never the slightest possibility that such a thing could befall *him*, but there's a very real chance it will happen to *me*.

CHAPTER XII

The Sprained Little Pinkie

Radio was a great teacher. Had it not been for my activities in that field I might never have had personal instruction in etiquette from Emily Post, nor been shown the way to successful living by Ann Delafield.

Miss Post's book on correct social behavior is probably the most widely read of any on its subject, but, as everyone knows, she did not invent etiquette—she simply took it over.

Miss Delafield's influence was not so widespread, but where it touched it penetrated deeply. In the first half of the 1940's thousands of women graduated from her DuBarry Success School on Fifth Avenue in New York and more than a hundred thousand subscribed to her "Home Course in Beauty." If you were lucky enough to enter the Fifth Avenue salon—a place where your fat, your freckles, and your gaucherie could be removed at one and the same time—you found a new beginning.

I broadcast several times with Miss Post at NBC and I joined Miss Delafield to make a series of recordings plugging the "Home Course in Beauty." On both occasions I learned something.

Most of the personalities featured from time to time on the radio shows were likely to remain aloof from the supporting cast. Dale Carnegie, author of "How to Win Friends and Influence People," seemed, when I appeared with him on "Maxwell House Show Boat," distant to the point of remoteness. I was surprised, therefore, as I sat marking my script for the Emily Post program, when a tall, handsome woman with a fine patrician face, and wearing a simple dress and a fur piece, rose from a seat on the opposite side of the studio and crossed to where I was sitting. She inclined slightly toward me and, looking down into my eyes,

141

smiled warmly. "I'm Emily Post," she said, and reached up to adjust her glasses, which had slipped out of place. "We are so happy to have you here," she went on, after I identified myself. Then she made a speech so agreeable that it gave me the impression that someone in NBC's production department must have spoken in advance about me. She left me feeling very buttered up, indeed. After the show was off the air, Miss Post made her way to my side of the studio once more and said a pleasant farewell.

The next week I was called for the program again. Miss Post rose from her chair and came over to greet me. She looked right into my eyes and smiled warmly. "I'm Emily Post," she said. "We are so happy to have you here." Then she repeated almost word for word the speech she had recited the week before. It had included some details about where I was to stand and which microphone I was to use, so when she got to that part I said, "I was here last week, Miss Post."

Her smile disintegrated. "Oh," she said. "Oh, I see—er—I see." She turned and walked away.

Twenty minutes later she was back. She leaned down and gave me a piercing look. "I think when people see *other* people wearing *glasses* they should *identify* themselves," she said. "Immediately! Before the conversation *begins.*"

I could see the point and to this day at the first glimmer of a spectacle I announce myself. "I'm Mary Jane Higby," I say, and in spite of an occasional reply like, "Big deal," or "So what?" I persist, secure in my knowledge that I am doing the Correct Thing.

My brush with the Success School came about several years after the "Etiquette" program had gone off the air. Ford Bond, a free-lance announcer, had gone into the production end of the business and had contracted to create a series of recorded spot announcements for the "Home Course in Beauty."

"I have a tricky job for you, Mary Jane," he told me over the telephone. "I need someone who can give me three distinctly different voices. Come along to the recording studios at two o'clock tomorrow afternoon."

I found the place in the East Forties, went down the hall to where a lighted sign indicated Studio B, pulled open the heavy, soundproof door, and entered the control booth. Inside I found Ford and the engineer deep in conversation.

"Let's try it again," Ford was saying. "You bring up the gain and I'll try to get her to put some *guts* into the thing." He pushed the button that allowed him to be heard over the talk-back in the studio. "We're not

142

getting quite enough voice from you, Miss Delafield," he said. "Can you speak up a little more?"

A low, breathy voice came over the talk-back. "I'll try," it said.

I looked through the glass into the studio. It was bare, save for a small table bearing a microphone and a reading lamp. The chairs had been placed by the table so that they faced one another. In one, a slim woman sat bolt upright. Her back did not touch the chair, her hands rested palms down on the table in front of her, and her feet were carefully placed, one slightly ahead of the other. Her chin was lifted at an angle that, except for the poise and placidity of the figure, might have suggested defiance. Ford turned to me and gave me three pages of copy.

"I want you to do three one-minute spots for me," he said. "It's a 'before-and-after' type of thing. Three women *before* they take the Success Course, then the same three *after*. Make the dames as different as possible."

As I approached it, the upright figure did not move, and as I got near I could hear the sound of rhythmic breathing. Her eyes were closed and the thought crossed my mind that she had fallen asleep there. Then, slowly, she began to move her chin up, down, and around, then up, down, and around the other way.

I sank into the chair opposite her and gave a good look. Miss Delafield was famous for the youthfulness of her appearance. Rumor had it that she was somewhere near sixty. What I saw was a very beautiful woman who might be in her late thirties. Her pale skin was flawless under a light make-up, skillfully applied. The lids were just touched with a lavender tint and the lips delicately outlined. The dark hair, falling softly around the brow, made a frame for the heavily lidded eyes. Her wonderful figure was encased in a perfectly cut navy blue suit. She wore the sort of hat that Lilly Daché then specialized in— a froth of tiny flowers and veiling, perched on the forehead.

A click indicated that Ford had again pressed the talk-back button.

"This is Miss Higby, Miss Delafield," he said. "She's going to do spots four, six, and eleven."

The eyes opened dreamily and the lips parted slowly in a yogalike smile. Her exquisitely manicured hand reached for her script, and I had an impulse to sit on my own grubby paws. I had got up at five that morning, and had spent half an hour hauling an anchor off the muddy harbor bottom before racing for the train to New York.

The scripts were short and simple. Each was to open with Miss Delafield saying, "Beauty—is a magnet!" Then would follow a speech from a customer *before* she took the "Home Course"—a speech that outlined her problems and insecurities. Then she would be heard *after*

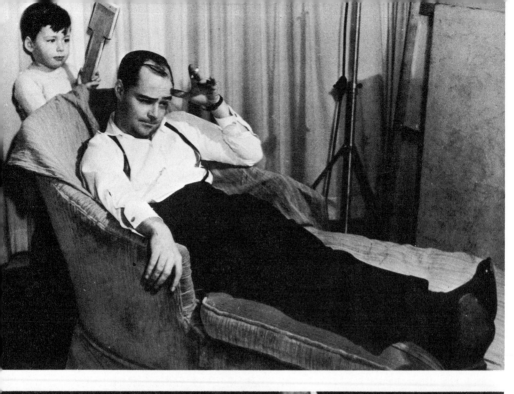

Luis Van Rooten, top, in publicity shot for "Editor's Daughter," a serial. Bottom, Les Tremayne and Claudia Morgan as Nick and Nora Charles on "The Adventures of the Thin Man" in 1945.

Ed Begley as the incomparable Charlie Chan in the early '40's.

she had taken the course. Miss Delafield would close with a plug that said in part, "You owe it to yourself to be vital, healthy, and beautiful— *And you can!*"

Ford threw us a cue and she began in a low, hollow whisper, "Beauty—is a mahgnet."

The engineer came bouncing out of the booth and started to move the table so the microphone would be closer to Miss Delafield's lips. The plug came out of the socket in the wall and he got down on his hands and knees to replace it.

I stood up and, as I did, I felt the strap of my slip break. I looked down. There was a lopsided fringe of pink hanging below my dark skirt. I smiled apologetically in the direction of Miss Delafield, but she was missing. I located her at the far end of the studio, standing with feet ten inches away from the baseboard, back flush against the wall, chin in, hands at sides—doing back stretches. As I drew near, *she* smiled at *me*, apologetically. "One gets so tired—just sitting there," she murmured.

She glided back to her chair and I stumbled after, still fumbling for the strap. I put on some lipstick. Then something came over me. Not since I broke the glass and sounded the fire alarm at Selma Grammar School had I felt such an irresistible urge. For the rehearsal I made the first of my three characters into a female wrestler: "Ahm agonna take the cawss. Effn it did so much for the other gals." The next one had hideous, Bronxian sibilants: "The otheh goils and the jumpmen in my awfiss." The last was a confirmed whiner. And, miracle of miracles, after taking the course they all spoke exactly like Miss Delafield. "I cawn't express my grahtitude," they said in deep, ghostly tones.

The talk-back button again. The voice was ominously sweet. "Miss Higby, will you come in here, please?"

In the booth, Ford turned on me with a snarl. "Now you cut that out!"

"Why, what, Ford?" I asked.

"*You* know what." His look became piteous. "Quit kidding. I'm in enough trouble as it is."

I went back to remove some of the muscle from the first character and the hiss and whine from the others.

"You have a right to be beautiful," Miss Delafield was saying. "Ahnd you cahn."

Ford was tactful. "Miss Delafield, for the radio audience, don't you think—it would be better if you said—'And you can?' "

"Yes, of course. Ahnd you cahn."

"No. And you *can!*"

146

"Ahnd you *cahn!*"

"Can! Can! *Can!* And you CAN!"

"Oh, I could never say that." She turned to me and made a face. "It sounds so *coarse,*" she whispered. "Ahnd you cahn," she repeated firmly and aloud.

Ford conceded. We made the three spots and I left, hitching at my slip.

Such an experience was bound to leave its mark. I took to drinking carrot juice (a Delafield recommendation) and painted my nails pink, and, although I had gone bareheaded all my life, I bought a Lilly Daché hat.

The informality of radio—everyone rushing from show to show, the women often in slacks, the men sometimes unshaven—did not encourage the social graces. But when the NBC Christmas party came around I thought I saw my chance. The affair, given each year in a different department (Spot Sales, Engineers, Announcers, and so forth) was to be held this time by News.

All the newscasters chipped in to give the most sumptuous party the network had yet seen. The many desks in the large Newsroom were pushed together to form a giant u, which was then spread with white tablecloths and covered with carved turkeys and hams, potato chips, buckets of ice, and bottles. There were no bartenders. Everyone helped himself. The fun started early in the afternoon and before long its incendiary sparks had lit fuses in every department in the building.

When I arrived for a soap opera rehearsal at four o'clock, even the elevator men had glints in their eyes. A page boy, herding a group of tourists through the studios, led them down the hall, trucking at the head of the line.

A soundman I hardly knew dashed up and kissed me enthusiastically. "I'm doing 'March of Time,' " he said. "Just one pistol shot. Keene's doing the rest. I been to the party three times already. It's in News, you know."

My last job that day was a commercial on the most high-powered news show on the air. Walter Winchell could announce the arrival of spring and make it sound like an invasion from outer space. There was never one dull news day as far as he was concerned. His frequently barked "Flash!" gave the impression that a dying messenger had just staggered in with final word from a beleaguered fort or that, at the very least, the reporter was translating Morse code as it came in hot over the wire.

As a rule, his programs were meticulously prepared well in advance and I never knew any real excitement to occur about anything except the phone book.

Most broadcasters demanded that the height of the microphone be adjusted to them. Winchell seemed to prefer to adjust himself to the mike. He sat at a table, the microphone before him, the phone book under him—and hell was to pay if anybody tampered with that phone book. NBC was only human, so a few times over the years the book was mislaid and another substituted. I, for one, never believed the story that he then tore out the pages, one by one, testing as he went, until he achieved the exact height.

If everything was in place, Winchell would loll gracefully back on his phone book until the clock showed air time. Then he would suddenly whip into fifteen minutes of journalistic brinkmanship, after which he would rise lazily to his feet with a cheerful good-bye and amble out.

I worked on his show a dozen times or so, and the only variation I ever saw in this routine occurred whenever he had guests. It seemed to me that an unusual number of admirals passed through the visitors' booth from time to time, but I'm no authority on braid and stripes, so perhaps they were merely captains and commanders. The newsman himself, you may recall, was commissioned a lieutenant commander during the war.

When I entered the small studio that day of the big NBC party, an assistant was standing nervously by, while Winchell, his hat pushed back on his head, feverishly edited copy. I looked into the visitors' booth. Sure enough, there was the navy blue.

"This may be too *long*," Winchell fretted. Then addressing the armed forces, "Time is *very important*, you know. Every word has to check out *exactly* on the dot." They nodded solemnly through the plate-glass window. "Ah, yes," he said briskly, as his eye fell on me, "you're here for the commercials." I stifled an impulse to say, "Aye, aye, sir," but snapped back to attention behind the mike. Only the young announcer, who had taken over while Ben Grauer was on vacation, seemed unaware of the tension around him. He smiled woozily at me across the mike and I thought he listed slightly to port, but he put us on the air in shipshape style. Then, his eyes at half-mast, he sagged over the chest-high desk that held the push buttons for the NBC chimes. In the middle of a "Flash! To-Mr.-and-Mrs.-America-and-all-the-ships-at-sea!" there came a resounding Bong-BONG-Bong! Winchell glared and the announcer hastily removed his elbow from the button.

My last chore done, I tilted my tiny hat over my brow and made for the Newsroom.

148

As I stepped off the elevator on the third floor, I saw the figure of a smallish man striding down the hall.

"Luis, wait!" I called. He stopped and I caught up with him. "Going to the party?"

"I'm just going to look in," he answered. "I've got a short rehearsal break. I'm doing 'March of Time.' "

We peered through an open door on a large and noisy crowd. One beautiful blond head rose high above the rest. It was a page girl (the war was already taking its toll from the ranks of NBC's pages)—a Dutch Brunhild, who must have stood six foot two in her stocking feet.

"Ach!" she trumpeted, spying my companion. "My little friend, Van Rooten." She picked him right up off the floor, gave him a smacking kiss, put him down, and went back to her drink.

A dignified and portly news commentator beamed down at me. I looked straight into his gold-rimmed glasses and smiled my new yoga-like smile. "I'm Mary Jane Higby," I said.

He bowed ceremoniously, pouring his highball on my shoes. "Give Betty Jane a drink," he roared.

A sharp stab from behind sent me plunging forward and the Daché creation slid over my eyes. Hands gripped my waist and propelled me swiftly through the mob in an impromptu Conga step, while a voice brayed in my ear, "Cha-cha-HOO! Cha-cha-HOO!"

We halted at the liquor-laden table. I looked around. What I remember is a room full of old, familiar faces. I must be wrong, though. I can't find anyone who will confess that he was there. (Correction: when I questioned George Ansbro, the announcer, he smiled. "Oh, yes," he said, and his eyes glazed as he looked down the twenty-three years. Then they widened suddenly and he flushed. "Oh, *that* party," he said. "But that was before I was *married*, don't forget.")

Be that as it may, I stayed on while the party explored new peaks of togetherness and camaraderie. At the end of an hour it seemed wise to depart.

Before I could go, however, I had to get my hat back. I tackled the brawny funster who was wearing it, with tactics learned not from Emily Post but from the IRT subway.

I passed the "March of Time" studio on my way out, and although it was close to their air time, I strolled in. Behind the sound-effects counter, Keene Crockett was fuming.

"For God's sake, where *is* he?" he groaned. "I can't do this all alone!"

Just then the door flew open and a rigid figure stalked to the sound table, grabbed a gun, pointed it toward the ceiling, and fired. Duty done

149

(but about three minutes too soon), the figure slumped down behind the counter, out of sight.

The actors somehow got through that first scene although they were bent double with laughter. Dwight Weist managed to give that portentous opening, "The March—of *Time!*" Then he, too, collapsed, his hand over his mouth.

Other regrettable events took place that night. A page boy backed out of a tourist-filled elevator, and, after calling out, "Will my tour step this way, please?" fell over another page boy who was stretched out on the floor with a glass in his hand. All evening, secretaries and page girls fled down corridors, racing for life and virtue, and someone doused the eighth floor with a fire extinguisher.

Such was the social whirl of radio's Golden Era. All in all, it was not a sight for Post or Delafield eyes. It was a party to end all parties, and end all parties it did. High in the echelons of NBC, the foot of authority was put down—firmly and forever. That was the last great interdepartmental blowout we ever had.

CHAPTER XIII

Rinso—What?

The play is not the thing. The sponsor's message is the thing, and no radio or television actor can ever forget it. The Commercial is here to stay. Vanished are "The March of Time," "We, the People," and "Cavalcade of America," but those one-minute blurbs about those little pills go on forever. Where now are Myrt and Marge, Lorenzo and Belle, and Mrs. Nussbaum of Allen's Alley? The stuff that gives you a whiter, brighter wash is still bubbling up on all the networks.

Although I played hundreds of radio characters over the years, I never became emotionally involved with any. My only sleepless nights and haunted days were caused not by some heroine's sad fate, but by that all-important Commercial Message. You, as listener or viewer, may turn down the sound when the talk begins about Crispy Crunchy Chunkies. But there is one man who does not. That's the man who foots the bill—the sponsor. He may laugh and chat through an adaptation of "King Lear," but let the product's name be mentioned once and he's all ears and nerves. Because he is at the top of a pyramid of big salaries, this neurosis drifts down through the advertising agencies and networks and invariably lands with accumulated fallout on the performer. He bears up pretty well, as a rule, because he has been chosen with all the care given to selecting an astronaut. Auditions go on sometimes for days. It was at one of these that my detachment from the world of reality began.

I arrived late and found the hall at CBS crammed with aspirants for the soap commercial. Lipstick-tipped cigarette butts overflowed the ashtrays and others had been snuffed out on the floor. The audition had been going on for a long time and about two dozen actresses were still

Richard Leibert, organist on many radio serials, including "When a Girl Marries."

waiting to be heard when I walked in. Some of them were restlessly pacing up and down. Others had lapsed into a gloomy stupor. Some had separated from the crowd and were humming "Mi, mi, mi" to themselves. From the ladies' room came the sound of someone vocalizing, "Ah-ha-ha-HAH-ha-ha-ha."

There were four studios on the floor. Every now and then a man would stick his head out of the studio door marked 22 and summon one of us, at the same time bidding her predecessor farewell. "Sorry. Not this time."

The vocalizing in the ladies' room had reached a remarkably high pitch. A's and B flats were bounding through the halls. A door marked 23 popped open and a young man with tousled hair flew out. He skidded to a stop before the ladies' room, then turned to the rest of us. "Tell whoever is in there to shut up. She's leaking into 'Backstage Wife.' "

That served to break the tension and it was several minutes before order was restored. Then my name was called.

The producer ushered me in and smiled kindly.

"Now, don't be nervous," he said, his voice trembling. "This is quite a challenge."

The producer, the sound-effects man, and I made a lone group at one end of the large studio. The microphone was surrounded by sound-proof boards, about six feet high, which were set up on wheels so that they could be moved about. Through the crack between two of them I could see the window that looked out on the control booth, where the engineer, who regulated the sound and voice levels, sat near his knobs and dials. He was dozing over a book. Behind him stood six men, each with the unmistakable "executive" look, and each staring at me frostily. The network, the advertising agency, even the high reaches of the sponsor, were represented.

"Now, Jimmy, here," said the director, looking at the sound-effects man, "has this whistle."

Jimmy Lynch didn't look up. He stayed perched on the high stool behind his effects counter and read on. Jimmy was always reading. The performers and, I'm sure, the producers and executives envied this aloofness of radio's technical staff. No matter what hell broke loose around them, the engineers and the soundmen preserved an almost mystic detachment. This is, perhaps, why they, of all of us, turned in the most consistently excellent work.

Jimmy groped around among the effects and brought out a whistle. He blew it thrice; twice on a low note, then leaping an octave for the third note. "Tweet-tweet—TWEET."

"What's that?" I asked. "High C?"

"F," said Jimmy.

That was no challenge to me. I can sing F on a clear day if the wind is right, and I said so.

"What do I sing?" I queried.

"But you musn't sing. That's the challenge. You must *say* it."

"OK," I said, less confidently. "What do I say?"

He handed me a paper on which was written, "Rinso—white."

"Now, just *speak* it," he said.

"Rinso—whaaaeet," I trilled.

"No, you're singing it." He looked resigned. He'd expected this all along.

Then I did it. I really did. I *spoke* it on F below high C. Jimmy dropped his whistle. My director looked as if he were going to gather me to his bosom.

"You're the first one," he murmured tenderly. "We've been at this all day. And you're the first one—the only one." He put his hands gently on my shoulders and pushed me to the microphone.

"Do it again," he pleaded.

"Rin-so—white," I chirped.

He did a little dance step and looked into the control booth. No sign came from there. Still Mount Rushmore in duplicate.

"The pots aren't open," said Jimmy. My admirer went over and rapped sharply on the control-booth window. The engineer jumped up and started twirling his dials.

"Do it again," whispered the producer.

I let them have it three or four times. The effect was seismic. Old Stony Faces broke up. They were grinning and pounding one another on the back. Even the engineer smiled. They came flowing out of the control booth and formed a circle around me. Could I, they implored, start the commercial next Monday morning?

"Sure," I agreed jauntily. "What time?"

"Eight-fifteen," they chorused.

I was hit by a heavy qualm. I'm a sound sleeper and a slow waker. I don't relate immediately with what is going on around me. My qualm must have showed, for one of the men added, "It pays double union scale." Still I hesitated. Another said, "Oh, we can do better than that." Now, I have a weakness. It's American money. I made a deal then and there.

It was with a light heart that I floated that afternoon toward NBC to portray one of about a half-dozen roles that I performed over the years on "Stella Dallas." At the time the plot concerned her brother (played by Frank Lovejoy) who kept seeing ghosts around his water cooler. Then I went on to "When a Girl Marries," where my baby was "being born under a cloud" (this phrase, which I repeated over and over for much longer than the normal period of human gestation, referred to the fact that my husband was on trial for murder).

There were no soap operas on Saturday so I had a day of rest. Sunday I awoke with a nagging depression. *Can* I be identifying? I asked myself. I ran over the plights of my various alter egos. True, I had broken a lamp over Helen Trent's head, but it was her concussion, not mine. I, the villainess, was safely on the lam in my Cadillac convertible. I felt I could rely on Stella Dallas to exorcise the water cooler. And that very Friday the light had broken through the cloud over baby's head. No, my thoughts were just those of any normal American girl. Then it dawned on me.

I sidled over to the piano and found F. "Rinso—wh. .," I began. But no sound came. Panic. I calmed myself with the thought that I hadn't even had breakfast yet. I ate a big one, waited a few hours and sauntered to the piano and there it was. Fine. Clear as a bell. "I'll get up early tomorrow," I thought.

I got up early, all right. I hadn't slept a wink all night. When I got to the studio, the cast of the serial for which I was to provide the commercial was assembled and had already rehearsed. All old friends, they greeted me with rousing cheers and warm embraces. Mount Rushmore was back in the control booth but wreathed in smiles. They waved at me gaily.

We were on the air. The organ droned out that the day's first soap opera was here. Then the announcer's brief blurb. Then Jimmy and his whistle. "Tweet tweet—TWEET." My throat was dry. My heart was pounding. "Rinso whi--," I croaked and flatted.

Heads jerked up in disbelief. Smiles faded. I gazed miserably down at my copy. "Yes," I read mournfully. "That's the happy little washday song."

When the show was over the actors filed out in embarrassed silence. A conference was being held in the control booth. All six executives and the producer were in a huddle. I stood forlornly by Jimmy while he put away his sound effects. I felt a strong hand under my elbow. It was the organist, Richard Leibert, a friend of many years.

"What are you hanging around for?" he whispered.

"To apologize."

"Get out. Always get out fast when you've made a mistake. Give 'em time to forget it."

Once in the hall, he rang for the elevator; then as the studio door moved slightly, he said, "They're coming," and pushed me through the door that led to the staircase. "Don't take the elevator. Walk."

I hid in the ladies' room on the second floor until I was sure everybody had left, then crept furtively out.

The following morning the actors were kind but subdued. I kept my eyes away from the control booth, but I could sense the tension coming from there. The half-hour before air time I spent pacing the studio saying, "Rin-so—white, Rin-so—white," over and over.

"You'll wear yourself out," Dick Leibert said. I paid no attention. I knew what I was doing. I had it and I meant to keep it. I had been up since six-thirty and, in spite of nasty phone calls of complaint, I had gone right on vocalizing from seven-fifteen to seven-forty-five.

On the air again. "Tweet tweet—TWEET." "Rin-so—White," I replied. Nice and clear. Perfect. I peeked into the control room. Men coming out from under a great strain were relaxing and lighting up cigarettes. I read my copy. "Yes, indeed. That little bird really has something. For a wash that's truly white—."

I settled back to listen to the actors play the soap opera. Suddenly I noticed Jimmy waving his whistle and pointing at me. I rushed hastily through my script and saw that I had a couple of tweets in the closing announcement, too. Caught by surprise, I flatted again. Once more I sneaked down the back stairs and out.

That night I thought it over. To resign . . . or to wait to be fired. Then it came to me. Yoga. I remembered my attendant at a gym in Grand Central Palace telling me that Lawrence Tibbett used to stand on his head in the steam room there and sing. "It starts the circulation," he said. "And clears the nasal passages."

I began standing on my head in the corner first thing in the morning. It did seem to wake me up a bit. Afterward I would bury the telephone in pillows so I couldn't hear it ring, and vocalize. At the studio I walked up and down for a full half-hour, saying "Rin-so—white" over and over until air time. The actors took to scowling when I came in.

"I can't study my part with *that* going on," the star said.

"I don't mind *her* saying it, as long as she doesn't get *me* to saying it," snarled the organist.

Friday I had the closing commercial. My neck was stiff from all those headstands. I couldn't turn my head but I got through the opening all right. Then panic seized me. Suppose my voice went to sleep again while the drama unfolded, as it had before. I decided to take steps to wake it up. I crept out into the hall, which was deserted, walked around the corner away from the elevators, pinned my skirt together between my knees, and did a quick headstand against the wall. "Mi, mi, mi,"

I chanted softly. A door squeaked and I heard an exclamation. I dropped to all fours and looked into the face of the head of network programming.

"Circulation," I babbled. "Tibbett stands in Grand Central." He crossed quickly to the door that led to the staircase and went out. Then the door creaked open again and I could see him peering at me through the crack, as if to confirm what he had just seen. I could feel that gaze on my back as I ran down the hall and into the studio. There, Jimmy tweeted, I flatted.

I hid in the ladies' room a long time. I had an unreasonable conviction that the head of network programming was lurking on the back staircase.

The weekend came. Oh, blessed relief. An old friend called up. He was not in show business and I felt that his type of fun was just what I needed. He had a sub rosa deal with a French champagne company (he was French himself) to roam the better night spots and order rare vintages just for the publicity value of it. The hitch was that he did not like champagne so his companion had to be prepared to down quite a bit of it. We made three of the nicer spots in town, ending up at the St. Regis for the supper show. I was brooding over you-know-what when it dawned on me.

"It's the soft palate."

"Pardon?" said Jacques.

"The soft palate. Look." I opened my mouth wide. "Iss izza hard palate." I pointed to the roof of my mouth. "The soft palate's behind it."

My friend moved my glass out of reach. "Let's dance," he murmured.

Out on the floor I tried to explain further but he wasn't listening. I was aglow with excitement. My troubles were over. It was all so clear to me now. Years of singing lessons had taught me that a yawn would lift the soft palate and allow one to emit one's highest possible note. All I had to do was to yawn wide at the back of my throat.

The orchestra stopped playing just as we reached their side of the floor. I caught the pianist's eye. "Sound your F," I called. He seemed surprised but laughed. He was a good sport. He sounded F. So did I.

The St. Regis doorman couldn't have been nicer when he picked me up, and the management never said a word to me. They may have spoken to my escort. I intended to ask him and I certainly should have if I had ever seen him again. It is true that I fell down the grand staircase, but I fell. I was not thrown out. I say this to scotch certain belittling rumors that were bruited about.

As I limped into the studio the following morning, still unable to turn my head, I felt that my fellow performers were a bit cursory in expressing their sympathy. Eyeing the bandage on my ankle, Dick Leibert smirked, "This commercial is taking a lot out of you, isn't it?"

"It's taking a lot out of all of us," snapped the leading lady.

The producer drew me aside. Here it comes, I thought. At last I was going to be fired. I was relieved. I had tried to quit several times but I was always held back by the thought of that lovely paycheck.

"We've been thinking this over," he said. "The girl on the Coast—."

"What girl on the Coast?"

"We are doing a similar commercial from Hollywood. The girl on the Coast doesn't seem to be having the same difficulty with pitch—."

Support came from an unexpected source. "The girl on the Coast," said Jimmy, with emphasis, "is not trying to *say* it. She *sings* it."

The director looked pained. "The Hollywood commercial is a singing commercial. Here in New York we want a *spoken* commercial."

I agreed to try to boost the pitch, although how I was going to do it I had no idea. I had used every method I knew. I gave it a try then and there. Pretty good, too. The trouble was I could never predict what a case of last-minute panic would do to me and my epiglottis. It was true even in the sober morning light that if I got my throat open wide enough I could hit it accurately. Never, of course, with the soaring abandon I had achieved at the St. Regis.

I started my practice period again. The actors groaned. The most I can say for that day's performance is that it wasn't as bad as some of the others had been. Maybe I was tired from the night before and thus more relaxed.

As Jimmy was putting away his sound effects, he turned the whistle over in his hand meditatively. "I wonder where they got this," he muttered.

"Isn't it yours?" I asked.

"No, they sent it over from the advertising agency," he replied. "They're very fussy about it. It had to be exactly like the one on the Coast."

Time dragged on and the executives quit getting up early enough to appear in person. It didn't help much because I had a picture of six men crouching and wincing in front of six radios at home or in their offices. Dick Leibert took to analyzing my errors. According to him I was finding tonal shadings unknown even to the Chinese. "Look," he would say. "She didn't hit this [pointing to the key of F on his keyboard], or this [pointing to E], she was somewhere in here [pointing to the crack between the keys]."

He was particularly evil over the affair of the fan mail. One day an unusually large stack arrived and the star was delighted. She opened the top letter and paled.

"That's not for *me*," she said. Dick shuffled through the letters. He brought them over to the corner where I was chirping. He gave me the nasty little smile he had developed lately.

"It's for you," he said. I glanced at it:

"If that's a record, break it. If it's a parrot, wring its neck. If it's a woman, cut her throat."

I was never replaced. It seems I was the only girl who could say "White" on F even occasionally. They decided that was not often enough and canceled the whole thing.

A few weeks later, when sudden noises no longer made me jump, I turned on my radio. There she was, the girl from the Coast, singing true as a pitch pipe, "Rinso white, Rinso white. Happy little washday song." I sang with her. Easy as pie. But there was something wrong. I went to the piano and touched the keys. Then I really did jump. She was in the key of D—three full notes lower than Jimmy's whistle.

I stormed over to the studio, teeth set, fists clenched. The program was off the air and the only person I could find was Jimmy.

"Yes," he mused. "I noticed that, too. Somebody goofed. They sent me the wrong whistle."

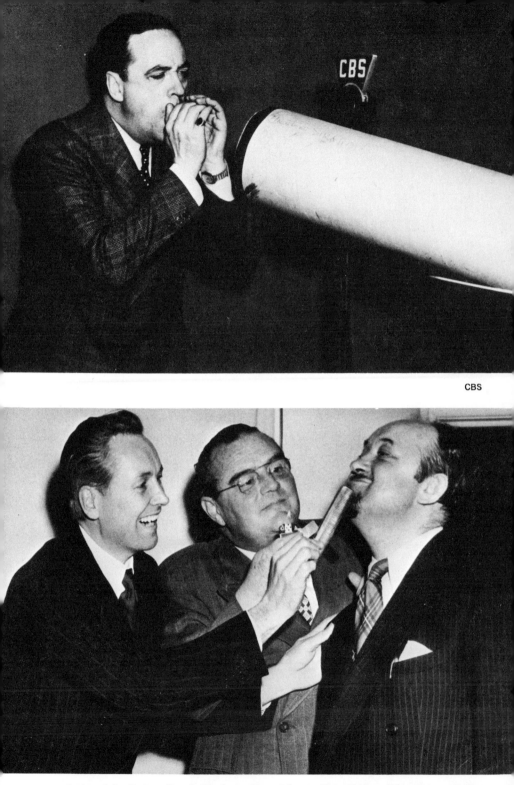

CBS

Animal imitator Brad Barker does his wolf call for "Renfrew of the Mounted," top. Combing director Ken MacGregor's goatee during rehearsal of "Show Boat," bottom, are Lanny Ross, star of program, and F. Chase Taylor (Stoopnagle).

CHAPTER XIV

Who's Who in the Zoo

It must have been sometime in 1939 that I first wandered into Studio 2 at CBS, where a group of actors had assembled to give to the small boys of America that day's episode of "Renfrew of the Mounted." My call was a purely social one. Radio actors with time to kill between shows would often drift into studios where other programs were in progress. We would chat with our friends and perhaps sit through the rehearsal or even the broadcast.

It was not unusual to find the cast clowning through the first reading of the script, and if you happened to catch a group that included, for example, Ed Begley, Art Carney, or Keene Crockett (soundman and possessor of the most wild and roving wit in radio), you could count on a few good laughs before you left. This visiting back and forth could make a day's work seem like one long kaffeeklatsch—all in all, a cheerful way to earn a living.

On this occasion, I glanced through the open door of the "Renfrew" studio, saw a few friendly faces, and went in and sat down. The last member of the cast to arrive was a stranger to me—a tall, substantial-looking man with a handsomely rugged face. He wore a pearl gray homburg and a chesterfield, its black velvet collar contrasting smartly with his white silk scarf. His shoes were discreetly polished and his nails neatly manicured. A perfect type for a bank president or a senator. I wondered what on earth he was doing in this blood-and-thunder saga of the Great Northwest. Before I had time to ask, the director signaled from the control booth that rehearsal was about to begin.

The newcomer went to the huge grand piano in the center of the room and lifted its heavy black lid. "A pianist?" I thought, "On 'Ren-

161

frew?' " But House Jameson, who played Renfrew, was also approaching the piano. He was carrying a metal tube that looked like a square stove pipe about six feet long. House placed one end on the piano strings and pressed his mouth to the other.

"Renfrew!" he called down the pipe, "Renfrew—of the Mounted!" His voice rolled and swirled back from the strings in a distant, unearthly cry and, as it did so, the gentleman in the chesterfield doffed his homburg, threw back his head, pointed his nose to the ceiling, and gave a long, hungry yelp. This sober fashionplate, I realized, was impersonating a timber wolf.

I learned later that, because he was part of the program's signature and the network ruling against recorded effects required him to be present in the studio every day, that howl brought him $10,000 a year. He was one of the busiest people in the New York radio world, going from studio to studio most of the day and much of the night—growling, howling, and barking as the case required. He specialized in the larger animals and could provide a magnificent trumpeting elephant. It is his voice you hear when the lion roars at the beginning of every MGM film.

I soon became better acquainted with him when he turned up on "When a Girl Marries." He was the mastiff guarding the house next door. This gentleman's name—and I can produce a cloud of witnesses to prove it—was Barker.

Bradley Barker had no monopoly in the animal imitation field. Many of the sound-effects men (Keene Crockett, for one) could bay very convincingly at radio's imaginary moon. Once, in Los Angeles, a soundman from KHJ was arrested for throwing rocks at the birds in the zoo. His excuse was that a peacock cry was coming up in a broadcast that evening and he had to learn to imitate it before nightfall. Peacocks are notably taciturn birds. He had lobbed a few stones at the creatures, not, as he explained, hoping for a direct hit, but only to startle them out of their aloof silence. He got a suspended sentence.

As far as the soundmen were concerned, however, animal noises were only a small part of an extensive repertoire of other effects. Brad Barker was a *specialist*. As such he had only one serious competitor, a man named Donald Bain.

Bain and Barker were opposites in nearly every respect. Brad was an old showman. He had come to us from motion pictures, where he had been an actor and director ("Grandma's Boy," an early talkie starring Morton Downey, was directed by Bradley Barker). Donald Bain, on the other hand, came to us (after a brief detour in Chautauqua) from the Department of Agriculture. Brad's unusual vocal talents had come

162

to light when the movies were first timorously grappling with sound (he gave voice not only to MGM's Leo, but to Pathe's rooster as well). Bain had developed his ability while roaming the hills and valleys of the Southeast on a barberry eradication campaign.

Where Brad was well-built and over six feet tall, with a strong, craggy face, Donald was short and tubby, with a round face, pale blue eyes, and sparse gray hair. Where Brad always arrived a picture of sartorial elegance, Donald would turn up wearing pants that sagged and a hat that was shapeless. His small feet, enclosed in scuffed brown shoes, were sometimes sockless. Where Brad was the epitome of conservative sobriety, Donald was an eccentric. He used to wander through the halls of NBC or CBS, absently clucking or cooing to himself. The smaller animals were his specialty—domestic and wild fowl, pigs, goats, small dogs, and so forth.

If Donald Bain was an eccentric, he was also a born showman, and it was not always evident which quality had the upper hand. He approached me on the third floor of NBC one day, an old-fashioned laundry basket under his arm. I could hear a chirruping noise coming from beneath a cloth that was thrown lightly over the basket. The little man said confidentially, "Baby chicks." The peeps continued very, very softly. "Want to see?" he whispered. When I nodded, he brought his fist down like a pylon and I screamed. He laughed and pulled back the cloth. The basket was empty, of course.

There was one setting that brought all of Donald's theatrical instinct to the fore—"The Theater Guild of the Air." Sponsored by United States Steel and produced by the theatrical company that had brought so many illustrious plays to Broadway, the program was broadcast each week from the Belasco Theater and always featured several Broadway stars.

The physical setup for the big "audience" shows was the same, whether for Hollywood's "Lux Radio Theater" or New York's "Cavalcade of America" and "Theater Guild of the Air." The orchestra was seated at the back of the stage and a microphone was suspended above the conductor's head. The announcers and cast used standing microphones at the front of the stage. When they were not on mike, the actors sat in a row before the orchestra, the stars near the center. Sound effects, contained in two or three movable counters, were put off to the side of the stage. This was advisable because often the spectators would show more interest in the rolling up of a window blind than they did in the drama. During breathtaking struggles to the death they had been known to shuffle noisily to their feet to peer at the soundman, who was beating his chest, throwing dishes to the floor, and smashing wooden boxes to simulate fist-to-fist combat. If something unusual caught their attention during a quiet scene their tittering could destroy the drama. "Sound" constituted a hazard whenever the public was allowed to watch a radio performance.

"The Theater Guild of the Air" was produced with an eye to the audience, so interruptions of this kind were unlikely to occur. Donald Bain appeared on the program often and gave a memorable performance in the sensitive and poetic drama, "The Barretts of Wimpole Street." An impressive cast was assembled. Madeleine Carroll and Brian Aherne played Elizabeth Barrett and Robert Browning. Charles Waldron was heard as Elizabeth's father. Donald was, of course, her little dog, Flush. The performances were always given in evening dress, and the stage was filled with as subtle a series of lighting effects as might have been seen at a ballet. Miss Carroll rose, beautiful and willowy, to take her place at the microphone. She brought a grave wistfulness to the scenes of the invalid poetess. Brian Aherne was vital and romantic as Browning, and Charles Waldron gave austere dignity to the part of Edward Moulton-Barrett.

Into this group shuffled wispy-haired Donald in his baggy tuxedo. "Grr-rr-yip—woof," he said. There was a hint of a stir in the audience. A gleam came into the animal imitator's eye. He straightened up and seemed to grow a little taller. Flush was an expressive dog. He yipped, growled, whined, panted, and barked as the scene progressed. When his moment was over, Donald made a long "fade," giving a farewell happy "Arf!" Then, as Flush should have trotted off, wagging his tail, Donald whipped around, faced the audience, and gave a low sweeping bow.

Chaplin, the Marx Brothers, and Bert Lahr never got a better laugh. After that, every time Flush was even mentioned, a titter ran through the house. At the end of the show, when the cast took their bows, Flush received an ovation.

It was some time before Donald was asked to appear again on "The Theater Guild of the Air." When he did, he found a special microphone set up behind the sound-effects section for his use alone. It was about three feet above the floor and he had to crouch down behind the sound cabinets to give his impersonation of a wild duck.

"I don't know why they're discriminating against *me*," he fumed. "*I* got the biggest hand they ever *had* on this show!"

Donald Bain got even more remarkable acclaim one day in Central Park, where he had gone to brush up on his birdcalls. It was during the mating season. Donald listened attentively to a couple of courting pigeons strolling by his feet. Then he repeated exactly what he heard the male say. The female cocked her head, gave Donald a sidewise look, and flew up onto his knee. The male took off in confusion. Donald continued the masquerade for awhile, then rose to go. But he couldn't get rid of the lady. No amount of shooing or flapping his arms discouraged her. She stuck to him all the way to the exit at Fifty-ninth Street. Suddenly he had an idea. He made the sound of another lovelorn female and that did it. She dropped off his shoulder in disgust and made for the zoo. As Donald turned toward Sixth Avenue, he spotted a couple of determined-looking male pigeons coming his way. He threw a few diversionary dog barks in their direction and sprinted out of the park and into the sanctuary of a nearby bar and grill.

Donald's dog barks were just as authentic as his pigeon coos, and there was a noise he could make that would set any dog whining and straining at its leash in hysteria. He used to drive my Cairn terrier, Letty, crazy. Once when he saw me walking on Fifty-second Street, he spoke to her in what must have been an outrageous way to canine ears from across the street. She slipped out of her collar and darted into traffic. I was nearly run down myself trying to catch her. When I did, I gave her a good spanking and then started stalking Donald Bain to tan his little hide for him, too. But with unfailing woodsy instinct, he had tracked silently away and lost himself in the wilds of Madison Avenue.

This odd little man never joked in the studio, however. He was in deadly earnest when it came to his work—or at least he seemed to be. Even there we were never sure where eccentricity stopped and showmanship began.

"Donald, you're going to be the star of this show," Earl McGill told him one time. "You have the leading part—a mosquito." Donald blinked his round little eyes. "Male or female?" he wanted to know.

It was a play about yellow fever and the discovery of its relationship to the mosquito. Several of the insects buzzed in and out of the story, and Donald made a conscientious effort to give each a distinctive personality. He reached his zenith in the death scene of one of the female mosquitoes.

The effect was written like this:

Mosquito: Zzzzzzzzzzzzzzzzzzzzzzzzz
Sound: SLAP . . . SILENCE
Donald Bain's version went like this:
Mosquito: Zzzzzzzzzzzz zzzzzzzzzzz zzzzzzz
Sound: SLAP
Mosquito: ZZZZZZ . . . ZZZZ . . . Zzz . . . zz . . . z. . . .
SILENCE
A veritable Duse among mosquitoes!

Brad Barker, too, liked to probe the psyches of the various fauna he was called upon to represent. Brad was often heard on "The March of Time," a program that dramatized the week's headlines and was therefore subject to hectic, last-moment changes. A couple of hours before air time, one night, word came that an escaped lion was terrorizing a Western town. New scenes were hastily written, parts were recast and Brad was called to come at once. He arrived minutes before air time and asked for a script. There was a shortage of newly typed pages so Homer Fickett, the director, told him, "Just roar when I give you a cue."

"I have to have a script," Brad insisted.

"No, you don't. Just roar when I——."

The big man drew himself up indignantly. "I *must* have a script," he said.

"What for?"

"How else will I know what the lion is *thinking?*"

It was inevitable that a certain amount of rivalry would grow up between Barker and Bain, but, because each had more work than he could do, it never became cutthroat competition. Donald used to express disdain because Brad employed "mechanical aids" in his reproduction of animal sounds. Brad had a sawed-off steamboat whistle into which he trumpeted or roared to achieve certain effects. Donald relied solely on his larynx and vocal chords to create the inhabitants of an entire menagerie. They both sounded breathtakingly perfect in any imitation they undertook to do.

During the season of 1945–46, Donald Bain was, in addition to his many radio shows, working in two Broadway plays at the same time. He was the cat in the first act of "I Remember Mama" and a mule in the last act of "A Bell for Adano." Never seen by the audience, of course, he stood in the wings and made appropriate sounds as they came up on cue. It was during this period that Ken MacGregor called him for the Ripley show, which demanded several days of rehearsal. Donald carefully took down all the hours of rehearsal in his notebook— 10 to 12 A.M. on Monday, 2 to 5 P.M. on Tuesday, 5 to 8:30 P.M. on Thursday. "That's fine," he said. "I'll be there for the rehearsals. The only thing is—I can't make the show."

Ken thought he felt a slight pull on his leg. "OK, Donald," he said. "We'll get Brad for the show. On second thought, maybe we'd better get him to do the *rehearsal,* too."

At about this time an important union membership meeting came up. It was called for eight in the evening. Two factions within the organization had been locked for months in what looked like a struggle to the death, and now the prospect of a really nasty fight had packed the hall. Donald came in late and walked down the center aisle to the front row, where he took a seat. He had just come from "I Remember Mama."

An hour later tension had reached the explosion point. The two extremes were at each other's throats in earnest, the rest of us cowering in our seats. Suddenly a jangled alarm rang out above the din. During the startled pause that followed, Donald got up, pulled a huge alarm clock from his coat pocket, silenced it, thrust it back, jammed his porkpie hat over his ears, and trudged solemnly up the aisle and out. Over the laughter that swept like a cooling wave of sanity across the super-charged emotions in the hall, the man behind me shouted, "Of course! He was afraid he'd be late for his cue in 'Bell For Adano!' " The little man got an even bigger laugh on his return to the meeting some forty-five minutes later.

Showmanship or eccentricity? We never quite knew. Brad Barker was different. He fitted right into the category that used to be known as "an actor of the old school." With Brad we knew where we stood. Or at least we thought we did until Keene Crockett staggered into NBC one day and gasped heavily, "My God! I just saw Brad Barker trotting down Fifth Avenue with Donald Bain in his mouth!"

CHAPTER XV

The Infernal Triangle

The sharp rivalry among the networks to acquire the highest ratings, the most prestigious orchestras, and the coveted public service awards, stopped cold when it came to décor. There was never any question of who *looked* best. When NBC moved from the opulence of 711 Fifth Avenue to the awesome splendor of Radio City, its competitors seemed to throw in the sponge. CBS's rented space in an office building, with its dull gray walls, its comfortable, middle-aged receptionists, and its small band of undistinguished messenger boys, had contrasted sadly with NBC's old quarters, where two of the studios were paneled drawing rooms furnished in faultless Chippendale. A visitor to NBC in those days trod through carpeting that tickled his ankles, and was greeted by receptionists who would have tickled a sultan. At nightfall these creamy-skinned beauties changed to high fashion décolletage, the entire announcers' staff switched to dinner jackets, and the page boys, a crack corps of elite guardsmen in snappy blue uniforms, doffed their four-in-hands for black bow ties.

As radio boomed, the industry felt a space shortage. CBS added to its premises a narrow seven-story edifice across the street from the main studios. A flaccid gesture was made toward modern architecture by installing a pale blue facade and heavy, but treacherously invisible, plate-glass doors. Twenty-five years later this former home of a music school was still known to the trade as the CBS "New Building."

A few years earlier, NBC had moved both of its networks (at that time it had two, the Red and the Blue) to the gargantuan sixty-eight-story RCA Building in Radio City. The last artists to leave the old quarters were Ben Grauer, NBC's top announcer, and Joe White, the

Silver Masked Tenor. Why a radio performer needed a mask, even a silver one, has always puzzled me. TV, by contrast, has no masks and as a result, we all know things about TV tenors that only their dentists should know for sure. The old, blind medium, however, had its masked tenor and, on that November night in 1933, he stood before a lone microphone in the already stripped studios of 711 Fifth Avenue.

"Kathleen Mavourneen," he began, "the gray dawn is breaking [here he switched to a portable mike and headed for the exit] . . . The horn of the hunter is heard on the hill. The lark from her light wing the bri-ight dew [out into the street now] . . . is sha-a-aking. Kathleen Mavourneen. What? Slumbering still? Mavourneen! [here he clambered aboard a vanload of NBC furniture] . . . Mavourneen! My sad heart is breaking to think that from Erin and thee I must part. It may be for years [he teetered away on his pile of desks and chairs] . . . and it may be forever . . ."

White lurched his way to Radio City, and, still singing, slid off the furniture, raced across the vast marble lobby, into the elevator, and up to the studios, where, casting aside his portable mike, he faced a shiny new one for his last and breathless high note.

Ben Grauer accompanied the Masked Tenor on that historic junket, explaining to the unseeing millions what they might have seen if they could have seen anything. And what they might have seen was impressive. Most of the staff seems to have been stunned by the sheer size of it. One announcer got so tangled up in the maze of corridors that he missed his opening cue. Not surprising, either, considering what he was up against. Although only 27 of the projected 35 studios were finished at the time, there were 296 double soundproof doors, 323 identical wall clocks, and 250 microphone outlets.

The studios ranged from cubicles, for one-man shows, to huge, two-story structures with glass-walled visitors' booths entered from the floor above. They were actually small auditoriums where the constant parade of NBC's Guided Tours could rest tired feet and watch a rehearsal or show. Out of our normal line of vision, these "goldfish bowls," as we called them, were easily forgotten. As a result, more than one tourist heard things never intended for delicate nonshow-business ears. I still squirm at the thought of the rehearsal of "When a Girl Marries" when the perennial sweetness of my soap opera heroine began to cloy. My three-year-old son in the story was having a tantrum. Instead of saying, as the script required, "Sammy, darling, be a good little boy, *please*," I turned on the thirty-year-old woman who played the squawling child and snarled, "Oh, shut up, you little bastard, or I'll kick your teeth in."

Ben Grauer, NBC's chief announcer, reading the news in 1940.

Something drew my eye upward to the goldfish bowl. A page boy stood frozen, his arm raised in a half-finished gesture, his jaw sagging. Mine sagged, too, when I saw behind him row upon row of black-robed nuns.

I lacked the presence of mind of Phillips Lord, owner and producer of "Gangbusters," when, after a profane and angry outburst, he noticed a brimming goldfish bowl. "And when *Mr. Lord* gets here," he added hastily, "we'll see what *he* has to say."

Studio 3B was out of bounds for tours when "The Gospel Singer" (Edward MacHugh) was broadcasting. The sweet singer was known among studio hands for conversation larded with one-syllable, four-letter, Anglo-Saxon words. Often the air around him would turn blue just before the engineer switched on the microphone and gave him the signal to edge throatily into the first line of his theme song: "If I have wounded any soul today . . ." NBC pages were under strict injunctions to see to it that he had not.

Arturo Toscanini allowed no tours through his prebroadcast rehearsals. It was just as well. During his NBC days, the great conductor was one of the most beautiful men ever to tread the earth. I used to hold my breath whenever I rode with him in the elevator to the eighth floor. He looked like one of God's own angels. But he cursed like one of Satan's own demons. In Italian, of course.

His concerts were broadcast from Studio 8H—a vast auditorium, three stories high, that seated more than 1,000 people—the largest radio studio ever built.

Almost as impressive was the second-floor reception room where aspiring actors were forced to wait for appointments with NBC directors. This artists' Gehenna resembled the main foyer of an ocean liner. A long desk ran almost the full width of the wall opposite a bank of elevators. Behind it, a giant plate-glass window revealed a flowing double staircase that led to the third-floor studios. The self-possessed beauty who presided at the desk was flanked by two rigid, white-gloved page boys.

NBC pages were, I am sure, unlike any other group of messengers anywhere. During the Depression, when applications swelled to the thousands, the network steadily raised qualifications for these $65-a-month jobs. At first, two years of college were necessary, but later, graduation was required. As a result, quite a few M.A.'s and even an occasional Ph.D. were to be seen in the daily four o'clock lineup behind the men's lockers. The whole brainy platoon would stand at attention, each left trouser leg raised to reveal NBC regulation black sock, each right hand extended to show immaculate white glove. A drillmaster, left over from the network's less scholarly days, would give a briefing. "Now, we don't want none of youse guys goin' into no clients' booths," he was known to say.

A partial list of former NBC pages would include actors Efrem Zimbalist Jr. and Gordon MacRae, TV producers Albert MacCleary and James Sheldon, announcers Don Gardiner and Gene Rayburn, singers Earl Wrightson and Ted Steel, and TV personality Dave Garroway.

Two of these sentries were always stationed on the ground floor to inspect each artist's pass before admitting him. Musicians carrying instruments were remanded to the freight elevators. A thoroughly briefed page once stopped a violinist on his way to Studio 8H.

"You can't come in here," he said brusquely.

"But I'm late for my broadcast."

"You have to go around to the other elevators."

"You don't understand," the man said patiently. "I'm Jascha Heifetz."

The page boy stared the virtuoso squarely in the eye.

"You can't bring that fiddle in here," he said. "Not even if your name is *Rubinoff!*"

The Columbia Broadcasting System's reply to all this spit and polish was to rent additional space in an office building at 799 Seventh Avenue—more gray paint and liver-colored, mock-leather wall benches.

Radio City, Madison Avenue, and Seventh Avenue, together with the Mutual Broadcasting Company studios at Fortieth Street and Broadway (much like those of CBS but smaller), formed a kind of triangular raceway for the busy radio actor. He could make from $10,000 to $30,000 a year on free-lance work alone, but it meant dashing from station to station, hiring stand-ins for portions of rehearsal periods, tipping starters to hold elevators, and chartering taxicabs.

Matt Crowley's case is typical. Matt was, at one and the same time, the announcer for "Pretty Kitty Kelly," John on "John's Other Wife," Jim on "Jungle Jim," and Doctor Brent on "Road of Life." Two of these shows had "repeats." (The difference in time between the East and West, together with the network ruling against recorded broadcasts, often made second "live" performances necessary.)

Matt's day began at 9 A.M. with a quick run-through of "John's Other Wife" at NBC. Leaving a stand-in to carry on there, he took a taxi to Seventh Avenue and "Kitty." This show, already rehearsed and broadcast to the Coast on the previous afternoon, was now to get its eastern airing—10 to 10:15 A.M. But at 10:15 Matt was due back at NBC and on the air as John. I can still see him at the CBS microphone, in hat, overcoat, and gloves, anxiously watching the clock. When it showed exactly fourteen minutes and thirty seconds after ten, he would say his last words for "Kitty" ("This is the Columbia Broadcasting System"), drop his script, and leap to the door, which Clayton (Bud) Collyer held open. An elevator car would be waiting. On the street he would race two blocks to Fiftieth Street, where a taxi stood with motor running. This took him just one block—to Sixth Avenue. For months a steel girder from the subway, then under construction, barred the way. He would jump from his cab, skip over the girder, dart through traffic, and trot half a block inside the giant RCA Building to the elevators. A greased palm held this one open and waiting, too. Up he would shoot to the eighth floor and "John's Other Wife."

That was what was known in the trade as a tight "conflict," and it was hard on the stomach lining. Matt held up pretty well—probably because the rest of his shows were more liberally spaced and left time for a quiet meal at Colbee's lunch counter. It was no epicure's delight, but it was better than adding to the studio clutter of half-chewed crusts and soggy coffee containers left by actors who had rehearsed with a script in one hand and a sandwich in the other. Track records between stations and how to beat them was a favorite topic at Colbee's. I once eavesdropped on a conversation between Santos Ortega (Inspector Queen and Nero Wolfe) and Walter Kinsella, one of the busiest of the free-lance actors.

"You can trim one minute forty-five seconds off your time from here to NBC," Ortega maintained, "if you cut diagonally through St. Patrick's Cathedral."

"One minute thirty," corrected Kinsella.

"One thirty," agreed Ortega, "if you stop to genuflect."

Ulcers were not the only hazards attending this split-second scheme of life. That infernal triangle had booby traps. Staats Cotsworth, rushing from CBS, where he was Casey, Crime Photographer, to NBC, where he was Front Page Farrell, once slipped on the shiny marble floor of the RCA Building and knocked himself out.

Jeannette Nolan, racing one day from CBS's "new" building to its old one, failed to notice those massive plate-glass doors. She hit them head-on with a force that sent her sprawling and bleeding to the floor.

Joe Latham, the hired man of "When a Girl Marries," will never forget the time he asked for and was granted a "conflict" to rehearse "Nick Carter" at Mutual. He planned to leave "Carter," speed by subway to NBC for the broadcast of our show, then back to "Carter" again. We waited until five minutes before air time, but he didn't show up. After the broadcast, the door flew open and Joe stumbled in.

"What happened, Joe?"

His usually cheerful round face crumpled and I thought he was going to cry.

"I got caught in a peanut machine," he said.

He had put a penny in a subway vending machine. The lever snapped back and caught his signet ring. A crowd of interested spectators gathered as the actor struggled to free himself. At last someone went for help. Joe begged a policeman to remove the machine and take both him and it up to "When a Girl Marries." When the gadget was loosened and tilted, he found himself suddenly free—but about fifteen minutes too late.

What did we do in such emergencies? Well, Jeannette picked herself up, charged through those doors (stopping this time to open them first) and went on the air with a quite literally stiff upper lip.

Staats, recovered from his fall, staggered woozily into the studio and clutched his director, Ed Slattery, by the lapels. "What did you *do?*"

"Oh, it went fine," Ed said easily. "Got Bart Robinson from 'Portia Faces Life.' He gave a great imitation of you. Your mother couldn't have told the difference."

Versatility was the key to success in radio. Most of us could imitate a few of our fellows, and some, like Art Carney, Bryna Raeburn, and Gil Mack could imitate almost anybody. When the director of "When a Girl Marries" (at that time, a young woman named Dodie Yates) wanted a replacement for Joe, she sent down to NBC's third floor, where a group of capable but, at the moment, unemployed actors hovered like birds of prey, waiting for just such a disaster. A similar pool of talent was to be found at Colbee's.

Of course, perfection was not always at hand. The rule then was to make do with whatever was available. That is how an elderly character actor, who usually played soft-spoken, fatherly types, was once suddenly called upon to replace the hard-riding, fast-shooting sheriff in a Western serial.

"Halt!" he shouted, as the desperados approached. The vigorous, aspirate "h" whistled its way up and over his upper plate and shot it out of his mouth. The resourceful old man fielded it deftly with his left hand about a foot in front of his face.

"Who are you?" demanded the outlaw.

"Shrfshrfshushunny," was the stern reply. Then, as he clicked the denture back into place, "The sheriff of Shoshone County."

For the most part, however, a clever substitute could slip by unnoticed. From my many years in New York radio I can recall only one occasion when a stop-gap performance caused any real dismay. J. Walter Thompson was handling the Republican campaign that year and had bought NBC time late at night for a woman who aspired to Congress. A young producer named O'Connor was assigned to the broadcast. He met his charge in the studio a few minutes before air time. She handed the announcer a two-page panegyric to be read as a preamble to her speech. The announcer declined. Network personnel, he explained, were forbidden to give any form of political endorsement.

"In that case," said the lady tartly, "I refuse to go on the air."

"It's too late to get an outside announcer now," said O'Connor.

"No introduction—no speech," said the woman, fishing in her bag for some knitting.

The producer insisted that NBC wouldn't permit it, the FCC wouldn't like it, and the Republican Committee wouldn't want it.

"Knit one, purl two," murmured the candidate.

O'Connor pleaded over the click of the needles that his job and, indeed, his entire future, depended on getting the show on the air.

"Nothing doing," was the reply.

He left the adamant woman and rushed out into the hall. The cast of a late mystery show was filing out of the studio next door. He hailed one of the actors.

"Ray, can you read an announcement for me?"

"Sure thing," said the actor, lighting up at the thought of an unexpected fee.

O'Connor handed over the copy. The actor put on his glasses and started toward the studio, reading as he went. Suddenly he stopped. "Just a minute," he said. "This is *Republican*, isn't it?"

"What of it?"

"I can't do it." He folded his glasses.

The producer looked at his watch. Three minutes to air time. "Double fee," he bribed.

"Sorry, old man." The actor rang for the elevator.

"A hundred dollars!" shouted O'Connor. He could pay it out of his own salary if Thompson or the Republican party balked.

"My conscience wouldn't permit it."

"I'm no Republican," the producer insisted. "I'm an Irishman. From Brooklyn. But I gotta get this dame on the air."

"Your conscience is your own," said the Democrat, and the elevator door slid shut.

The hall was deserted now. The rest of the mystery cast had already left. The door of the men's room creaked open and O'Connor whirled around to see Arthur come out. Arthur was an ex-child actor who had recently progressed to playing moronic adolescents. His high nasal whine would frequently break in the most unexpected way.

Shirley Booth and Lawson Zerbe in the late 1930's, top. Actors Arnold Moss and Michael FitzMaurice reenact a scene from "Grand Central Station" for publicity purposes, bottom.

Jan Miner and Staats Cotsworth, top, on "Casey, Crime Photographer."
Hugh Marlowe, bottom, was star of mystery "Ellery Queen" when he
was fingerprinted at New York City Police Headquarters. In center is
Santos Ortega (Inspector Queen), at right is Marian Shockley (Nikki).

"Arthur," said the worn producer, "are you a Democrat?"
"I can't vote yet, Mr. O'Connor," he said in that hideous little voice.
"Will you read a political announcement for me?"
"Political announcement? *Meee?*"
O'Connor pushed him into the studio, the NBC announcer gave his permitted laconic introduction, and Arthur broke into what sounded like a political tirade from a drunken gremlin.

All the telephones in the control booth started ringing at once. The candidate's husband was sputtering on the long-distance wire; the man from J. Walter Thompson came through loud and clear. But from Republican headquarters came only an inarticulate roar.

The next morning, after a stormy interview at the agency, O'Connor slipped quietly out of his office and joined the Marines.

The greatest single cause of disaster for actors and directors alike was the "repeat." There was a sense of accomplishment about a broadcast that made it easy to forget that it all must be done over again a few hours later. I don't know what the salesgirl in Saks Fifth Avenue thought the day I suddenly tore off the dress I was trying on and raced for the exit, pulling my mink coat over panties and bra. I made it to NBC in time to snatch the script away from my replacement and say the first line, but I kept a wary eye on the goldfish bowl. The mink was a buttonless wraparound, and whenever I let go to turn a page, all was revealed. The morality clause in my contract did not mention stripping, but I had a strong hunch that the men from Post Toasties would not be amused.

The midnight repeat of "Gangbusters," with its large casts, was always a source of anxiety to Leonard Bass, the director. One evening Lawson Zerbe (a gangster on the show) began playing with the sound effects and somehow managed to handcuff himself. Everyone thought it a good joke when the soundman claimed to have no key. As air time drew near, however, Lawson wanted out. The truth dawned slowly. NBC really had no key.

"How am I going to hold the script?" Lawson began howling.
"Quick! Get him a music stand," Leonard bawled.

Another actor stood by to turn the pages, and Lawson played the entire show in his handcuffs. The rest of the night was spent trying to extricate him. First they bundled him into a taxi and off to the police station. The officers were amused but helpless. Each pair, they explained, had its own key.

"They're the best handcuffs made," a detective offered admiringly. "You'll never get out of those."

178

The Infernal Triangle

Back at NBC they went to work in earnest. Hammers, chisels, pliers —every tool available was brought into play. But the handcuffs were designed to resist just such effort. With every blow the manacles tightened. The victim's hands began to swell and he was musing on gangrene, amputation, and other grisly paths to freedom when at four in the morning a last, stunningly painful blow snapped the beautifully tempered steel and he was released.

A newly hired page boy at CBS's Seventh Avenue studios sprang into action one day when the elevator door opened and a human derelict stumbled out. Disheveled gray hair fell over her dirty face and she was outfitted in what looked like gleanings from a dustbin. Staring wildly, she shot past him and down the hall. The alert young man overtook her just under a sign that marked the studio as "On The Air."

"You can't go in there," he said as he grabbed her.

She put up a good fight, but he had her shoulders firmly pinned against the wall when the studio door opened and a white-faced director peeked out.

"Leora! For God's sake, you're on!"

She gulped out something about "Taxi—traffic—had to run three blocks," and staggered through the open door. The director threw a nasty look at the dismayed page boy.

"You damn nearly made her miss the repeat," he said.

It was Leora Thatcher, dressed for her role as Ada Lester in "Tobacco Road." There had been no time to change after the matinee.

It seems incredible that any actor caught in the maelstrom of radio would attempt the hysteria of a Broadway opening, but others, beside Leora, did and managed to cling to their programs as well. The audience at a midnight repeat of "Cavalcade of America" must have been more perplexed than that page boy when Abraham Lincoln appeared dressed as George Washington. The actor was Ed Jerome; the play, Sidney Kingsley's "The Patriots."

Dick Kollmar once played Jack Orpington, millionaire playboy, in bloomers. The program was "Kitty Kelly"; the play, "Knickerbocker Holiday."

Such frenzied activity during the working day was sure to bring on equally vivid nighttime adventures. Most of us, it seemed, spent the small hours tossing, turning, muttering, and even crying out in our sleep. My own recurring dream concerned a conflict. Night after night, in trying to get from CBS to NBC, I would be caught in a parade of Japanese Boy Scouts. Once I fell, and the whole Nipponese phalanx was tramping over me when I woke whimpering in the night.

It was a dream with realistic foundation. Fifth Avenue parades were a major threat to the conflict-ridden radio actor. Orson Welles solved the dilemma one St. Patrick's Day by hiring an ambulance to take him from CBS's Seventh Avenue studios to its Madison Avenue building. You can imagine the surprise of passersby when the vehicle clanged to a halt and a nonchalant young man emerged to walk away smoking a pipe.

Not many of us went that far, but we did what we could to prevent mishaps. We hired telephone services and kept pocket diaries in which we entered our every program, its time and its place. The abbreviations used in those books became part of our vocabulary. "When a Girl Marries" was known to its cast as "Wag'em," and "Life Can Be Beautiful" was known throughout the trade as "Elsie Beebe."

There were some errors beyond our control—those that originated in the casting offices. The whole crew of "When a Girl Marries" was once called for the wrong day—Tuesday's actors turning up on Monday. Dodie Yates met that crisis by sending, not for Monday's actors, but for Tuesday's script. Thanks to Mrs. Carrington's "Meanwhile, back at the ranch" technique, such a switch was possible and no one was the wiser.

It was an office error, too, that sent Michael FitzMaurice speeding through the New England countryside in his new Mercedes-Benz. When the erring secretary noticed her mistake she called him at his country place in Vermont. The show in question went on late in the evening. He could make it, they decided, if he hurried. Mike determined to give it a whirl. He had whirled as far as Connecticut when a state trooper intervened and escorted him to a police station to explain his haste. Among other things, Mike mentioned that he was radio's Superman. There must have been a reporter present, because The Associated Press carried the story coast to coast. "Who can go faster than Superman?" read the headline. "A Connecticut cop!"

There was one office where no such lapse ever occurred—Air Features. This perfect record was due to a handsome but serious young blond named Frances Von Bernhardi. Hers was the nerve-shattering job of go-between to the meticulous Hummert operation and what she considered, perhaps rightly, a bunch of harum-scarum, irresponsible actors. She developed the attitude of a harassed and overwrought school teacher. She refused to deal with the telephone services, but insisted on talking to us each day, personally.

"I'm not hiring your service," she once snapped when I suggested a relaxation of this rule. "I'm hiring *you*."

The conflict problem was solved with dispatch at Air Features. They allowed none. Their directors, however, working on a free-lance basis themselves, were inclined to be sympathetic. Occasionally one of them would go out on a limb for an actor. One season the International Silver Company selected me as the star of the opening program of their "Silver Theater." It was a great honor, and I wanted to do it. I was dismayed, though, to find that it cut right across "Helen Trent." I went to the director, Ernest Ricca, with tears in my eyes. He agreed to let me go on "Trent" cold—with no rehearsal whatever.

I only had to run across Fifty-second street from CBS's old building to the new, but Ernie began sweating the day before. I tipped elevator boys in both buildings, but Fielden Farrington was already in "Trent's" opening commercial when I skidded breathlessly into the studio. Ernie's hand was shaking when he handed me my script. A few seconds more and he'd have lost his job.

When I asked Richard Leonard to excuse me from part of a rehearsal of "Mr. Keen, Tracer of Lost Persons," he refused. I couldn't blame him. Television had by then set nerves jumping throughout the industry. The Hummerts were keeping a close watch on shows and ratings. As for the director, himself, his days were evenly divided between producing "Stella Dallas" and Arturo Toscanini. God alone knows what *he* dreamed about at night.

There was one Air Feature director whom I would never have dared ask for a conflict—Martha Atwell. Over the years I learned that she was a kind, generous, warmhearted person, but for a kind, generous, warmhearted person she had the stoniest face I had ever seen. She smiled rarely, and when she did it always seemed to me to be the smile of someone whose feet hurt.

My first show for Martha was a recorded series, "Linda's First Love." I arrived at the studio early but Miss Atwell was already seated at a table—script and a stopwatch in her hands. The cast, which included some of the most frolicsome madcaps in radio (Karl Swenson, Arline Blackburn, and André Baruch), sat in a silent solemn row before her. I could only conclude that someone had died or been fired, so I joined the row of mourners.

At the exact second set for rehearsal, Martha clicked her watch and André began the narration. The first reading of a soap opera was usually pure camp. This one proceeded with the tension associated with opening night at La Scala.

When it was over I relaxed and smiled around at my friends. No one smiled back. I started out to get a glass of water but Martha had flipped her script back and was reading with the rapidity of a machine-gun.

"Page two, line fourteen . . . 'Now Linda' . . . through line seventeen . . . 'any more.' Page seven—."

TUNE IN TOMORROW

She was giving cuts. I sat down and grabbed for my script. What was that? Page two, line what?

"Page eight, line two—," I heard her saying.

"Excuse me," I said. "I didn't quite get—."

"Please pay attention," she said. Then, stenciling out each word, "*Page—two—line—fourteen—'Now—Linda'—.*"

There were a couple of things I missed but I decided to pick them up during the next rehearsal or the "dress." Martha had gone into the control booth and the cast gathered silently around the microphone.

"The *dress?* Already?" I whispered to Karl.

"There is no dress," he hissed. "This is the *show.*"

I got through it—reading partly from my own script and partly from Karl's. Afterward I sank weakly into my chair, but Martha bounced right out of the booth, picked up the second script, and with a click of her watch we were off again.

We made five fifteen-minute recordings in three hours. Any other director would have taken a minimum of five hours. When it was over, Martha dropped her watch in her bag and left the cast of "Linda's First Love" for NBC and "Young Widder Brown."

Wauna, Joey, and I had rented a cottage in Atlantic Highlands, New Jersey, that summer. There was a good beach and, best of all, we could commute by boat. I love the water, and every trip was a joy—every trip but one. That time I had done what I thought was my full day's work, so I boarded the steamer for the two-hour voyage. Hardly had we pulled away from the dock, when I clutched the arm of the startled man next to me—" 'Linda's First Love,' " I cried.

I sprang to the ship's rail. The first mate who plucked me down probably still thinks he prevented a suicide. Two facts emerged from the conversation that followed: they were not going to turn around and go back, as I urged them to, and if I moved one inch from my deck chair I would be locked in a cabin till we reached the Jersey shore. My employers didn't take it lightly, either. It was four years before I worked for Martha Atwell, Frances Von Bernhardi, or Air Features again.

I seem to be the only actor who had the abysmal luck to miss an Atwell show, although Cliff Carpenter came near it. Driving to work one day, he had entered the narrow, two-way underpass running beneath Park Avenue from Thirty-third Street to Fortieth when his northbound line of traffic slowed to a stop. The whine of a grinding starter told him someone's car had broken down. Rehearsal time was drawing near. He waited as long as his nerves would stand it. When the thought of a steely eye and a clicking stopwatch became more than he could bear, Cliff watched the unbroken flow of southbound cars whizz by for a second, then closed his eyes and swung the nose of his car boldly into the line of opposing traffic. A screech of brakes and a blare of horns roared through the tunnel. The frantic actor made a U-turn and shot out of that tunnel. He got to Martha on time, all right, but it cost him $20—a fine for what the police considered a too casual job of parking his car.

Later, Cliff was one of the first of our group to go to war, and wound up in the Battle of the Bulge. His unit was ordered to dig in. Cliff and a young southerner obediently dug a foxhole and there they spent ten hideous, cold, sleety days and nights.

Each dawn the enemy laid down an earth-shaking barrage. The soldiers tried to sleep in alternate hitches, and occasionally one of them would manage to slip into an uneasy half-slumber.

Once, when it was Cliff's turn to rest, he curled up in the mud. His legs ached. His heart was pounding. He couldn't get his breath. "I've got to. I've *got* to," he gasped. The harder he ran, the farther it seemed to be. Got to get there! Run. Harder. *Harder.* He flung himself forward and sudden pain ripped through his chest. But the CBS Building remained cold and distant as before, its leaden windows showing dully against the sky, and behind them a steely-eyed woman with a relentlessly clicking stopwatch. "Got to get there. Got to. *Help!*"

"You havin' a dream or somethin'?"

The actor stared stupidly into the face of his companion in the foxhole. A giant blast shook the earth, and he smiled as a wave of icy mud engulfed him.

"Oh, thank God," he said with a happy moan of relief. "Thank God, you woke me up."

183

Richard Widmark and Betty Garde in "Front Page Farrell."

Arlene Francis and Van Heflin as "Betty and Bob," about 1940.

NB

Wendell Corey and Barbara Weeks, top, on "Inner Sanctum," about 1950. Lawson Zerbe, Flora Campbell, and Frank Lovejoy, who later became a film star, rehearsing for "Texas Village" in 1944, bottom.

CHAPTER XVI

I Hit the Fan!

Radio never brought to an actor the acclaim it offered a Vallee or a Crosby. The list of former radio actors who found fame in other media is impressive (Don Ameche, Richard Widmark, Van Heflin, Richard Quine, Mercedes McCambridge, Agnes Moorehead, Martin Gabel, Ann Francis, Gale Gordon, Dane Clark, John McIntyre, Macdonald Carey, Gary Merrill, Tony Randall, Paul Ford, Art Carney, among others), but the only actor ever to achieve such renown through radio alone did it not by acting, but by causing a panic.

In Halloween week, 1938, Orson Welles' "Mercury Theater" was interrupted suddenly with what seemed to be a series of news bulletins. It was, in fact, a version of H. G. Wells' "War of the Worlds," made up largely of "flashes" in the style of bona fide news broadcasts. To a nation jittery with threats of war, it was like printing bogus copies of *The New York Times* with scare headlines and circulating them in the streets.

When the good burghers of New Jersey learned that Martians had captured the Pulaski Skyway, a lot of them hit the road without waiting for Orson's cunning disclaimer, ". . . just Mercury Theater's way of saying boo."

It was not the first inflammatory episode in Welles' career. While making the rounds in the early days he had an interview with Knowles Entriken, a CBS producer. On leaving, Orson shook the contents of his pipe into the wastebasket. Later, as Mr. Entriken beat out the flames, he remarked that here was an actor he would not forget in a hurry.

But most of us, lacking the Welles panache, were dismally aware that we had mounted what Fred Allen was later to name the "Treadmill to Oblivion." If we were not sour about it, we curdled slightly. During my Hollywood years, we had been too busy scratching out a living from the local shows and the network programs that came to us, one by one, to think much about it. The movies were the lodestone that had drawn most actors to the Coast, however, and in the film studios their hearts, if not their treasure, lay. When starred on the local radio shows (networks *always* featured film names), they felt sheepish. It was hard to feel like much of a star at $5 a throw.

Chicago actors, on the other hand, had no chimerical movie world to lure them, and little theater. They had only radio. But that they had aplenty. (In the thirties, 75 percent of all dramatic programming came from Chicago.) They seemed less like ambitious young actors than Forty-niners whooping it up after a Big Strike.

One of the first of our Hollywood group to leave for Chicago was Bret Morrison. The last time I saw him he was borrowing a sports coat from Ted Osborne to wear to an interview in a film studio the next day.

"If I ever get any money," he was dreaming, "I'm going to have a *wardrobe*. My cupboard may be bare but my closet will be *full*."

Two years later he won the Chicago Retail Merchants' award as the Best Dressed Man of the Year. In addition to his investment in elegance, he kept saddle horses (he and Barbara Luddy, another arrival from the Coast, liked to take an occasional canter along the lakefront) and a secondhand but chauffeur-driven Rolls-Royce. That sort of thing made it easier to feel like a star in Chicago.

There were even signs of a budding class system among the performers. I am told that when Bess Johnson, radio's highest paid actress, entered a studio, the other players rose to their feet.

New York radio actors, by contrast, wouldn't have risen to their feet for Marconi. Colbee's was filled with displaced Barrymores and Duses, lamenting that a funny thing had happened to them on their way to the theatah (and you miss my point if you sound that final "r"). My first impression was of sharply dressed, bored young men, lounging about in a deadpan, wisenheimer imitation of a Humphrey Bogart or George Raft movie. A deprecating sneer would greet a request by the director to drop the newspaper and turn to the script. "Well, back to the hogwash," one of them used to say.

Indifference and swaggering self-assurance, like the mink coat, were badges of success. Only beginners, it seemed, took radio seriously.

Most of us behaved like particularly arrogant cases of delayed juvenile delinquency. In my first week in New York an actor approached an announcer in mid-commercial, took out his cigarette lighter, and set fire to the poor man's script. Holding first one corner of the page and then another as the flames crept toward his hand, the victim managed to get the last word out just before he dropped the smoking remnants to the floor.

Someone else at NBC pulled an announcer's pants off while he was on the air. Luckily, no tourists were goggling in the goldfish bowl at the time.

Every face in the room blanched when Orson Welles dropped the hour-long Philip Morris script just as he got his opening cue. People lunged forward from every side to offer substitutes. Welles smiled angelically and pulled the *real* script from his pocket. What he had dropped was a dummy.

A crisis in world affairs always reflected itself in disrupted radio schedules. We were never sure we would get on the air, and if we did we were likely to be cut off for news. In the uncertain days just before World War II, I was selling Lux Soap on a program called "Doctor Susan." The organist, Richard Leibert, used to pepper the commercials with musical effects, and the announcer, Frank Luther, would sing a little jingle. Someone tripped over an electric cord one day and the organ went dead. Frank paled but sang bravely on, unaccompanied. Dick leaped for the piano and fell into a huge Chinese gong with a loud "bon-n-n-ng." Frank's eyes now popped out but he never missed a beat. Dick picked up the tune on the piano in a higher key. Frank shifted to a squeaky falsetto. Someone snatched the microphone from under his nose and raced to the piano. Frank ran after, neck outstretched, squealing the praises of Lux. Dick gave way to hysteria, and collapsed over the keyboard with loud guffaws.

I had watched the disastrous sequence in frozen horror. Now it was time to act. I ran to the shrieking organist, whispered, "Shut up!" and belted him one.

"Hey," he said, rubbing his reddening cheek, "we're not on the air. This is a gag."

I should have guessed. It was a custom to keep the news of a possible cancellation from anyone unlucky enough to be out of the room at the time—and then try to scare him out of his minimum daily requirement of vitamin B. It was a scary thing to feel a show passing the point of no return that way. Fortunately, it rarely happened. The old-timers could weather any mishap. Barbara Luddy and Gale Gordon went on talking when the lights went out during "Coronets." Afterward, Barbara said, "We never could understand why, if there was a power failure, the mikes stayed on and only the lights went out." Having been the victim of more than one irresistible impulse, I think I can guess. But whatever the cause, Barbara and Gale saw to it that there was no dead air.

TUNE IN TOMORROW

Bill Lipton made a remarkable recovery during a show called "Counterspy." He was supposed to be a scientist demonstrating the functioning of an extremely noisy, computerlike machine. NBC was, by then, permitting the use of recorded sound, but the electric turntable suddenly went dead.

Without a second's hesitation Bill tossed in, "These are specially constructed baffles. By throwing that switch, I deadened all noise. I can start it again by throwing the same switch"—he looked at the sound-man, who shook his head frantically—"but I won't." And Bill reworded his entire part, describing silence where the author had written about deafening din.

It required less quick thinking but equal self-control for a CBS announcer to give a convincing tobacco commercial after his unfortunate opening, "Well, folks, it's smipe poking time."

During the days when NBC had two networks, the Red and the Blue, an announcer once signed off with "This is WEAF, the Red—No, this is WJZ, the Bl—No, by gosh! This *is* WEAF, the Red Network of the National Broadcasting Company."

Paul Douglas (later a stage and screen star, but then announcer for "Buck Rogers—in the 25th Century") kept his poise even though the director's wife bounced in while the show was on the air, caroling, "Hello, everybody." Realizing her mistake, she shrank back abashed. After Paul had given his closing billboard, "Tune in again for Buck Rogers—in the 25th Century," she ran to him to apologize.

"Oh, Paul, is my face red," she began.

Douglas played it cool. "It *ought* to be," he said. Then he added into the still functioning microphone, "*This* is the Columbia Broadcasting System."

The self-possessed casts of various programs managed to keep calm even after such remarkable statements as:

"He fell for it—hook, line, and stinker."

"Jump into the squid car and catch those smur fugglers."

"The suspect was sitting on the floor playing with his kidneys."

I know of only one show that went completely and unredeemably to hell—"When a Girl Marries"—starring you know who. The trouble was that after the initial slip, the unusually doleful dialogue built into a snow-balling gag.

Rosemary Rice began it all by saying that she was "worried about the potahto crap." She stopped, flushed, and a broad grin spread across her face. Ann Burr countered with, "Why, what's happened to the potahto—er—potato—ha,ha—crop?"

"It's some sort of *disease*," said Rosemary, gleefully, "and my poor husband [here she doubled up with laughter], my poor husband has put—teehee—has put—ha,ha—his *all* into potatoes."

A period of silence followed, punctuated by explosive little giggles. Ann was waiting until she thought it safe to try again.

"That's too bad," she said. (She stared hard at her script but strangled on the next line.) "Coming so soon after—[Whoops, she was off again]—the house burned down."

"That's not the worst," Rosemary tittered wildly on, "I'm afraid he'll have another nervous breakdown." (They both convulsed at this.)

When Jeannette Dowling entered the scene she began firmly enough. "Thank goodness, Kathy, I've found you. I have dreadful news." But when she heard Rosemary's voice, tremulous with merriment, ask "Why Mother, what *is* it?" she let out a roar of laughter. "It's little Sammy," she chortled. "The doctor says he won't live through the night!"

And so it went. Disaster piled on disaster, hilarity mounted. In the control booth, Oliver Barbour, the director, had thrown his script in the air and sagged forward, head on desk, shoulders shaking convulsively. The engineer slumped out of sight. I edged up to the mike, eyes averted. The others greeted me giddily.

"Here comes Joan," they snickered. "Poor darling—heh, heh—she looks miserable."

I, too, began bravely. "Irma, I must talk to you." (Inadvertently I caught a glimpse of those contorted faces.) "Harry," I quavered. "Harry—." Then, with a loud guffaw, "Harry's in *jail!*"

We shrieked out woe upon woe until, as each one came to the end of her part, she collapsed in a chair, tears streaming down her face, and limp with laughter. With this sight before him, Charles Stark tried valiantly to deal with Chocolate Chip Cookery.

The next day Ann Burr took me aside before rehearsal.

"I saw Tom last night," she whispered. Tom McDermott was an energetic young man who had progressed from running the Benton & Bowles mimeograph machine to Assistant Director, to Producer of TV Sports Events, to Creative Head of Radio and Television. Later, he left Benton & Bowles to join Four Star Productions in Hollywood, where he was made President, and a cloud received him out of our sight. At this time, though, he was in his Creative Head period.

"He asked me how the show went yesterday," Ann said. "They had a new product on and the sponsor was listening!"

I never heard a word about the incident from the agency, sponsor, or—strangest of all—from my fans. From all those millions of daily listeners came not one letter of complaint. It was a phenomenon that

191

TUNE IN TOMORROW

always mystified us. Our mistakes were never reflected in our mail. The wildest fluffs, the most egregious inconsistencies of plot were simply ignored.

This indifference to logic and good sense was not the result of failure to "suspend disbelief." We had abundant evidence of that. On December 30, 1947, John Crosby, radio editor of *The New York Herald Tribune*, ran the following item:

"A Mrs. Davis of Hillsborough Township, near Somerville, N.J., recently received a note on which was scrawled: 'Steve killed Betty MacDonald. Irma has him on her farm. I hope you will come out of this with flying colors.' Mrs. Davis turned the letter over to the police, who traced it without difficulty to a woman in Brooklyn, from whom they wrung a remarkable confession.

"The writer told police that she listened every day to a soap opera called 'When a Girl Marries.' On this program recently a Betty Mac-Donald was killed and Harry Davis of 'Somerville' was arrested. The Brooklyn letter writer went on to explain that Harry Davis was really innocent. The real murderer, she told the startled cops, was a man named Steve, Betty's lover, who was now hiding out on Irma's farm. (Irma loved him, too.) She had written the letter to Mrs. Davis to reassure her that everything would come out all right and to assure her that her faith in Mrs. Davis and Harry remained unshaken.

"That's all there is to the story. The police presumably told the Brooklyn lady not to write any more letters and may even have advised her against taking soap opera so seriously. The reaction of the Brooklyn addict to a visitation from the police remains unknown. Does she still listen to 'When a Girl Marries'? What went through her mind when she discovered that Harry and Irma and Steve were people of fancy, not fact? Was she outraged at the betrayal of her implicit trust and if so, has she found anything to take its place? Or to put it more plainly, are there any other anodynes so satisfying and undemanding as soap opera for credulous ladies from Brooklyn?

"The psychiatrists will have to take it up from there. This column is out of its depth."

In dealing with the fans, I was *always* out of mine. A comfortable, motherly woman approached me one day on the third floor of NBC.

"Your husband has not run away with another woman," she said. "I've walked all the way from the Bronx to tell you."

"Thanks," I said. "but it's just a story. It has nothing to do with me, really. I'm an actress."

"You must go to him. I know where he is."

I gave her my real name, my husband's name, and a list of radio

192

characters (about seven) that I was impersonating at the time. She listened patiently, then went right back to the plot of "When a Girl Marries."

Dolores Gillen came by just then, and I introduced her to the woman.

"You know in the story I have a little boy?" I said.

"Oh, yes," said the woman, beaming. "I love Sammy."

"Well, *this* is Sammy. Miss Gillen plays Sammy. See? We're actors." There was a silence. "Dolores," I said, "talk like Sammy."

Standing right in front of the fan from the Bronx and wearing a smart blue suit and a chic feather hat, the finest child imitator in the business obligingly started with Sammy, aged five, and worked back through the years until he was wailing in his crib, gurgling and burping.

The woman frowned, but it was a passing thing, like a shadow cast by a falling leaf. She turned to me. "Your husband still loves you. He's lost his memory. You must go to him."

"OK," I said at last. "I'll go to him."

After that interview I felt the need for a cup of tea. There were always a few radio actors in the NBC drugstore, killing time between shows. Don MacLaughlin (Chaplain Jim and David Harding, Counter-spy) was sympathetic. He had not yet recovered from a long-distance call that had come in after a "Chaplain Jim" broadcast.

"I have a big problem," the caller had begun. "I'll have to talk fast because I used all the money I had for this call."

He was a farmer whose son had deserted from the Army. The father was convinced that if the authorities caught the boy they would shoot him. He had hidden him in a coal bin on the farm and driven into town to "call the only person I can trust." Don tried to make it clear that he was not a man of the cloth but an actor. He gave up when he heard the note of despair in the man's voice.

"I'm sure they won't shoot him," Don said, finally. "They'll discipline him, but they won't shoot him. Talk to your own minister." The man didn't know a minister. The conversation ended with the man crying, "What am I going to do? What am I going to do?" and then the impersonal voice of the telephone company: "I'm sorry. Your three minutes are up. If you wish to continue—." Click. Silence.

"Does this sort of thing happen to you, too?" I asked Bill Lipton (Nick Carter, Boy Detective).

"No," he said, grinning. "My fans are teen-agers—girls who get me on the phone and then don't say anything—just giggle."

Staats Cotsworth (Front Page Farrell and Casey, Crime Photographer) brought a letter out of his pocket. It was from a man who had followed Staats' career for years and was acquainted with his work both on stage and in radio. He considered him one of the finest actors the world had ever known, comparing favorably with Edwin Booth, Lawrence Barrett, and the elder Salvini. He signed himself, "Your devoted listener," and added a postscript. "Please forgive the pencil. We're not allowed anything sharp."

Mason Adams (who had taken over the part of Pepper Young when Lawson Zerbe went to war) produced a letter from a woman who included a snapshot of herself with a proposal of marriage. She had a genius, she claimed, for writing titles. Not stories—just titles. "We can make a fortune together," she insisted, and enclosed two sample titles as come-ons: "The Passersby" and "The Pot."

I was feeling more cheerful. "It just shows," I said. "The world is full of nuts."

"It shows the terrible loneliness of these people," Virginia Payne (Ma Perkins) said. I knew Virginia answered personally and in longhand every bit of Ma's enormous mail.

"Do you answer all these letters?" I asked the others. Most of them said they tried. I thought guiltily of my chest of drawers bulging with yellowing envelopes. I resolved on the spot to turn over a new leaf, put my best foot forward, and brighten up the corner where I was. That's how I got mixed up with Ethel.

Every afternoon, as I left Radio City, there was a pleasant moment on the ground floor when I was surrounded by a cluster of admirers, seeking autographs. A woman detached herself from this group one day, and followed me toward the street.

"Miss Higby," she said shyly, "may I walk a little way with you?" She had come to New York from a college in the Middle West, she told me, and was here for further study. She had always admired me. I was a truly great artist. When I left her it was in a tipsy glow of self-satisfaction.

At four o'clock on the following day, she was waiting on the eighth floor of NBC. Although I was late, I took time to chat with her. She followed me to the studio door.

"I'm sorry. No visitors allowed," I said. "You can't come inside."

When I arrived the next afternoon, she was already inside.

"*He* said I could," she whispered, and nodded toward Tom McDermott, then in his Radio Director period.

That was Friday. Monday my admirer, whose name I now knew to be Ethel, sat through the program again, then clung to me all the way home. She was lonely. She couldn't seem to make friends in New York, though she'd been in the city six months. "I guess I'm too shy," she said.

I made a sticky speech to the effect that in order to have friends we must take an interest in the other fellow. "You're so *sweet*," she murmured, and followed me right up to my door.

"I must leave you here," I said.

"Oh, I wasn't coming in," she said. "I just wanted to find out where you lived," she said.

The first thing I saw when I returned to the show was Ethel's pudgy figure.

"Ethel, we're not supposed to have visitors—."

"Mr. McDermott is helping me with a paper I'm writing," she explained.

After that she became as much a part of studio equipment as the microphone. One day Tom called me into the control booth.

"Is that girl *really* a close friend of yours?"

"No, she's just a fan who—."

He shot into the studio, crossed to the corner where Ethel sat, and pointed to the door. She left.

But she was waiting for me in the hall after the show.

"Ethel, this has got to stop," I said.

"I just want to walk a little way with you. That's all right, isn't it?"

"No," said Tom McDermott, and taking my arm, he led me away.

That night Ethel telephoned.

"How did you get my number, Ethel?"

"Can I meet you tomorrow?"

"How did you get my number?"

"I thought you were my friend."

"How did you get my number?"

"Your telephone service gave it to me."

A few days later, the telephone rang at 7 A.M.

"Why do you hate me?" asked Ethel.

"I don't hate you, but I don't like you very much either."

"You said we should take an interest in each other's problems."

"I did, I did. And I was wrong."

"Well, it's good to know who your friends really are!"

She hung up on me and I thought that was that.

About this time the tenth anniversary of "When a Girl Marries" came up, and Benton & Bowles went all out to snare the attention of the press. Among other things, they prevailed upon Mrs. Frank Henderson, a member of Manhattan's wealthier set, to give a party in my honor in her Park Avenue apartment. Ethel read about it and was back on the phone at dawn. She was upset because she hadn't been invited. I explained that it was a publicity stunt, that I had no control over the

195

guest list, and that it was not my habit to rise with the birds. I hung up but she called again in a couple of days. The drippy phone conversations continued until the eve of Mrs. Henderson's reception.

I enjoyed those business parties about as much as I would a hanging—my own. I always awoke on the day with no stomach and two left feet. For this occasion I had bought, as a morale booster and at the cost of a week's salary, a midnight blue chiffon evening dress. Standing with a small group of important-looking strangers waiting for the elevator to take me to the Henderson apartment, I heard the familiar, soft whine in my ear. I jumped, and something ripped.

"Oh, I'm sorry," Ethel said, and took her foot off the hem of my skirt.

"*Go away.*" I gave her a shove that sent her spinning. She did not fall but looked at me reproachfully. Then she walked sadly away, leaving me to ride hot and shamefaced to the fifteenth floor in a car filled with VIP's and icy silence.

The next day my little nemesis turned up once more outside our studio door. The sight of her sent McDermott into orbit. He stomped right up to Ethel and put his nose about an inch away from hers.

"I have never hit a woman in my life," he said, slowly and deliberately, "but I don't want anybody to think I won't. Now, you get out—and stay out!"

That's the kind of thinking that makes a Creative Head, *and* a President!

I was not the only serial star to suffer unwelcome attentions from a fan. For three weeks a uniformed policeman was posted at CBS to protect Florence Freeman of "Wendy Warren and the News." A listener had "identified" in some mysterious way with this hybrid program—half newscast, half soap opera—and thought that Wendy was out to get her. She wrote threatening letters: "I'm on to you, you bitch. If you mention my name in your filthy column . . ." Finally, she took to lying in wait for Florence outside the studio. When she stalked her from CBS to NBC one day, Florence appealed to Benton & Bowles, and the Creative Head called the cops.

Elspeth Eric's spirited portrayal of gangster's molls in "Gangbusters" excited the admiration of convicts all over the country. Incipient fan clubs sprang up in Leavenworth and Sing Sing. Elspeth's troubles began when one of her fans got out. She solved the problem herself with some colorful gangbusting language and a threat to notify the police.

Less menacing, but embarrassing in her own way, was the fan who, recognizing our voices, followed Julie Stevens and me stark naked

Ralph Locke (Papa David) with Clayton "Bud" Collyer, top, on "Life Can Be Beautiful." Everett Sloan and Shirley Booth, bottom, before air time in the early 1940's.

from gym to showers to hot room to steam room and back to showers, trying to get our autographs.

In all fairness, though, I must add that there was another side to the question. Cliff Carpenter's hideous winter warfare in Germany was brightened somewhat by an angel food cake—a gift from a fan who had the good sense to pack it in popcorn so that it arrived in perfect shape. Some of Bill Lipton's giggling teen-agers matured into responsible young women and wrote him regular and welcome letters while he was serving in the armed forces.

For several years, Toni Darnay (Nona From Nowhere and Evelyn Winters) received a gift of an orchid each week from a woman in Boston. Me? I was big with the potholder-antimacassar crowd.

Of course, all the fans, even our loyal weirdos, were important to us, for without them we would have been of little interest to our sponsors. We thought of the networks as selling time, and the agencies as selling programs, but what the sponsor actually *bought* was the audience. It was for the attention of those very fans that he put down his money, and he was neurotically keyed to their reactions. A misspelled, pencil-written letter from Keokuk or Sand Lake has sent many a Brooks Brothers suit shinnying up the board room walls.

We rarely saw these nervous men in person. We knew them by their memos—such as the last-minute message delivered by panting messenger to the director of "Pretty Kitty Kelly":

"Urgent! The difficult word crystalline will not be understood by the audience. Cut it!"

We frantically combed the script, but in vain. Then somebody spotted the word, not in the dialogue at all, but in a sound effect:

Sound: Crystalline object falls to floor.

I often complained, as did most radio actors, about the top-heavy acting instructions that preceded some of our speeches. The page might look like this:

Freda: (Deeply terror-stricken but realizing that she must put up a front.) Hello.

Jim: (Has been drinking but there is no thickening of his speech, only a slight unsteadiness, coupled with the bitterness he feels.) Hi.

Freda: (A note of gaiety to hide her terror but with deep sincerity, nonetheless, and no trace of shrillness.) How do you want your egg?

Jim: (Getting control now but the struggle with self goes on.) What?

Freda: (Patiently, the earth mother able to absorb all woe.) Your egg.

Jim: (Compassionately.) Oh.

I used to go over the scripts first thing and black out these parenthetical acting lessons. One day at CBS, though, I blew up.

"Earl," I yelled at the director, Earl McGill, "look at page thirteen! 'Tempestuously, brokenly, but with pride.' All I have to say is 'How?' *You* say 'How' tempestuously, brokenly, but with pride if you can. Tell that idiot author he'll be lucky if I say it without sounding like an Indian! I'm going to have to *talk* to one of these writers some day!"

"Here's your chance," Earl offered drily. "He's right here beside me. Miss Higby, may I present Mr. _____?"

A stranger rose from the shadows of the control booth and leaned over the talk-back button.

"Those directions are not intended for *you*," he said. "I assume that you can probably understand the dialogue. But the sponsor probably can't. I save myself a lot of his memos by explaining it in parentheses as I go along."

It made sense, because it was, of course, on the heads of the writers that the bulk of the memos fell. Shortly after World War II, Mrs. Carrington tried to bring the subject of racial integration into "When a Girl Marries." She knew that the millions of women, many of them mothers, who tuned in to "When a Girl Marries" daily, not only listened to what I said but also seemed to accept it at face value with frightening simplicity. When Mrs. Carrington got to brooding about the responsibility involved, as from time to time she did, she would insert bits of her own personal philosophy into the dialogue. Because her view of life was one that would have been acceptable to *Good Housekeeping* and *St. Nicholas* magazines, she rarely ran athwart her sponsors. She had only two concepts that in those Joe McCarthy-ridden days might have been considered "controversial." She liked people—all people, regardless of race, color, or creed—and she yearned for world government. Mrs. Carrington was much too realistic to try to trouble the torpid air with a blast at national sovereignty, but she did try to strike a blow at the roots of racial prejudice.

She outlined a sequence in which my son, Sammy, brought home a colored child as a playmate. Exhaustive voice tests brought to light a splendid Negro child actor. He appeared only twice. Then the memos came tumbling down and the plot line with them. The memos might well have come from the executive who later made the famous defense of The Blacklist. "We have to be careful," he is supposed to have said. "We don't want to offend the bigots."

Other sponsor-inspired script editing, although on the pixie side, was more defensible. I can see, for example, why Westinghouse wanted to change the title of Kipling's "The Light That Failed." And why Alka

TUNE IN TOMORROW

Seltzer flatly rejected "The Storm Within." But mere corporate pettiness seems to have forced the writer of the Philip Morris show to strike the phrase, "I'm just *lucky*, I guess."

Such points might be argued with an ad agency, but to a decision handed down by the sponsor there was no appeal. This power of life and death, coupled with the fact that they were responsible for our paychecks, was probably what made the "business" party such a nightmare.

Elaine Carrington seemed to be aware of the strain these affairs were on actors and always tried to put them at ease—sometimes a little too much at ease. There was, for example, the supper party in her penthouse for the top personnel of a great soap manufacturing concern. Early in the evening the kitchen door opened and a strong vapor entered, followed by a maid bearing a punch bowl—the only punch I've ever smelled at fifty paces. Soon, the actors were not only at ease, but were sprawling. A big man from a soap company went to the piano and gave his rendition of Debussy's "Clair de Lune." Raucous conversation continued as usual until it dawned through the drunken haze that this was the *sponsor* performing, by God, and somebody'd better sit up and take notice. A sound like steam from a broken radiator raced round the room—"Shshshshshsh!" A voice, thick yet piercing, piped up from the terrace.

"Why the hell should *I* shush?" it said. "I ain't in radio."

To cover the situation, Elaine prevailed upon Shirley Booth to sing. In the voice of her famous Miss Duffy of "Duffy's Tavern," she gave us "Siam! It's So Lonely Where I Am!"

Through it all, an actor from "Pepper Young's Family" lay on the back of his neck in a big chair, mumbling. After Miss Booth had finished and the applause subsided, the sponsor leaned over the muttering young man.

"I'm sorry!" he said, politely, "I didn't quite get that."

"Grrrrff!" said the actor, and, springing suddenly to life, bit the sponsor on the neck.

The culprit was not, under normal circumstance, a heavy drinker. The proximity of the men with power of life or death over his contract had produced an edginess that led too often to the vaporous punch bowl.

The actors who seemed best able to cope with a covey of sponsors were the ones who had been through those posh days in Chicago, when the great men had become familiar figures, turning up every couple of weeks to check on their radio shows. Chicago was then the acknowledged center of commercial broadcasting, probably because it was only an overnight train trip from the manufacturing centers, Battle Creek,

Detroit, Cincinnati, and Kansas City. The day of general air travel had yet to dawn. When it did, the soap operas slipped away to New York, just as, with the reversal of the Round Robin in 1937, most of the night shows left both Chicago and New York and settled on the Coast.

I never met a sponsor until I moved to New York, and even there a visit from one was a rare occurrence. I would get truly splendid presents from General Foods at Christmas, though. Very often it would be a series of gifts—a brace of pheasants, an enormous box containing all their products, as well as some minor objet d'art, a vase holding chocolates or a huge handwoven Mexican basket full of assorted chocolate bars.

All in all, radio provided a pleasant life and the easiest money actors had ever known. Richard Widmark, referring to his radio days in a *New Yorker* interview, said, "I was probably the first actor to *leave* a house with a swimming pool to go to Hollywood."

Radio actors, for the most part, were careful to keep the news that they had found the show-business equivalent of the key to Fort Knox under their hats. They were not eager to encourage competition. Broadway people tended to look on the medium with contempt. My husband, Guy Sorel, in the early days of his career, made a substantial success on Broadway. He was named by George Jean Nathan as having given the best character performance of the year, and the other critics had been unanimous in their praise. The play ran five weeks. During the six months that Guy waited around for something else to turn up, somebody gave him a ticket to see a radio program. His heart bled when he saw those competent actors, some of them elderly, working—as he thought—for five or ten dollars a show, struggling to get by. It wasn't until he got into radio himself that he realized the show he had seen, DuPont's "Cavalcade of America," employed only the top people, and that everybody on that stage could count on an annual income of at least $20,000.

Sooner or later, some smart reporter was bound to sniff out the gravy on our train. In 1948, Staats Cotsworth was asked by a *Newsweek* reporter how it happened that an actor who had started with Eva Le Gallienne in her repertory theater and who had played on Broadway with Judith Anderson, Flora Robson, and Maurice Evans, was now devoting his time to "Casey, Crime Photographer" and "The Second Mrs. Burton." Staats poured the writer a drink and settled down on the terrace of his penthouse to explain.

He was delighted when the article appeared in the magazine. A full page in a national publication is not to be sneezed at. But the title gave him pause: "Cotsworth in the Chips." The writer pegged Staats' average weekly salary at $1,000, arriving at the figure by deduction. He knew what union scale was at the time ($18.15, plus $7.26 for each hour of rehearsal, for a fifteen-minute show), and Staats had unguardedly said he was getting $250 for "Casey" (a half-hour once a week). The article said in part, "Currently he is Front Page Farrell and Wolfe Bennett in 'Lone Journey.' . . . About three times a week he appears . . . as Dr. Jack Mason in 'The Second Mrs. Burton.' An average Cotsworth week also includes free-lancing on one or two nighttime shows—without billing—which pushes his cash total up to the weekly $1,000 . . . Why does he toy with soap operas? 'Giving up a daytime show,' he says, 'is like turning in your insurance policy.' "

Staats had not intended to offer a financial statement to the press. He had just answered a simple question. The result was a gathering of the Cotsworth clan such as had never been seen before. Staats was hearing from Cotsworths whose existence he had never suspected. His new relatives all had one thing in common: they needed money.

One day my phone rang and a voice asked me bluntly how much money I was making. Before I could say anything, the voice explained that the information was for a national publication. "Would you mind telling if it's under or over fifty thousand?" the inquisitor went on. I said I *would* mind. Later I learned that some others had not minded. One young man had given a figure of thirty thousand, another of fifty thousand, and one actress had said she was making forty-eight thousand.

What happened to all the loot?

Well, there were the running poker and gin rummy games on the balcony of one of our favorite restaurants.

There were the apartments furnished in antiques, with Cadillacs nestling in the garages below.

There were the mink coats, the custom-made clothes, and the small yachts, riding at anchor in Long Island Sound.

Everything, as they say, was coming up roses. For morale boosters, there were the eager fans waiting outside the studio doors, and the gorgeous presents from the sponsors.

But about 1948 a wind began to blow that was destined to reach gale force. Under its hot breath, the cluster of fans melted away. We learned that it was easier to acquire an estate than to sell one. And the largesse of our sponsors slowly declined. One year General Foods sent me a frozen turkey. The next, a small assortment of products—cake flour, cocoa, salt, and so forth. In 1951, when TV had reached hurricane proportions, their last memento came—a small, lone box of nuts.

CHAPTER XVII

Help Stamp Out TV!

"Help stamp out TV!"

About 1948 some wag posted this sign in a prominent spot in the New York office of the Young & Rubicam advertising agency. Radio was already on the wane, TV had raised its fuzzy head, and we had entered what is now wistfully called the Golden Age of Television.

It is easy to say when it came to an end—in mid-1958, when the New York District Attorney got wise to those rigged quiz shows. Amid the flames of a great public scandal, TV's Golden Age was reduced to a slag heap. Everybody settled down to crime and comedy and tried to fly straight.

The end of the Golden Age of Radio is harder to pinpoint. It left us in no such grand Immolation Scene, but rather in a series of spine-jangling bumps.

For me, the first jolt came when the television set went up over Colbee's bar and my picture, which for years had occupied a prominent place in the restaurant, gave place to Lassie's. I sat in the semigloom of the bar with a group of actors, staring at the flickering light in the little box.

"Why didn't I buy A.T. & T. instead of that damned yawl?" someone moaned.

Art Carney started mournfully reeling off the names of radio shows that had been canceled the previous week.

"I did a TV show last month. Rehearsed for a whole week and made fifty dollars," Cameron Andrews said. "Those lights'll roast you. It must be a hundred and two on those sets."

"We'll all have to get into it, though," Tony Randall said.

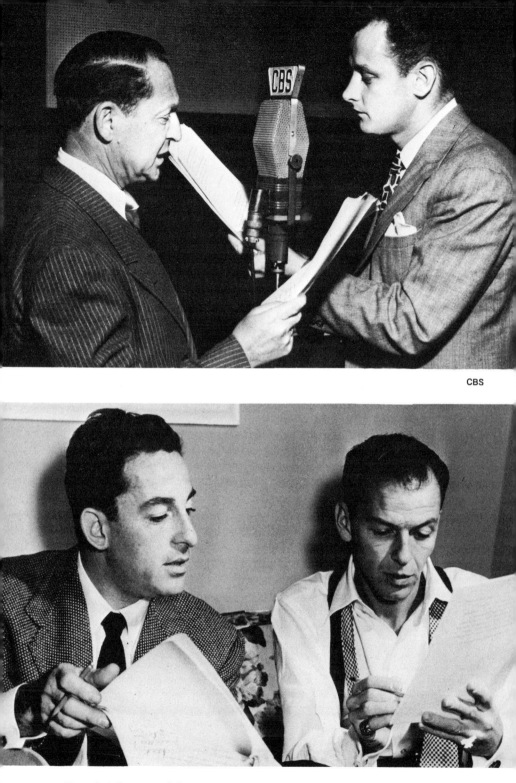

**Top, Art Carney, right, and Phil Kramer in 1948 on "Mr. Ace and Jane,"
a sequel to "Easy Aces" written by Goodman Ace. Bottom, Frank Sina-
tra studies one of his first dramatic roles with Himan Brown, producer
of "Inner Sanctum," in 1949.**

"Not me," said James Meighan. "My mind is made up. I'm looking for a good location for my apple stand."

Don MacLaughlin was serious. "Of course, we knew it was coming," he said, "but not so soon."

"It's too late," said a former movie actor who had drifted into radio when his film career had waned. Now he examined himself in the bar mirror. "I'm getting gray."

He had a few gray hairs, all right, but that wasn't his main problem. John Raby couldn't resist the temptation.

"Alas, yes," he said. "Silver threads among the bald." And on that note the kaffeeklatsch broke up.

As a matter of fact, John Raby and I were not so worried as some of the others. "When a Girl Marries" was still going strong, and Benton & Bowles had put John back in the lead when he returned from the Army—although I doubt that he got the salary his wartime replacement, Bob Haag, had managed to wring out of them. If so, he might not have taken the lead on TV's first soap opera, "A Woman to Remember." It was a local show from the Dumont studio in New York and featured John, Patricia Wheel, Ruth McDevitt, and Frank Thomas Jr.

The Teleprompter, standby of modern live TV, was as yet unknown. Memorizing a fifteen-minute show every day was no joke. John left the Friday broadcast of "When a Girl Marries" with a bright eye and a fast quip. He returned to us Monday, after his TV appearance, pale and pensive. He shook slightly when he picked up our script.

John had played a scene with an actress who had panicked and tried to walk right off the set. John grabbed her and pushed her into a chair. She stared up at him witlessly.

"I can *guess* what you came to tell me," he ad-libbed. Then, holding her pinned firmly in place, he repeated her lines as well as his own. He could feel her struggling all the while, hell-bent to get out of there. When it was over, John went outside and threw up.

"Are you getting enough to make this worthwhile?" I asked.

"A hundred dollars a week," he said bitterly.

John stuck it out for over a year. By that time he, too, had silver threads among the bald. Then, in 1951, he landed the ANTA show.

The American National Theater and Academy is a government-chartered institution for the promotion of live theater. When ANTA put on a TV program for the Dodge Motor Corporation, the greatest stars of the theater were available for the enterprise—Henry Fonda, Carol Channing, Alec Templeton, Helen Hayes, and the Dancing Hartmans appeared on the first show. John Raby told me he had been given the largest salary of his life as spokesman for the sponsor.

When you come right down to it, TV is radio with pictures—except for one thing. It is hellishly more expensive. The most insignificant show has a small fortune riding on it. The ANTA program was the biggest thing yet to hit television, and it affected the Madison Avenue boys—never a calm lot—like hives superimposed on shingles. The control booth looked like the subway at rush hour. NBC, the Academy, the Dodge Brothers, and the Ruthrauff & Ryan advertising agency were all fulsomely represented. But the stars on that first broadcast were doing acts they had done many times in the theater. The brashest V.P. would not dare tell Helen Hayes how to play "Victoria Regina" or Carol Channing to wait for her laughs. That left just one spot on which to pour the overflow of eager executive talent.

John stood alone under the sizzling lights, his recently acquired toupee pasted in place, and his make-up running. From the control booth, high above the giant stage, he could hear the click of the talk-back button.

Click. "John, if you'll just take the opening again and this time try—."

Silence.

Click. "Now John, the feeling here is that if you would—."

Long pause.

Click. "John?"

"Yes, sir?"

"It's a little bit too slow. If you—."

Prolonged stillness, while thought in the control booth was changed, rechanged, modified, remodified, disassembled, reassembled, and codified.

Click. "Yes, we feel it's a little too slow, John—well, not just—."

Click. "We don't want you to rush it—."

Click. "It's more sell we need—."

Click. "Of course, we don't want you to push it *too* hard—."

Minds were obviously changing too rapidly for the talk-back to get out a sentence. John turned to the only other thing on the set beside his weary self, the Dodge sedan, opened the door, and sat down on its front seat.

Click. "John?"

"Ye-e-ess?"

"It's about your hairpiece—." *Click.*

A decision finally survived. The hairpiece should be a little unkempt. Not too much, mind you. Just a trifle—a bit more informal. John asked permission to wait until the last moment to avoid getting it too rumpled. Permission granted.

Next came the commercial dealing with the interior of the car. John struggled through a welter of clicks to the sentence that described the slope of the seat. It was another hour before he got past that. V.P.'s descended from the control booth to supervise the gliding of his index finger along the Dodge upholstery. It was crucial that his finger reach an exact spot on a certain word.

"No, your finger moved too fast. It's got to be *right here* when you say 'gentle.' No, you passed it again, Johnny. Too slow, old man. Too fast . . . too slow . . . fast . . . slow . . . Whoa! Ah, ah, *ah!* That's it. Well, *almost*. Try again."

John stayed on after they left, in order to practice. When he knew he had it, he went back to his dressing room, where he smoked half a pack of cigarettes and sent out for coffee he was too nervous to drink. During the next hour a series of people stuck their heads in the door.

"Mr. Raby, they want you to ruffle your toupee slightly."

"John, don't forget about the hairpiece."

"Your hairpiece is to have a wind-blown effect, Mr. Raby."

Finally, when a stranger knocked, entered, and said, "Has anyone told you that your toupee—?" John turned on him like a wounded animal.

"Yes, yes, *yes*," he snarled. "The doorman has told me, the floor manager has told me, the director has told me, the assistant director has told me—."

"And now," said the man quietly, "the *producer* has told you."

John ruffled his toupee and went out in the hall. He sidled around gay, confident Carol Channing, elbowed past carefree, jovial Paul Hartman, and made his frightened way to the stage.

The royalty of show business packed the theater. This was "Broadway's own" and they turned out en masse. To a young actor, just out of the Army, it was one step short of appearing before the Almighty on Judgment Day. Once he was on the stage, however, fear left him and he swept through his opening spiel with brilliance. He went to his dressing room to practice sliding his finger over an imaginary line. "Notice the soft, gentle curve . . ."

His heart skipped a beat when, once more on stage, he stepped up to the Dodge. Lips screwed into his salesman's smile, he opened the door. There was somebody in the car!—a sexy, skimpily clad showgirl, her chin nestling coyly on her raised left shoulder, a dimply, provocative smirk on her lips. She wore a fluffy tutu like a ballet dancer, and her round young thighs were visible through black fishnet stockings. John knew what had happened. In a last-minute spurt of creative thinking this houri had been hired to embellish the décor. But no one had warned

him! When he reached the line about the curve of the luxurious upholstery, he ran his finger along the exact arc prescribed. It happened
also to be the exact arc of the young lady's bottom. Every word about
the beautiful seat took on new meaning. Myopically preoccupied with
the progress of his index finger, John let the roar from the spectators
take him by surprise. All the great minds of show business opened their
big mouths and sent up a shout that shook the rafters.

When John's heart started beating again he was still pointing at the
young lady's behind, but he couldn't remember what car he was selling.
Buick? Studebaker? Ford? . . . *Dodge!* But that carefully written, sponsor-
approved copy was gone from his mind forever. He faced the camera and
in simple sentences of his own devising said some nice things about the
automobile. When he could see by the clock that his time was up, he
walked off the set, out to the street, into the nearest bar, and had a
stiff one. Then he took the long way home—a trail that led him
through every bar in lower Manhattan.

Four days later, when he stomped belligerently into the inner
sanctum of the advertising agency and stared through bloodshot eyes
at the somber-faced executives before him, there was the terrible hush
that precedes the storm. Then one of the men spoke.

"It was our fault."

"All our fault," another said.

"You did a great job, Raby. In spite of—difficulties."

"We want you to sign a new—and better—contract."

John sank weakly into a chair. Why, these guys—these *wonderful*
guys—loved him!

When he got home his wife, Adele, was waiting for him at the door.
Smiling gamely, she tossed him a mocking salute. "Hi, Captain," she
said. She started whistling reveille, and handed him a paper. Uncle Sam,
it seemed, loved him even more than did Ruthrauff & Ryan. Reserve
Officer John Raby was back in the Army again.

The showgirl-in-the-Dodge is a perfect example of the thinking at
the period. "Is it *audio* or is it *video?*" That was the question of the
day. Every "idea man" was terrified of being thought "audio," that is,
"old hat."

In 1937, when my wondering eyes first lit on the titanic temple of
sound known as Radio City, it was impossible to imagine that one day
the magnificent double stairway would be plugged up to provide storage
space for scenery, that beautiful Studio 8-H would be dismantled and
converted (at the cost of $1,000,000) to the uses of TV, and that, more-
over, those fabled halls would resound to the roar of the lion and the
bear. (Not Brad Barker and Donald Bain this time, but the real thing.)

What better source of the purely "video" than the circus? I recall struggling for ten minutes to wrest the third-floor phone with its ten-foot cord from the paw of a chimpanzee.

I was alarmed another day when I heard loud squeals coming from a studio on the third floor. I went to investigate. A quiz show was in rehearsal, and TV lights had converted the place into an inferno. Bob Dryden was standing by to do the commercial.

"What's going on?" I asked. He grinned and pointed to the prizes set aside for the lucky contestants. Among the luggage and the toasters was a piglet in a box. Over it stood a burly stagehand, directing an electric fan toward the little pink hide.

"This is Buck," said Bob, happily.

"Forty years in show business," growled Buck. "I never thought I'd wind up playing nursemaid to no pig!"

Many an actor would have welcomed the tender ministrations of Buck. Cameron had not exaggerated the blistering blaze of those lights. A common ailment during TV's Golden Era was sunburn along the part of the hair.

Before TV some of my best friends had been blonds. Now they all were. Word had gone out that, for television, "the lighter the better." Brunettes might as well come on with their heads in a shopping bag, according to those early cameramen. Suddenly above every mink in Colbee's there gleamed a crown of gold.

One afternoon, as I hailed a taxi in front of NBC, I heard a plaintive voice behind me.

"Mary Jane, can I share it with you? I'm dead!"

It was the star of a half-hour weekly radio drama that had been adapted for TV. Still in his early twenties, he played a teen-ager, but today he looked forty. His thin, distinguished face showed lines of fatigue, and there were dark spots under his eyes. Above his heavy brows his normally patent-leather black hair had turned a brassy pink. It was dry and bristly, as though it had been dyed with a mixture of lye and peroxide and trimmed with pinking sheers. He dropped his head on my shoulder as we rode along, tears of exhaustion and anger in his eyes.

"TV," he whimpered. "The worst thing that ever happened to actors."

As for the small-screen offerings themselves, there was a "spontanooity" about TV's Golden Age that we'll never see again—a show-biz-with-its-pants-down effect. I remember my seven-inch screen lighting up to reveal an announcer standing alone against a backdrop. He stared solemnly at me. Then he curled his lips back in a half-smile. He let his face sag again, then smiled broadly and inclined his head. He became serious, then broke into a broad grin and bowed. Suddenly the scene shifted to the show that should have been on in the first place. They had somehow picked up an announcer practicing his new TV smile. It recalled one of radio's first symphony broadcasts, when a ghostly voice had been heard over the music, "Hello, everybody—hello-o—hello —o—o." An announcer was practicing his new radio "hello." A lot of phone calls came in to the network suggesting that outer space was trying to contact earth.

Another high point in TV's Golden Age was the death scene of "Camille," featuring the backside of a stagehand, as he wriggled around under her bed, adjusting a cable.

Never to be forgotten was Ralph Locke's first TV appearance. Ralph, who had for years played Papa David in radio's "Life Can Be Beautiful," was cast as a passenger on a plane flying over the African veldt. He went up in his lines, floundered for a few seconds, then said, "This is my station. I've got to get off," and stepped out of the plane.

Writers were having as much, if not more, trouble in adjusting to the new medium. One of the authors of the soap opera world took over the scripts on an interplanetary tale called "Captain Video." Her highly developed radio technique worked perfectly for the small screen fantasy —until the day she made the mistake of writing a scene between two invisible people.

Television is at its best, though, in public events. Who can ever forget the broadcast of the Republican convention in 1948? For the first time the nation saw its prospective lawmakers in action. Leaflets had been circulated, giving standards of behavior under TV's piercing eye, but as *Variety* later remarked, the delegates seemed not to have read them. It was summer. They lounged about in shirt sleeves with open, rumpled collars. There was inattention—people read newspapers during the important speeches. The microphone would occasionally pick up background profanity in the middle of a commentator's remarks. There was some hooting and catcalls. In fact, a bit of drinking seemed to be going on. The camera panned nervously from one unkempt group to another, while the announcer kept up a running patter, trying to suggest that everything was just fine. At last the lens reached a group of neatly attired people, sitting upright on their chairs and chatting politely. The announcer's voice took on new life.

"Ah, yes," he said with a happy sigh. "Here we have—er—I believe —Senator and Mrs. _____. With them is Governor _____."

"Hst!" came an urgent whisper. "Hsst!"

"The Governor's wife is wearing a beautiful—."

"Hst!" the voice insisted. *"That's* the *quartet!"*

Sure enough, the "governor" and "senator" were soon on their feet singing the "Star Spangled Banner." It was interesting that the best-looking, best-behaved group in sight were the AFRA members. There was a lesson here, but it dawned on the two parties very slowly.

The Democrats promised, somewhat smugly, to look better at *their* convention, but as *Variety* wistfully noted, riding herd on hundreds of fun-loving delegates is a thankless job. The Democrats proved just as messy as their opponents had been.

It was fifteen years, however, before the full implications of 1948 dawned. In the interim, both political parties made every effort to create an image that any candidate's mother could be proud of. Make-up men and lighting experts were employed. Aspirants to office sought aid from actors, taking lessons in deportment, speech-making, and sincerity.

Then in 1964, the Republicans came up with what had been obvious from the first. Instead of converting a lawyer, a soldier, or a rancher into an actor, why not call an actor and just hand him the part? They tried it, and shooed a movie star into a senator's seat like a breeze.

In 1966 they provided us with a governor who could not only be seen presiding with dignity and sincerity from Sacramento but playing a hot love scene on "The Late Show" as well. As a confirmed suffragette, I await with eagerness the time when one of the parties plumbs the yet untapped vote-getting potential of Doris Day. We shall no longer elect our representatives. We'll cast them.

If TV wrought changes in the political arena, think what it did on the athletic field. The probing lens took to sneaking in on the huddles between players and umpires and referees. The hitherto discreet microphone went along to pick up the sound. The sounds it picked up threatened to shatter the image of the wholesome, Wheaties-fed athlete forever, until the powers-that-be came to and hastily washed out some mouths with soap.

Meanwhile, back at the old, blind medium, radio, ratings plunged and memos avalanched down Madison Avenue demanding change of plot, change of cast, change of writer—change—change—CHANGE! The Hummerts sent word to their writers, requesting "action." I don't know whether they specified general conflagration or whether the writers just happened to spark simultaneously, but to a man they responded with "Fire!"

Keene Crockett, NBC soundman at the time, describes it this way: "Within one week Just Plain Bill's barber shop burned, Mrs. Wiggs' bakery was razed to the ground, I forget what it was of John's Other Wife that lay smoldering, but I do know that the sound department had but *one* good electric fire gong and it was the first piece of equipment ever to have conflicts. Often as not, it was pushed out of Lorenzo Jones, into Amanda of Honeymoon Hill, down to Stella Dallas, and across the third floor to where Young Widder Brown's tearoom was ablaze."

In a reverse play, Benton & Bowles tried to heal rating wounds on "Perry Mason" by converting that action-packed daily melodrama into a slow-moving, sentimental soap opera. They expanded the part I was playing until it was the virtual lead (I think they craftily dreamed of snatching some of the still fanatically loyal audience of "When a Girl Marries") and turned the stony-faced detective into a male Elderly Agatha Anthony, on whose shoulder I for two whole years shed the unavailing tear. Unavailing because "Perry Mason" went off the air anyway.

Nighttime shows were rapidly being replaced by disc jockeys, but the soap operas were doing pretty well. "When a Girl Marries" held remarkably firm—still leading the daytime field. A cheery man from General Foods made an unexpected visit to our studio one day. "Your show is a mainstay of our advertising," he told me. "It's doing a great job for us. We wouldn't dream of letting it go."

With those comforting words ringing in my ears, I took my first long vacation in ten years. It was really a honeymoon. I had been married to Guy Sorel for six years, but, show business being what it is, we had never found time to get away together. The new electronic tape made it possible. Benton & Bowles taped a month of the show in advance, Guy returned from Hollywood, where he had been making a film for Otto Preminger, and we took off for Paris.

Quick as a flash, General Foods dropped "When a Girl Marries." Tom McDermott did not cable. He let me dream on in my Parisian idyll, but the day I returned he rushed to my apartment to explain what had happened.

"What I want to know," I said, "is where is that sanguine chump who told me they'd never let go of 'When a Girl Marries'?"

"Oh, him," Tom said, mournfully. "He died. Then somebody else allocated the whole budget to—."

"Let me guess," I begged. "Television."

"By the way," Tom added as he left, "the show goes off June 29."

"It figures," I said. "It's my birthday."

CHAPTER XVIII

When a Girl Commutes

Colbee's was Forest Lawn without the flowers. General Foods had canceled not only "When a Girl Marries" but also "Portia Faces Life" and "The Aldrich Family"—both shows with high ratings.

"I feel as though the main pillars had been knocked out of the house," Virginia Payne ("Ma Perkins," still on for Procter & Gamble) said nervously.

Many other shows had been dropped in my absence. Only Air Features tried to hold the line. They fought a slow retreat—grimly battling over each show, switching to better time as cancellations made it available, and experimenting with plot line and giveaway. Now they threw up a sudden, brilliant, rear-guard action. They put a brand new radio serial on NBC, "Nona From Nowhere," starring Toni Darnay. They cast me as the "heavy." The opening date was July 1 but we rehearsed the week before—on June 28. A telephone call was waiting for me when I got out of the Hummert rehearsal. It was LeRoy Bailey, who for years had been writing "When a Girl Marries." The old girl was not dead, after all. She was just moving—to the American Broadcasting Company as a morning show. Could I clear the time? It meant telling the Hummerts that the strongest program on the air was going on in direct competition with "Nona," and asking to be released for it.

I was sweating when I came out of that NBC telephone booth. Fortunately, I walked right into Mr. and Mrs. Hummert. They listened, smiled, and let me go with a pat on the shoulder. With tears of relief, I called Roy back again.

"It's too late," I said, "to get to Benton & Bowles and sign a new contract—."

213

Bennett Kilpack, left, played the title role in the longest-lived of detective programs, "Mr. Keen, Tracer of Lost Persons." James Kelly was Mike Clancy.

"Oh, they have nothing to do with it," he said. "John Gibbs is packaging the show now."

My sweat broke out again. John Gibbs and I had had a brief but unromantic encounter years before, when he offered me scale to play a lead on one of his programs. I explained that I did not play a lead for scale.

"Lots of others do," he replied, and proved it by putting somebody else in the part.

John Gibbs started in Chicago, selling a program written by his wife, Sandra Michael. That was an achievement, because she wrote outside the accepted soap opera formula. Her first daytime serial, "Against the Storm," however, won the Peabody Award for Radio Excellence.

From radio Gibbs swung easily and profitably into television and by the time he took over "When a Girl Marries" he controlled both the Robert Montgomery TV show and "Schlitz Television Playhouse." In a spectacularly short time, his hole-in-the-wall office had grown into a large establishment with East and West Coast branches.

I called the New York branch. I couldn't reach Gibbs, but a henchman explained that there was no particular need for my services. I could come along if I liked—at scale, of course.

For reasons known only to the Janus-god of advertising, General Foods had bought "When a Girl Marries" right back again, but on a short-term contract. Although Benton & Bowles no longer produced the show, they still represented the sponsor, so the next day I called the Creative Head. I couldn't get through to Tom, but while I was trying, a masculine voice broke in on the wire.

"I hope you've signed your contract," it said. "They're breathing down our necks about it. The sponsor won't take the show without you."

He was cut off, and I never did learn who he was. I hope he reads this book. To you, sir, Hosanna! Live forever!

By now I was a far different girl from the one who had been cowed by Mr. Darland. I sat tight and waited for the phone to ring. A series of calls came from the Gibbs office late that afternoon. Finally, the Big Man himself got on the wire, and we made a deal. Not my old fee, but a lot better than scale.

Moving both time and network was the most debilitating thing that could be done to a program. The following excerpt from *Variety* indicates the formidable strength of "When a Girl Marries":

"ABC's new morning soap opera lineup, which kicked off two weeks ago, has boosted the web's ratings for the 11:30 A.M.–12 noon period and brings it right behind the leading chain, CBS.

TUNE IN TOMORROW

"Special Trendex report made last week (July 9) gives ABC's 'When a Girl Marries' a rating of 5.4 with a 23.2% share, just behind CBS' 'Grand Slam' with a 5.8 and 24.9%. NBC's Jack Berch follows with 4.0 and 17.2% and MBS' 'Queen for a Day' gets 3.2 and 13.7%. Indies get 3.6 and 15.4% while TV took 1.3 and 5.0%.

"Study indicates that ABC's soapers-in-the-morning pitch may give CBS, including the latter's Arthur Godfrey, a run for its money as the airers get established."

We continued to climb, pulling our new network with us. When in spite of this brilliant showing, General Foods soon canceled, Carnation Milk picked us up. A few months later the new sponsor tossed a bomb. They were moving the show to the Coast, where they could supervise it. Not Mr. Gibbs, but ABC cagily approached and asked if I would go with it. I refused. I felt no emotion at leaving Joan and all her friends and enemies. My emotions had been spent when General Foods canceled that first time and I lost my fat salary. The radio gravy train, I could see, was pulling into a siding, and the sooner I jumped off and found another mode of transportation, the better.

Then Jan Miner came for a weekend on my boat. This energetic young blond had come from a local station in Hartford, Connecticut, in 1946 and had made an immediate success in New York. She quickly became a soap opera star ("Lora Lawton") and later replaced Bess Johnson in "Hilltop House." These shows were now off the air and Jan was working on the Robert Montgomery TV program.

When she heard that I had responded to the ABC offer with a flat refusal, she told me, "*Never* do that. Always *negotiate*. You can't tell what might come of it. The publicity is wonderful. It will run through the industry like wildfire that they are trying to get you on the Coast. It'll make you *important*."

"But she doesn't want to go to the Coast," my husband said.

"She's *not* going to the Coast," Jan said. "She's just going to *negotiate*. Call them right now—on the marine telephone—from your *yacht*. Oh, that's a marvelous idea," she gurgled on. "It'll bowl them *over*. The most *Hollywood* thing I ever heard of. Say casually, 'I'm calling you from my yacht.' "

"Oh, bilge!" Guy said. It reminded him, and he went below to start the pump.

The marine operator got through quicker than she usually did, and I soon had a V.P. on the wire.

"Ahoy there," I said. "I'm calling from my—er—boat."

"Yacht," whispered Jan.

"My yacht," I amended.

216

"You *are?*" Sure enough, he sounded impressed. "I didn't know you had a phone on it. Where are you?"

"Cold Spring Harbor."

"Open sea," Jan prompted.

"*Off* Cold Spring Harbor," I said. "I thought we might talk this Carnation thing over again."

"Tell him you might be willing to *commute,*" Jan urged.

"I thought I might commute," I said.

"That's an idea. Come into my office Monday. Say, how *big* is your yacht? Do you ever do any *fishing?*"

I honestly tried to follow Jan's advice during the next two weeks. I said yes-and-no-but-don't-quote-me until I hated myself. There was no advantage in my spending every third week in Hollywood to tape "When a Girl Marries." I couldn't keep my other New York work anyway.

"Maybe you *ought* to commute," Jan said one day. "Think of the *publicity.*"

"But I'd lose *money.*"

"Get more for it. Then when the show comes back east you'll have set a precedent. And think of the *publicity.* You'd be a big shot."

"Look here," Guy said that same evening. "This is a lot of damned nonsense. You're not going. March over there and tell them so—and mean it!"

And that's what I did. I'm no snooper, but as I was leaving the office my eye fell accidentally (I swear it) on a letterhead: "Erwin Wasey." I knew the Wasey agency handled the Carnation account. It was the signature at the bottom—a huge, angular thing I couldn't help seeing—that made me catch my breath: "Robert Redd." The man who years before had given me that $100 to stooge with the Marx Brothers. The man who said I was the best talent on the Coast. I was ashamed of my shilly-shallying, and felt I owed him an explanation. I went home and called him in Hollywood.

"I'd love to be back with you, Bob," I said. "But I can't afford it."

"Don't you realize you're contractually obliged to come?"

"I have no contract, Bob. I never signed—."

"What?" The shout hurt my ear. "I understood that you—I can't talk to you any more. This is taking on legal implications. You'll have to deal with somebody else. But it shouldn't cost *you* anything."

The next day John Gibbs invited me to his office. He was all charm. "I feel in a case like this that little people like you and me shouldn't have to lose anything," he said modestly. "So I'm going to get the network to pay your expenses. Of course, you can go tourist class."

"No, I can't," I said.

I have never been able to explain just what happened after that—at least, not to Guy's satisfaction. I felt pretty foxy about it until I faced my husband that evening.

"What do you mean—'good deal?' " he demanded. "You were just *negotiating*, remember? Have you *signed* anything?"

"Sort of. But Carnation won't keep the show long. They'll cancel. And the *publicity* . . ."

I must confess that ABC made every effort to provide me with the greatest publicity break of my life on my first junket to the Coast. Cameramen stood by—even a newsreel photographer—and I was escorted to my plane by a public relations man from American Airlines. Important people like me, he explained, were not made to stand waiting to go through the gate. My luggage was already aboard. After the other passengers were all settled in, we would walk out in a leisurely fashion, take the pictures, and I would step into the plane.

I felt good. Important. Sophisticated. I felt like Jan Miner.

I stood on the boarding stair and waved. Guy kissed me good-bye. The cameras whirred and clicked. Then somebody handed me some roses and we started the whole scene over again. Suddenly, the airlines representative caught sight of a sign near the tail of the plane and let out a howl.

"This is the wrong plane! It's going to San Francisco! There's *your* plane over there."

I could see it a good block away, its propellers already whirling.

"I'll have your luggage sent on from San Francisco," cried the man, and he dragged me across the field, shouting "Hold that plane! Hold that plane!"

They never showed the newsreel. How could they, with that big sign, reading "Golden Gate," in it.

Six months later, I had collected eight one-line squibs in *Variety*, a bad case of flight fatigue, and lasting friendships with three airline hostesses. I had lost my part of ten years' standing in "Helen Trent" and all the rest of my New York radio work, and was holding onto my husband only by the power of positive thinking.

Then came the horrid moment when I had to tell Guy what had really happened in John Gibbs' office.

"You agreed that if Carnation kept the show—after six months— you would settle down out there?"

"Well, sort of. I was so sure they'd cancel. I still think so, but maybe we ought to move out there, anyway. It stands to reason TV is the thing now and they're all set up to handle it—equipment and space and weather and everything—and simply all the actors are going out and—."

"Not this actor!"

In the end, Guy let himself be talked into taking the Christmas holidays to "look the field over." During the month of December he made three TV films in California.

"Much as I hate it," he said, as he left to fly back to New York, "I guess you're right. There *is* more work out here."

He sublet our New York apartment to three airline hostesses and I rented a furnished house in Westwood.

We had been married since 1945. I had learned through the years that although Guy had come to this country as a very young child, certain characteristics of his native France still clung to him. He appears an average, open-faced American actor. He'll give you the shirt off his back, but he'll break your arm if you touch his omelet pan. He is as attached to hearth and home as a house cat and likes to have his own things around him. I never understood how he managed to fill a cross-country moving van and still leave a furnished apartment behind, but he did. With the sprawling hi-fi equipment and his 2,000 old-fashioned, heavy 78 r.p.m. recordings and other such bare essentials thundering expensively down Highway 66, there was still an overflow.

"We'll need two cars in Hollywood," I told him on the telephone. "Buy a secondhand station wagon. Drive it out, and bring Camille with you."

Camille is our elderly French housekeeper. She was my husband's nurse when he was a baby and looks upon us not so much as her employers as her charges. That is probably why, despite sullen Gallic misgivings, she agreed to come to California. We, on the other hand, agreed to keep her apartment in New York, so that at any moment she could cut and run.

A few days before Guy and she were to leave, his agent called me to say that "Lux Video Theater" wanted Guy for its next production.

"He'd have to fly here tomorrow," the agent said, "but it's a prestige show. I hate to see him miss it."

"What's the part?" I asked.

"Clemenceau."

Clemenceau—that was the role in which Guy had made such a success on Broadway. He *must* be seen in it on TV. I called New York.

"Hell, no," Guy said. "The car's all packed. Camille is packed. We're leaving Tuesday."

"Fly out," I begged. "I gave them my word you would. They're depending on you."

219

TUNE IN TOMORROW

I felt a delicious surge of excitement as I dashed to the airport to race my husband straight to the TV station.

"You know," I said, as we breezed along, "say what you will, it means a lot having your name in *Variety* every week—saturation advertising. 'To the Coast Mary Jane Higby . . .' 'To New York Mary Jane Higby . . .' 'To the Coast Guy Sorel . . .' 'To New York . . .' "

Guy was haggard and silent. I felt I could read his mind, "To hell . . ."

Several hours later, after his rehearsals, he stalked out to the car, got in without a word, and slammed the door.

"How'd it go?" I asked timidly.

"Did you *read* that script?"

"Why, no, I—."

"It's not the play I was in at all. It's a *movie script* of the life of Zola, and it's lousy. And I haven't a damned thing to do in it. Nothing. I wouldn't have touched this part in New York. And you dragged me out here."

As rehearsal week crawled on, our little gray home in the West got grayer and grayer. At last, there was nothing for me to do but get out of there. I decided to go to Flagstaff, Arizona, where Mother and Rita were now living.

The air was bracing and I was beginning to feel like myself again when the owner of the local radio station telephoned me. "I hear 'When a Girl Marries' is going off the air," he said.

They wouldn't! They couldn't! Not without telling me. Or would they?

I dashed back to Los Angeles. They would. They *had*.

I moped around the bungalow for two days trying to summon courage to tell Guy. Calls started coming in from ABC in New York. They had sold the show, for six weeks only, to a chemical company, and the sale would fall through without me. *Please* would I come back—just for six weeks?

The day Guy finished with "Lux," I picked him up at the studio and told him the news.

"We can't go home," he said. "There are airline hostesses in our bed. Half our things are somewhere around St. Louis and the rest in a garage on Sixty-fifth Street. Camille is packed, sitting on the edge of her chair with her hat on, growing an ulcer."

I told him about the chemical company. "I may as well go back and pick up the money just for six weeks," I said.

"Don't *sign* anything," he begged.

Guy's agent called that night. "I've put you up for a feature film at Fox and they're definitely interested. In the meantime, would you like to do a 'You Are There'?"

The upshot was that I left Guy rehearsing a TV show, flew to New York, stuffed Camille into the already overstuffed stationwagon, and headed westward again for California.

A tire blew after the first ten miles. The headlights didn't work properly. The tarpaulin holding our assortment of pots and pans came loose heading into Oklahoma City. And another tire blew in the Mojave Desert.

Six days later, I limped into Los Angeles. Guy gave me a cup of soup and tucked me into bed.

"You have time for a two-hour nap before your plane takes off," he told me. He had booked me a nonstop flight to New York, which, of course, stopped in Chicago after we lost an engine. The "slight wait" there took most of the day. I was still groggy when I tottered into rehearsal the next morning.

My New York director, Warren Somerville, was jubilant. "Somebody in the Sales Department here," he told me, "has just come up with the greatest idea since Marconi. They're going to sell radio as they do TV, on a participating basis. Several sponsors for each show. We ought to get a few more months out of 'When a Girl Marries'—at least."

"Not me," I said firmly. "Six weeks, and back to Hollywood."

A few days later the head of Sales asked me to call on a prospective sponsor with him.

"No, back to the Coast for me," I said.

"We just want you to give him the background on the show. Mrs. Carrington is sick and nobody else knows it as well as you."

That was the nicest sponsor I ever met. "We listened to every woman on two networks and picked you—because of your naturalness and sincerity. We want *you* to do the commercials—instead of an announcer. We'll pay you an extra fee."

"You'll pay her for writing them as well, won't you?" said the salesman.

He added that a reducing salon was also buying time on the show, and wanted me on the same basis. In radio's last, tragic, Götterdämmerung glow, my salary seemed about to balloon up close to its old, healthy size. I agreed.

It took several hours for me to screw up courage to telephone Guy, although strictly speaking, I had been obedient. I had not signed anything. He was about to start work on the film for Fox. When I reached him he had just learned that Fox had decided not to make the picture after all. He was desperately homesick and lonely. We decided to try to close the California chapter forever.

Well, Virginia, I don't know about Santa Claus, but there is *something* going on. The airline hostesses in our apartment were all suddenly transferred to other cities, and the owner of our house in California, a staunch Mormon woman, truly a saint, airily dismissed a two-year lease.

The new system of participating sponsorship had its own peculiar delights. It brought small companies into the field. Contact between sponsor and artist, hitherto impersonal and remote, now became personal and intimate. One client was in litigation over his product's name. He asked us to slur and mangle its pronunciation until the legal problem was ironed out. So for three months both our announcer, Don Gardner, and I sounded slightly drunk. The reducing salon was snatched abruptly off the air. The FCC had raised some questions about the claims it made. The producer of a laxative (networks never took such ads in the old days) called a meeting and gave us a long talk on the virtues of his preparation. It had been thoroughly tested on convicts down South with dramatic results, which he hastened to describe, categorizing them as Mild, Mean, and Explosive. He passed out a booklet he had written on the subject. Gertrude Warner, star of "Whispering Streets," sent her copy, chapter by chapter, to ABC's script editor, who was vacationing in Europe at the time. As he arrived in each new capital—Paris, Rome, Madrid—he found waiting for him a new episode in "The History of Constipation—Starting With the Egyptians."

At this point I think we can safely say that the Golden Age of Radio had passed.

In all, we managed to squeeze six years out of "When a Girl Marries" after General Foods canceled, giving me a total run of eighteen years as Joan. When I wheezed out her last line, it was almost with relief. Hers had been such a slow, bumpy decline. Nearly all her contemporaries had gone on long before. Only Ma Perkins, Our Gal Sunday, Nora Drake, and Helen Trent were still alive—four out of a one-time high of fifty-four—the survivors all on CBS. The day "When a Girl Marries" left the air I returned temporarily to my old part in "Helen Trent," while my replacement, Andrée Wallace, had a baby.

For years there had been a steady migration of radio actors to the Coast. Now, Joan Tompkins (Nora Drake) gave notice to CBS, and she, too, headed into the setting sun. The network held what was destined to be the last of the great radio "auditions."

It was a whopper. Eighty-four contestants from every branch of show business tried out for the part of Nora. Arthur Hanna, the director, made a speech to the actresses. It went like this: "Nora is not the usual soap opera heroine. This is an adult story of a nurse in a psychiatric clinic. What CBS wants is an honest, straightforward performance and above all, a quality that is *different.*"

I studied the material. Nora, I found, did use a lot of high-flown pseudopsychiatric jargon, but her real preoccupation seemed to be which of the several neurotics she had sweet-talked into a stupor she was going to marry. I thought I detected, too, hints of amnesia, and the loss of the use of both legs—traditional soap opera ailments—among her suitor-patients. Nonetheless, I took CBS at its word and jumped into the audition with a dramatic fervor that would have stunned David Belasco. Then I marched my tear-stained, perspiring self home and waited for the glad tidings.

Nothing.

Finally my phone did ring again, but only to hail me back to another huge audition. As I listened to the "no-soap-opera, new-different" speech again, the pages of memory flipped back. I was on top of an old Fifth Avenue bus. A soft voice spoke in my mind's ear, "A nice girl. A nice, *nice* girl."

A few weeks later I met a successful young Broadway leading woman at a party. She approached me with a look of frustrated disbelief.

"I hear *you* won the Nora Drake audition," she began. "I've never been so *mad* in my life. They told me they wanted something *new—*something *different.*"

"I know," I said. "And when you heard the old, stereotyped—."

"*Yes.* I can't understand it."

"Well, darling," I said in the prevailing cliché of the day, "that's the way the *old* cookie crumbled."

A little more than a year later (January 2, 1959), Nora and Our Gal Sunday bit the dust. Eighteen months later (June 24, 1960), Helen Trent and Ma Perkins breathed their last.

So came the end of radio as we knew it—a unique chapter in the annals of Show Business.

Back in those zany, hectic years of the unseen actor the most coveted role was that of the murdered person in a mystery show. There would be a brief first speech:

"Who's there? Come out from behind that bronze Buddha! What's that? A knife! No! No! Get away from me! Help! Help! Help! He's kill—." (Sound: Body falls.)

After that, you could retire to a corner and read *Variety*—while the rest of the cast tore a passion to tatters—cozy in the knowledge that you had made as much money as any of them.

When we were lucky enough to capture that part, we spoke of it as "getting the brass ring." And I think that sums up the entire radio story. For awhile there, from his notoriously shaky seat on life's merry-go-round, the Actor had copped the Brass Ring, and now and then it looked almost like genuine, 24-karat gold.

Bibliography

Allen, Fred, *Treadmill to Oblivion*, Boston: Little Brown, 1954.

Berg, Gertrude, *Mollie and Me*, New York: McGraw-Hill Book Co., Inc., 1961.

Buxton, Frank and Owen, Bill, *Radio's Golden Age*, New York: Easton Valley Press, 1966.

Cantril, Hadley, *The Invasion From Mars, a Study in the Psychology of Panic*, Princeton: Princeton University Press, 1940.

Cantril, Hadley and Allport, Gordon W., *The Psychology of Radio*, New York and London: Harper & Brothers, 1935.

Chase, Francis Seaburg, Jr., *Sound and Fury, an Informal History of Broadcasting*, New York and London: Harper & Brothers, 1942.

Cook, Whitfield, "Be Sure to Listen In," *American Mercury*, March, 1940.

Crosby, Bing, as told to Martin, Pete, *Call Me Lucky*, New York: Simon & Schuster, 1953.

Crosby, John, *Out of the Blue*, New York: Simon & Schuster, 1952.

Dennison, Merrill, "Soap Opera," *Harper's Magazine*, April, 1940.

Gibson, Worthington, "Radio Horrors for Children Only," *American Mercury*, July, 1936.

"Gore Criticized for Making Children's Hour a Pause That Depresses," *Newsweek*, November 9, 1937.

Gould, Jack, "Rise and Fall of the Quiz Empire," *New York Times Magazine*, September 28, 1958.

Green, Abel and Laurie, Joe R., *Show Biz From Vaude to Video*, New York: Henry Holt & Co., 1951.

Gross, Ben, *I Looked and I Listened*, New York, Random House, 1954.

Harding, Alfred, *The Revolt of the Actors*, New York: W. Morrow & Co., 1929.

Head, Sidney W., *Broadcasting in America*, New York: Houghton Mifflin, 1956.

Klapper, Joseph T., *The Effect of Mass Communication*, Glencoe, Ill. Free Press, 1960.

Landry, Robert J., *This Fascinating Radio Business*, Indianapolis, Bobbs-Merrill Co., 1946.

Lazarsfield, Paul F., *The People Look at Radio*, Chapel Hill: University of North Carolina Press, 1946.

Lerner, Max, *America as a Civilization*, New York: Simon & Schuster, 1957.

Mann, Arthur, "The Children's Hour of Crime," *Scribner's Magazine*, May, 1934.

Mannes, Marya, *But Will It Sell?* New York: Lippincott, 1964.

Murphy, Walter, "1,000 a Week—Who Are They?" *American Magazine*, August, 1945.

Phillips, Irna, as told to Markel, Helen, "Every Woman's Life Is a Soap Opera," *McCall's*, March, 1965.

Rosenberg, Bernard, editor, *Mass Culture: The Popular Arts in America*, Glencoe, Ill., Free Press, 1957.

Seldes, Gilbert, *The Great Audience*, New York: Viking Press, 1950.

Seldes, Gilbert, *The Public Arts*, New York: Simon & Schuster, 1956.

Siepmann, Charles A., "Further Thoughts on Radio Criticism," *Public Opinion Quarterly*, 1941.

Slate, Sam J. and Cook, Joe. *It Sounds Impossible*, New York: The Macmillan Company, 1963.

Smith, Ralph Lewis, *A Study of the Professional Criticism of Broadcasting in the United States, 1920–1955*. Thesis for the degree of Doctor of Philosophy, University of Wisconsin.

Steinberg, Charles S., *The Mass Communicators*, New York: Harper, 1958.

Thurber, James, *The Beast in Me and Other Animals*, New York: Harcourt, Brace and Co., 1947.

Vallee, Rudy, and McKean, Gil, *My Time Is Your Time*, New York: Ivan Obolensky, Inc., 1961.

Warner, W. Lloyd and Henry, William E., "The Daytime Radio Serial: A Symbolic Analysis," *Genetic Psychology Monographs*, Vol. 37, 1948.

White, Llewellyn, *The American Radio*, Chicago: University of Chicago Press, 1947.

Zolotow, Maurice, "Washboard Weeper; Foremost Enemy of the Daytime Serial," *Saturday Evening Post*, May 29, 1943.